The X-Rated Bible

Leviticus 19:27

Do not cut the hair at the sides of your head or clip off the edges of your beard.

hemorrhoids p161

Deuteronomy 28:27

ISBN 0-922915-55-5

Design by Linda Hayashi

10 9 8 7 6 5 4 3 2 1

Feral House
2532 Lincoln Boulevard, Suite 359
Venice, California 90291

www.feralhouse.com

Originally published 1985 by American Atheist Press

The X-Rated Bible

Bible

AN IRREVERENT SURVEY
OF SEX IN THE SCRIPTURES

Ben Edward Akerley

FERAL HOUSE

Dedication

This anthology is dedicated in general to the countless number of persons whose efforts have served as an antidote and a counterforce to the all-too-numerous militant pro-censorship groups trying desperately to impose their narrow moral views on everyone and to curtail our priceless heritage of freedom of expression in the first republic in history founded on the bedrock principle of the absolute separation of state and church.

In particular, it is dedicated to: Adam Parfrey for his foresight, encouragement and enthusiasm. And to the Trevor Helpline. This hot line provides the nation's first toll-free suicide prevention service for gay, lesbian and uncertain youth (800 850–8078). May its continued success help negate the Bible's pernicious influence and save the lives of troubled teens who might otherwise succumb to the myth that homosexuality is truly "an abomination in the sight of the Lord."

Contents

"Bible, little girl?"

INTRODUCTION

N SEPTEMBER 25, 1976, DURING THE FERVOR OF THE PRESIdential election campaign, the following Gallup Poll results appeared in newspapers across the nation:

The Gallup Poll

1 In 3 Claims To Be A 'Born Again' Christian by George Gallup
PRINCETON, NJ—The dramatic rise to political prominence of Jimmy Carter, a "born-again" Christian, has focused attention on the evangelical movement in America.

The latest nationwide Gallup survey shows thirty-four percent (one in three) saying they had been "born again"—that is, had a turning point in their lives when they committed themselves to Jesus Christ. This figure projects to nearly fifty million Americans, eighteen and over. Among Protestants alone, nearly half (forty-eight percent) say they are "born-again" Christians, which projects to forty-three million adults.

"Born-again" Christians, accounting for one-third of the electorate, represent the core of Carter's support. Although these people tend to be more conservative in political ideology than the electorate as a whole, they currently support Carter over President Ford by a fifty-eight/thirty-three percent margin.

Although a wide range of churches define themselves as "evangelical," a "born-again" fundamentalist has an outlook or state of mind that pervades the membership of many churches, including the Roman Catholic Church. About one in five (eighteen percent) of Catholics says he or she has had a "born-again" experience.

Bible Seen as God's Word

The survey shows four in ten persons nationwide (38%), nearly one-half of Protestants (46%), and about one-third of Catholics (36%) believing the Bible to be the actual word of God and to be taken literally.

To measure conversion efforts, or witnessing, the Gallup Poll asked a sample of the nation's adults if they have ever tried to encourage someone to believe in Jesus Christ or to accept Him as their Savior.

A high proportion answered in the affirmative—47%. The figure is even higher among Protestants alone—58%.

A far higher proportion of persons of the evangelical group of churches than among the nonevangelical or mainline denominations have had a "born-again" experience, hold a literal interpretation of the Bible, and witness to their faith.

This question was asked first:

Commitment to Christ

"Would you say that you have been 'born-again' or have had a 'born-again' experience—that is, a turning point in your life when you committed yourself to Christ?"

Here are the results nationwide and by key groups:

Have Had "Born-Again" Experience

Nationwide	34%
Protestants	48%
Catholics	18%
Men	28%
Women	39%
College	27%
High School	36%
Grade School	42%
18–29 years	29%
30–49 years	33%
50 and over	39%
East	23%
Midwest	34%
South	55%
West	20%

The following question was then asked to determine the respondent's interpretation of the Bible:

Respondents Make Choice

"Which one of these statements comes closest to describing your feelings about the Bible?" (Respondents were handed a card with the following statements: **A.** The Bible is the actual word of God and is to be taken literally, word for word; **B.** The Bible is the inspired word of God but not everything in it should be taken literally, word for word; **C.** The Bible is an ancient book of fables, legends, history and moral precepts recorded by men.)

The X-Rated Bible

And here are the results:

	ACTUAL WORD OF GOD	INSPIRED WORD OF GOD	BOOK WRITTEN BY MEN	NONE OF THESE	CAN'T SAY
Nationwide	38%	45%	13%	1%	3%
Protestants	46%	42%	8%	na	4%
Catholics	31%	55%	10%	1%	3%
Men	33%	45%	16%	2%	4%
Women	41%	46%	9%	1%	3%
College	17%	58%	22%	na	3%
High School	42%	45%	9%	1%	3%
Grade School	60%	23%	7%	3%	7%
18–29 years	32%	45%	17%	2%	4%
30–49 years	34%	50%	13%	na	3%
50 and over	45%	41%	9%	1%	4%
East	27%	52%	15%	1%	5%
Midwest	42%	43%	9%	1%	5%
South	49%	39%	9%	na	3%
West	30%	48%	20%	1%	1%

na is less than 1%

The poll was a surprising revelation not so much for its information on the so-called "evangelical" experience, but for the light it cast on contemporary attitudes toward the Bible—eighty-three percent of those polled view the Bible either as the actual or inspired word of God.

Since I number myself among the thirteen percent of the populace who consider the Bible to be nothing more than "an ancient book of fables, legends, history and moral precepts recorded by men," my thesis in this book is that nothing in the Bible more forcefully or compellingly reinforces this viewpoint than an objective and impartial examination of the Biblical passages which relate to sex. It is an unpopular position, to be sure, but I am convinced that the eighty-three percent of the population who revere the Bible do so from a lack of familiarity with its contents in general and its passages relating to sex in particular, for the Bible enjoys a twofold, albeit paradoxical reputation. On the one hand, it is the world's undisputed, number one, all-time best-seller with more than two billion copies extant in at least 1,800 languages. On the other hand, it is one of the least read of books and certainly one that few ever venture to read through from cover to cover. Most Bible reading, therefore, centers on selected passages or favorite portions which are usually the same excerpts heard from the pulpit.

That much of the Holy Writ has a decidedly salacious flavor comes as a surprise, consequently, to the average layperson. This is also due in no small part to the majestic sweep, the grandeur and the melodic ring of the great King James Version—the 1611 translation which is the one most familiar to the English-speaking world. The lofty seventeenth-century idiom masks most of the bawdy narrative by its plethora of obsolete and archaic forms, the literal meaning of which escapes the modern reader. It has been estimated that more than five hundred words used repeatedly in the King James Version have altered radically in meaning since 1611.

My interest in writing a book about Biblical sexual practices dates back to my college freshman year as a theology major when I studied the Bible formally, my approach then being both reverent and uncritical. I was astounded to discover the great amount of sex in the Good Book, for until that time, I had viewed it as the literal word of God. I was soon to learn that this view is held only by fundamentalist religious groups.

After changing my major to education, I read Thomas Paine's scathing indictment of the Bible in his *The Age of Reason* and began to reflect on the validity of some of his observations. Shortly after earning my university degree, I saw the provocative play *Inherit The Wind* and greatly admired the stirring defense of evolution which Clarence Darrow gave in that Dayton, Tennessee courtroom, where he represented school teacher John Scopes in the famous "Monkey Trial." Darrow's daring in using the Bible itself to challenge fundamentalist William Jennings Bryan left an indelible impression on my mind. I soon adopted the view that the Bible is just another history or collection of histories.

In the early 1970s, while serving on the faculty of the University of Southern California, I was disturbed by the trend of the campus newspaper, *The Daily Trojan*, in giving frequent space to evangelicals who were mostly members of the Campus Crusade for Christ. When these religious zealots objected in print to official university recognition of the Gay Liberation Forum on the basis of homosexuality being condemned in the Bible, I expressed my concern to the editor of the paper who, in turn, invited me to write a rebuttal article expressing my views. My article "Bible Sex" soon evolved into a series in the form of a dialogue between me and the newspaper staff writer who represented the Campus Crusade for Christ. The controversy created over this series proved to me what little tolerance fundamentalists have for anyone who has the temerity to criticize or challenge the Bible or, more especially, their interpretation of it. It also gave me the impetus to write this book.

The fundamentalists' position is truly contradictory: they hold to a narrow moral code which they base squarely on the Bible, yet they are on shaky ground indeed since, by the very standards of these conservative religious groups, much of the Bible might be considered obscene.

Not content to keep their myopic, Biblical-based morality to themselves, fundamentalists are notorious in forming pro-censorship groups, in objecting loudly when evolution is presented in school textbooks without giving "equal time" to Adam and Eve, and in staunchly opposing and lobbying against any form of sex education or the dispensing of abortion and birth control information.

America has an incredible array of more than 300 of these pro-censorship, anti-evolution and anti-life groups with such picturesque names as Americans to Stamp Out Smut, Youth for Christ, The Knights of Columbus, Campus Crusade for Christ, The Guardians of Morality in Youth, Operation Moral Upgrade, The Christian Force for Our Righteous Christian Environment, The Moral Majority, American Christian Cause and Morality in Media.

Of course, it is always instructive to examine the psychological motives of these self-appointed guardians of everyone's morality and no one has penned a more perceptive or a more penetrating analysis of the censorial mind than have Harvey O'Higgins and Edward Reede in their spellbinding book, *The American Mind in Action*. They were writing about that archetype of all anti-vice crusaders, Anthony Comstock, but the description certainly applies to all smut-hunters of Comstock's ilk. On page 15 they state:

> The Puritan lived in a state of war with his instinctive self, which he regarded as his evil self tempting him to live according to the law of the flesh when he wished to live according to the Pauline law of God. He hated the flesh in himself and he hated even more fiercely that flesh appearing as the vices of others. Hence he was a great persecutor, a strong vice-crusader, the best of witch hunters. The more puritanical the modern American is, the more he has of these vice-crusading qualities. It is useless to tell such a man to love his neighbor as himself; he hates so much of himself. His hate, reservoired within him, gets its drainage in raids on vice, in the prosecutions and suppressions carried on by anti-vice societies, and in the campaigns of reform that call for the punishment of evil-doers. Nowhere else in the world could modern life produce such characters as America's Anthony Comstock.

But few have been the voices raised in opposition to these do-gooders and even fewer have been those who have dared to suggest that the Bible is anything but inspired.

One voice raised loud and clear against the Bible was that of America's great patriot-by-adoption, Thomas Paine (1737–1809). As a child, he was exposed to the Bible and its teachings and, at the age of seven or eight, heard a sermon on redemption in which there were frequent allusions to the Holy Scriptures. Paine recounts how he left the church and went outside into the churchyard garden completely revolted by what he had just heard. In *The Age of Reason,* published in 1784, Paine's recollection of this event was still vivid and undiminished with a lapse of nearly forty years. After describing his traumatic childhood experience, Paine concludes: "I moreover believe that any system of religion that has anything in it that shocks the mind of a child cannot be a true system."

Here is autobiographical evidence of at least one person who, as a child, felt that the Bible had a corrupting influence. Yet, judging by the very names of many anti-vice societies which are deeply rooted in the Bible, it is the protection of the morality of youth that is their primary concern.

Paine waxes even more vitriolic, again in *The Age of Reason,* and he pens an excoriating indictment of the Bible:

> Whenever we read the obscene stories, the voluptuous debaucheries, the cruel and tortuous executions, the unrelenting vindictiveness, with which more than half the Bible is filled, it would be more consistent that we called it the word of a demon than the word of God. It is a history of wickedness, that has served to corrupt and brutalize mankind; and, for my part, I sincerely detest it, as I detest everything that is cruel.

A famous contemporary of Thomas Paine who also was personally contemptuous of the Bible was Thomas Jefferson (1743–1826). It is a little-known but fascinating historical fact that he was so disgruntled with the New Testament in particular that he wrote his own "Jefferson's Bible" in which he radically altered most of the four Gospels dealing with the life of Christ. He rearranged them to suit his own interpretation of the events and entitled the work *The Life and Morals of Jesus of Nazareth.* Since Jefferson had once written in a letter to Charles Clay: "I not only write nothing on religion, but rarely permit myself to speak on it," his Jefferson's Bible was presumably never intended for publication. Nevertheless, since Jefferson's death, it has been published in several editions and it makes engagingly interesting reading.

Another fearless critic of the Bible was D. M. Bennett, a freethought publisher whose journal *The Truth Seeker* came under fire during the heyday of the most fanatic anti-obscenity crusader America has ever produced, Anthony Comstock (1844–1915).

Comstock was successful in getting Congress to pass the notorious Comstock Act of 1873 and it is to America's great discredit that this despicable law is still on the statute books today. This law gave Comstock unlimited power as Chief

Inspector of the Post Office Department and it allowed him to be the sole arbiter in obscenity and pornography cases. Concurrently, he was the chief agent of New York's Society for the Suppression of Vice.

Comstock arrested Bennett in 1877 for publishing a heretical tract entitled "An Open Letter to Jesus Christ" and a biological essay "Why Do Marsupials Propagate Their Kind?" When the Government decided to drop its case against Bennett, Comstock became so frustrated that he resolved to get Bennett by any means available to him.

In 1878, Comstock finally managed to get another indictment against Bennett for distributing a free love tract entitled "Cupid's Yokes." It was written by E. H. Heywood of Boston who himself had been arrested by Comstock. Much to the chagrin of Comstock, President Hayes had personally intervened in the Heywood case, having granted Heywood a presidential pardon.

The method Comstock used to entrap Bennett was a favorite with him: he sent a decoy letter through the mail requesting the tract from Bennett's publishing office, and upon receipt of the tract, he had Bennett arrested for mailing "obscene" matter. Bennett served one full year in prison. What had particularly enraged Comstock was Bennett's audacious suggestion that Comstock should also consider indicting the American Bible Society for obscenity for distributing the Bible.

The most famous and most outspoken American critic of the Bible was the great agnostic orator, Robert Green Ingersoll (1833–1899). At the zenith of his career, he once offered one thousand dollars in cash to any minister in the city of Cleveland who would agree to read to his congregation, from his pulpit on a Sunday morning, passages from the Bible to be selected by the agnostic. The offer was never accepted, and this in a day when one thousand dollars was a considerable sum.

Ingersoll once wrote in a letter to a friend:

> Nobody holds in greater contempt than I the writers, publishers, or dealers in obscene literature. One of my objections to the Bible is that it contains hundreds of grossly obscene passages not fit to be read by any decent man; thousands of passages, in my judgment, calculated to corrupt the minds of youth. I hope the time will come when the good sense of the American people will demand a bible with all obscene passages left out.

Ingersoll's eloquent anti-theological lectures "Some Mistakes of Moses" and "About the Holy Bible" are masterpieces of oratorical defamation of the Scriptures.

Mark Twain, a great admirer of Robert Ingersoll, once had occasion to take a jab at the Bible. A young woman superintendent in the Children's Depart-ment of the Brooklyn Public Library charged that *Tom Sawyer* and *Huckleberry Finn* were corrupting the morals of children. Twain's answer, as recorded in volume two of his autobiography, page 335, was:

> I am greatly troubled by what you say. I wrote *Tom Sawyer* and *Huck Finn* for adults exclusively, and it always distresses me when I find that boys and girls have been allowed access to them. The mind that becomes soiled in youth can never again be washed clean; I know this by my own experience, and to this day I cherish an unappeasable bitterness against the unfaithful guardians of my young life, who not only permitted but compelled me to read an unexpurgated Bible through before I was fifteen years old. None can do that and ever draw a clean, sweet breath again this side of the grave. Ask that young lady—she will tell you so.
>
> Most honestly do I wish I could say a softening word or two in defense of Huck's character, since you wish it, but really in my opinion, it is no better than those of Solomon, David, Satan, and the rest of the sacred brotherhood.
>
> If there is an unexpurgated [Bible] in the Children's Department won't you please help that young woman remove Huck and Tom from that questionable companionship?

Another outstanding example of open criticism of the Holy Writ where even its divine authorship was brought into question is the famous Scopes "Monkey Trial" of 1925.

William Jennings Bryan, a devout Christian fundamentalist who ran for president three times but was defeated all three times, had been successful in drafting legislation which prohibited the teaching of evolution in the public schools of America. John T. Scopes, a school teacher in Dayton, Tennessee, challenged this law and was charged and brought to trial.

Bryan volunteered to represent the prosecution, but he had a most formidable opponent in the person of Clarence Darrow, the prestigious criminal trial lawyer from Chicago who had volunteered to represent the defense.

Darrow brought the Bible right into the courtroom and brilliantly challenged Bryan's troglodyte fundamentalist views in a stunning and eloquent exegesis of the opening chapters of Genesis. Although Bryan won the case, the trial proved to be such a strain on him that, worn and haggard, he died five days after the termination of the trial. The panoply of events has been freely adapted and splendidly dramatized for all posterity in the superb drama *Inherit The Wind* which was authored by Jerome Lawrence and Robert E. Lee in 1955.

In my criticism of the fundamentalist interpretation of the Bible, I wish to focus only on sex. Anyone who doubts that there is much sex in the Bible need only read Genesis to find in just that opening chapter explicit and graphic examples of several varieties of incest, rape, adultery, indecent exposure, pimping, homosexual assault, bigamy, ritualistic circumcision, attempted seduction of a youth by an older woman, prostitution, baby-making by proxy, use of both an aphrodisiac and a fertility drug, fornication with devils, women punished with sterility, husband-swapping, masturbation/withdrawal and a fertility contest with four female contestants.

I insist that if the Bible is inspired, the passages relating to sex should reveal great enlightenment and exceptionally advanced knowledge and understanding. What we encounter instead are superstition, fear, primitive thinking and gross misunderstanding of even the most basic sexual functions.

Several other books have been written about Biblical sexual practices, but they have always been authored by apologists who rationalize anything and everything to conform to their theological orthodoxy. My approach is different because I do not consider the Bible as sacrosanct or above even objective criticism.

Once we disabuse ourselves of the notion that the Bible is inspired, we see it in a new light and delving into its sexual mysteries becomes real fun. But please don't take my word for it. This is what a noted contemporary theologian has to say about the subject: ". . . the Bible contains much racy material, fully as sexy as the works of Jacqueline Susann, only better written." (Rev. Charles Merrill Smith writing in *The Pearly Gates Syndicate or How to Sell Real Estate in Heaven.* Doubleday, 1971.)

Modern versions of the Bible are selling today as never before, but even in these easy-to-read and understand translations, many passages which refer specifically to sex are either glossed over or left without any explanation. In *The X-Rated Bible,* I leave nothing to the imagination since I am providing a comprehensive anthology of sex as we find it in the Scriptures.

I sincerely hope that this anthology will have the additional therapeutic benefit of helping readers learn not to take sex so seriously. Masters and Johnson, the sex research team from St. Louis, estimate that fifty percent of all marriages suffer from some form of sexual dysfunction. They go on to add amazingly that "the factor of religious orthodoxy still remains of major import . . . in almost every form of human sexual inadequacy." (*Human Sexual Inadequacy,* p. 229.)

Let us now explore the "racy material" which Rev. Smith mentioned in his book and get a fresh perspective on the Bible and its many interesting, colorful and very human characters.

Ben Edward Akerley
Glendale, California
January, 1984

PREFACE

INCE THE PUBLICATION OF THE ORIGINAL VERSION IN 1985, the rise of the Religious Right and the resurgence of Protestant fundamentalism have exerted a tremendous impact on three critical areas of American life: 1. sex education, 2. creationism vs. evolution and, 3. family values vs. gay rights.

Despite America's dubious distinction of having the highest unwed teenage pregnancy rate in the world, abstinence-only sex education has been aggressively subsidized by both state and federal governments. The best known curriculum, *Sex Respect*, previously titled *Love and Life: A Christian Sexual Morality Guide for Teens*, is currently in use in at least 1,500 public school districts with the blessing of religious extremists everywhere. Planned Parenthood has evaluated the program as follows: unrealistic, misleading, medically inaccurate and nothing more than fear and shame-based indoctrination.

Fundamentalist religious gurus have successfully intimidated public school boards and even textbook publishers into giving creationism equal time with evolution in the classroom. Their coinage of the neologism and oxymoron "creation science" reveals the absurdity of their anti-evolution campaign.

By far, the extremely lucrative and unrelenting anti-gay propaganda machine has been much more insidious in its disastrous consequences. Employing such inane slogans as "God created Adam and Eve, not Adam and Steve," televangelists have lavishly filled their coffers with generous contributions from sincere but misguided followers led to fear that the Gay Agenda includes not only seducing and corrupting American youth, but also in special, not just equal rights for gays and in undermining the Bible-based moral fabric of any God-fearing nation: the heterosexual nuclear family.

It has been seductively easy to convince most true believers that AIDS is the death sentence promised in Leviticus as a reward to those who "lie with mankind as with womankind." But what about AIDS victims who are heterosexual or intravenous drug users or recipients of a contaminated blood transfusion?

When then-presidential candidate Bill Clinton promised during his 1992 campaign to make lifting the ban on gays in the military a top priority of his new administration, he encountered overwhelming opposition from religious conservatives.

Also militating against lifting the ban was the UCMJ (Uniform Code of Military Justice) enacted in 1950 in part to enforce Biblical morality on all soldiers. Like the topsy-turvy morass on which it is based, it creates this confusing but amusing paradox of federal crime: cheat on your spouse and you get a one-year maximum sentence for adultery; give your spouse head or attempt anal sex and you get a maximum sentence of five years! Like the sodomy laws of nearly half of our states, these proscriptions apply to both gays and straights and include married couples.

It should boggle our minds that as we stand on the threshold of the twenty-first century, these antiquated statutes confuse sin with crime and survive as prudish relics of a particularly shameful period of our puritanical heritage. It took from 1786 to 1873 to repeal capital punishment for sodomy in all of our states.

Think of it! Just a little over 100 years ago, you could have been executed for performing a non-genital sex act in our own land of the free and home of the brave.

Another decisive factor in defeating Clinton's resolution came from the Southern Baptist Convention. They sent a memorandum directly to the White House reminding Clinton of his Baptist roots which teach the Scriptural condemnation of homosexuality as immoral, perverted and sinful behavior and demanded that he retain the ban. These same Baptist brethren commanded their followers in 1997 to boycott all Disney enterprises because the corporation had the temerity to offer full domestic partner benefits to unmarried and same sex couples and to sponsor the TV sitcom *Ellen* with real-life lesbian Ellen DeGeneres playing her openly gay namesake. With the charitable spirit of true Christian love, the Rev. Jerry Falwell denounced the program calling its star Ellen Degenerate.

Since abhorrence can and does beget violence, hate-spewing evangelicals deserve a large part of the credit for the meteoric rise in gay-bashings and murders despite their hypocritical protestations that "God hates the sin but loves the sinner." Fortunately, PFLAG (Parents, Families and Friends of Lesbians and Gays) serves as an increasingly visible antidote to the venomous anti-gay rhetoric of the Religious Right radicals. With chapters in more than 400 U. S. communities and in eleven foreign countries, their mission is to educate and lobby for acceptance and celebration of diversity. And in a wonderfully ironic twist on the pious platitudes of fundamentalist religious bigots, PFLAG has adopted the motto: Hate is not a family value.

It is axiomatic that the more fundamentalist-oriented true believers are, the more homophobic they become. It should come as no surprise, then, that the Religious Right has urged its followers to boycott the King James Version of the Bible solely because they have finally discovered what historians have known for centuries: King James I lived as an openly gay monarch.

Therefore, in today's climate of rampant homophobia, is it any wonder that although gay teens comprise no more than 10% of the overall adolescent population, nearly one third of teen suicides are gay kids? I myself could easily have become just another gay teen suicide statistic. When I chanced upon the Leviticus decree of death for gay sex at age 13, I was both devastated and traumatized. As an impressionable teenager, I suddenly realized that my sexual orientation was condemned by the one book I had been taught to revere as an infallible moral guide; that what was perfectly normal and natural for me was called unnatural and sinful by God's Holy Word. Consequently, if my *X-Rated Bible* can spare only one gay teenager from going through the guilt, shame, self-hatred, remorse, self-doubt and torment that I suffered, then it will have been well worth the effort.

Ben Edward Akerley
Los Angeles, California
November, 1998

King James I takes a Bible belting.

News item in *Out* magazine June, 1998

RIGHT-WING MAINSTAYS the Family Research Council (FRC), the Christian Coalition, and Americans for Truth About Homosexuality (ATH) have urged their members to cease using the King James Bible, first published in 1611 by James I of England. It appears that scholars of the period are in agreement that King James might better have been named Queen Mary. "James had a number of 'favorites,' such as the Earl of Somerset and the Duke of Buckingham, with whom he undoubtedly had sexual relationships," said biographer David Harris Willson. Here's evidence that the leaders of the Right need a serious reality check:

▼ Gary Bauer, the rightist stalwart who recently announced his presidential candidacy for 2000: "Anything that has been commissioned by a homosexual has obviously been tainted in some way."

▼ Peter LaBarbera of ATH: "I would ask Christians to check who is responsible for both the translation as well as the editing of their Bibles. We all need to be vigilant."

▼ Christian Coalition head and televangelist Pat Robertson: "It is very important that we stand up to the homosexual wherever and whenever he appears."

PROLOGUE

HEREAS THE FUNDAMENTALIST CONTENTION THAT THE BIBLE is the literal word of God merely expresses an opinion, it is illuminating indeed to discover that the Bible itself makes the claim that it is inspired and that it is an irreproachable guide in moral conduct:

> II Timothy 3:16–17 ¹⁶All scripture is inspired by God and profitable for teaching, for reproof, for correction, and for training in righteousness, ¹⁷that the man of God may be complete, equipped for every good work.

With the above quote uppermost in mind, let us now embark on our ribald romp through the nitty-gritty of an astonishing amount of Biblical hanky-panky.

Part I
INCEST: IMPLIED, SINGLE, DOUBLE AND MULTIPLE

IN THE BEGINNING WAS INCEST

ITERALISTS CONTINUOUSLY REFER TO THE STORY OF ADAM and Eve. They should more properly allude to the "stories" of Adam and Eve since Genesis contains two parallel but decidedly divergent versions of the creation legend.

In the first account, man and woman were created simultaneously.

> **Genesis 1:27**   So God created man in his own image, in the image of God created he him; male and female created he them.

In the second account, a man was created out of dust and named Adam and then later a woman was created from one of his ribs.

> **Genesis 2:21–23**   ²¹And the Lord God caused a deep sleep to fall upon Adam, and he slept; and he took one of his ribs, and closed up the flesh instead thereof. ²²And the rib, which the Lord God had taken from man, made he a woman, and brought her unto the man. ²³And Adam said, This is now bone of my bones, and flesh of my flesh: she shall be called Woman, because she was taken out of man.

But in both renderings of the mythical epic, Jehovah's edict to be fruitful and multiply was obeyed. That command alone has resulted in our present ecological mess with overpopulation ravaging our fragile planet.

> **Genesis 4:1–2**   ¹And Adam knew Eve his wife; and she conceived, and bare Cain, and said, I have gotten a man from the Lord. ²And she again bare his brother Abel. And Abel was a keeper of sheep, but Cain was a tiller of the ground.

The word translated here as "knew" is the Hebrew verb *yada* which, in this context, could best be rendered in modern English as "had sexual relations with." The next passage relating that Cain "knew" his wife is the one from which we can infer incest, for he would have had to cohabit either with his own mother Eve or with one of his unnamed sisters.

> **Genesis 4:17**   And Cain knew his wife; and she conceived, and bare Enoch: and he builded a city, and called the name of the city, after the name of his son, Enoch.

It is only an inference, of course, for it is possible that there existed another couple in the creation fable, but that they were simply omitted from the narrative. Under this hypothesis, Cain would have married one of their daughters.

The fundamentalist explanation is that Jehovah did not see fit to create more than one couple and that the usual eugenic objections to incest simply do not apply here because of the pristine purity of the race at that time.

To be sure, incestuous liaisons were to become quite commonplace throughout the Bible. Moses, the great leader of Israel, was himself a son of incest.

> **Exodus 6:20**   And Amram took him Joch'ebed his father's sister to wife: and she bare him Aaron and Moses: and the years of life of Amram were a hundred and thirty and seven years.

Surely an omnipotent deity could have avoided even the suggestion of incest by including at least two couples in his plan of special creation and thus precluding any speculation about what has since become the strongest universal taboo.

Many Biblical interpreters of the modern school also see sexual overtones in the expulsion of Adam and Eve from Eden. They insist that their original sin was not just in partaking of the forbidden apple but rather the story of forbidden fruit is simply an allegory for sexual intercourse.

Theologians who oppose this theory of sexual original sin make a persuasive case for their argument by stating that if Jehovah had indeed given the edict to be fruitful and multiply, he would hardly have condemned Adam and Eve for obeying his explicit instructions.

At any rate, the fragmentary and ambiguous narrative leaves room for speculation about incest having occurred either on a mother and son basis (Eve and Cain) or on a brother and sister basis (Cain and his sister). It cannot be ruled out as unlikely since other episodes in the Holy Writ reinforce the notion that there's nothing wrong with incest as long as it's kept in the family.

AMNON RAPES HIS SISTER TAMAR

MNON'S INFATUATION WITH HIS HALF-SISTER WAS OF SUCH magnitude that he became physically ill as a result of his amorous ardor. He didn't know exactly how to get to Tamar since she was still a virgin and seeing her privately was very difficult because of the custom of segregating young men and women from one another.

II Samuel 13:1–2   ¹And it came to pass after this, that Ab'salom the son of David had a fair sister, whose name was Tamar; and Amnon the son of David loved her. ²And Amnon was so vexed, that he fell sick for his sister Tamar; for she was a virgin; and Amnon thought it hard for him to do anything to her.

Amnon had a cousin Jonadab who was very crafty and it was his suggestion that if Amnon wanted so badly to see Tamar in private, he should feign sickness and then ask his father David to allow Tamar to minister unto him.

II Samuel 13:3–5   ³But Amnon had a friend, whose name was Jon'adab, the son of Shim'e-ah David's brother: and Jon'adab was a very subtle man. ⁴And he said unto him. Why art thou, being the king's son, lean from day to day? wilt thou not tell me? And Amnon said unto him, I love Tamar, my brother Ab'salom's sister. ⁵And Jon'adab said unto him. Lay thee down on thy bed, and make thyself sick: and when thy father cometh to see thee, say unto him. I pray thee, let my sister Tamar come, and give me meat, and dress the meat in my sight, that I may see it, and eat it at her hand.

Amnon followed Jonadab's advice and his father David granted his request and sent Tamar to wait on him. Amnon sent all the men away from his chamber so that he and Tamar would be alone at last.

II Samuel 13:6–10   ⁶So Amnon lay down, and made himself sick: and when the king was come to see him, Amnon said unto the king, I pray thee, let Tamar my sister come, and make me a couple of cakes in my sight, that I may eat at her hand. ⁷Then David sent home to Tamar, saying, Go now to thy brother Amnon's house; and dress him meat. ⁸So Tamar went to her brother Amnon's house; and he was laid down. And she took flour, and kneaded it, and made cakes in his sight, and did bake the cakes.

⁹And she took a pan, and poured them out before him; but he refused to eat. And Amnon said, Have out all men from me. And they went out every man from him. ¹⁰And Amnon said unto Tamar, Bring the meat into the chamber, that I may eat of thine hand. And Tamar took the cakes which she had made, and brought them into the chamber to Amnon her brother.

When Tamar entered Amnon's bedroom with the food, he asked her to go to bed with him. She refused saying that it was a crime of incest. She then suggested that Amnon speak to David and ask him for her hand in marriage so that there would be no scandal about the affair.

II Samuel 13:11–13

¹¹And when she had brought them unto him to eat, he took hold of her, and said unto her. Come lie with me, my sister. ¹²And she answered him, Nay, my brother, do not force me; for no such thing ought to be done in Israel: do not thou this folly. ¹³And I, whither shall I cause my shame to go? and as for thee, thou shalt be as one of the fools in Israel. Now therefore, I pray thee, speak unto the king: for he will not withhold me from thee.

But Amnon would not listen to reason. He forcibly raped Tamar and then hated her for having refused him, his hatred exceeding the love he had felt for her. Amnon had his servant put Tamar out of his quarters. As Tamar left, she rent her clothes, put ashes on her head and went away weeping.

II Samuel 13:14–19

¹⁴Howbeit he would not hearken unto her voice: but, being stronger than she, forced her, and lay with her. ¹⁵Then Amnon hated her exceedingly; so that the hatred wherewith he hated her was greater than the love wherewith he had loved her. And Amnon said unto her, Arise, be gone. ¹⁶And she said unto him, There is no cause: this evil in sending me away is greater than the other that thou didst unto me. But he would not hearken unto her. ¹⁷Then he called his servant that ministered unto him, and said, Put now this woman out from me, and bolt the door after her. ¹⁸And she had a garment of divers colors upon her: for with such robes were the king's daughters that were virgins appareled. Then his servant brought her out, and bolted the door after her. ¹⁹And Tamar put ashes on her head, and rent her garment of divers colors that was on her, and laid her hand on her head, and went on crying.

In this narrative, there emerges a hierarchy of sin which will run throughout the entire Bible. In verse 16, Tamar complained more about Amnon's rejection of her afterwards than she did about the actual acts of incest and rape. Her own words to Amnon were: "This evil in sending me away is greater than the other that thou didst unto me."

When Tamar's full-brother Absalom learned of her being violated by Amnon, he tried to console her by saying that since it was all in the family, it was not really such a terrible thing. But David was very upset by what Amnon had done.

Absalom said nothing to Amnon about his violation of Tamar, yet inside himself, he detested Amnon for his nefarious act.

II Samuel 13:20–22   ²⁰And Ab'salom her brother said unto her, Hath Amnon thy brother been with thee? but hold now thy peace, my sister: he is thy brother; regard not this thing. So Tamar remained desolate in her brother Ab'salom's house. ²¹But when king David heard of all these things, he was very wroth. ²²And Ab'salom spake unto his brother Amnon neither good nor bad: for Ab'salom hated Amnon, because he had forced his sister Tamar.

Absalom seethed with rage for two years and finally gave vent to his anger by having Amnon murdered so that Tamar's honor could be avenged.

II Samuel 13:23–29   ²³And it came to pass after two full years, that Ab'salom had sheepshearers in Ba'al-ha'zor, which is beside Ephraim: and Ab'salom invited all the king's sons. ²⁴And Ab'salom came to the king, and said, Behold now, thy servant hath sheepshearers; let the king, I beseech thee, and his servants go with thy servant. ²⁵And the king said to Ab'salom, Nay, my son, let us not all now go, lest we be chargeable unto thee. And he pressed him: howbeit he would not go, but blessed him. ²⁶Then said Ab'salom, If not, I pray thee, let my brother Amnon go with us. And the king said unto him, Why should he go with thee? ²⁷But Ab'salom pressed him, that he let Amnon and all the king's sons go with him. ²⁸Now Ab'salom had commanded his servants, saying, Mark ye now when Amnon's heart is merry with wine, and when I say unto you, Smite Amnon; then kill him, fear not: have not I commanded you? be courageous, and be valiant. ²⁹And the servants of Ab'salom did unto Amnon as Ab'salom had commanded. Then all the king's sons arose, and every man gat him up upon his mule, and fled.

It is a fascinating commentary on human nature that after Absalom's revenge for Amnon's incestuous bond with Tamar, Absalom himself was to be guilty of the same act of incest, except that in his case, it was to be a multiple act of incest against his own father David (see Chapter 4).

When Amnon approached Tamar, he undoubtedly already knew of the legal prohibitions against copulation with his own sister, even though she was only his half-sister. When he first accosted Tamar, she forcefully reminded him that what he was asking of her was against the Hebrew law.

Leviticus 20:17   And if a man shall take his sister, his father's daughter, or his mother's daughter, and see her nakedness, and she see his nakedness; it is a wicked thing; and they shall be cut off in the sight of their people: he hath uncovered his sister's nakedness; he shall bear his iniquity.

Deuteronomy 27:22   Cursed be he that lieth with his sister, the daughter of his father, or the daughter of his mother; and all the people shall say, Amen.

Tamar's suggestion that David might be willing to give her to Amnon in marriage indicates that matrimony between a brother and a sister was not out of the question at this stage in Israel's history. But what remains unclear is whether this was traditional or merely an exception because they were both from a royal family or because they were only half-brother and half-sister.

Lot Knocks Up Both His Daughters

OT'S WIFE APPARENTLY YEARNED FOR WHAT SHE HAD TO LEAVE behind in Sodom (see Chapter 11) and Jehovah's penalty for her looking back as the city of the plain burned was to turn her into a pillar of salt.

Genesis 19:26–29   ²⁶But his wife looked back from behind him, and she became a pillar of salt. ²⁷And Abraham gat up early in the morning to the place where he stood before the Lord: ²⁸and he looked toward Sodom and Gomorrah and toward all the land of the plain, and beheld, and, lo, the smoke of the country went up as the smoke of a furnace. ²⁹And it came to pass, when God destroyed the cities of the plain, that God remembered Abraham, and sent Lot out of the midst of the overthrow, when he overthrew the cities in the which Lot dwelt.

Lot was fearful of the people of Zoar and he and his two daughters headed for the nearby mountains where they decided to live in a cave.

Genesis 19:30   And Lot went up out of Zo'ar and dwelt in the mountain, and his two daughters with him; for he feared to dwell in Zo'ar: and he dwelt in a cave, he and his two daughters.

Because of the fate of their mother, Lot's two daughters were determined that their clan should continue uninterrupted and since their father was seemingly unwilling to let them marry any of the local men, before Lot was too old to father any more progeny, they decided literally to take matters into their own hands. It is also not unlikely that they still harbored some resentment toward their father for having proffered them both to that lustful mob of men clamoring outside of their home in Sodom (see Chapter 11). Had those Sodomites been willing to accept Lot's proposition, it is entirely possible that both of them would have been fatally abused by that lecherous mob. Therefore, Lot's daughters decided to get their father thoroughly soused before screwing him. Maybe the young women were concerned that if their dad was sober, he would not have been able to get it up with his own daughters. So they felt that by pouring wine into him until he got stiff (both figuratively and literally), they would at least solve the problem of temporary impotence.

𝔊enesis 19:31–33 ³¹And the firstborn said unto the younger, Our father is old, and there is not a man in the earth to come in unto us after the manner of all the earth: ³²Come, let us make our father drink wine, and we will lie with him, that we may preserve seed of our father. ³³And they made their father drink wine that night: and the firstborn went in, and lay with her father; and he perceived not when she lay down, nor when she arose.

The following day, the elder daughter suggested that her younger sister repeat the incestuous act and that night, they got Lot drunk once again and this time the younger daughter took her turn lying with her father. In both cases, Lot's drunken stupor was so great that he didn't even realize he was having sexual relations with his daughters.

𝔊enesis 19:34–35 ³⁴And it came to pass on the morrow, that the firstborn said unto the Younger, Behold, I lay yesternight with my father: let us make him drink wine this night also; and go thou in, and lie with him, that we may preserve seed of our father. ³⁵And they made their father drink wine that night also: and the younger arose, and lay with him; and he perceived not when she lay down, nor when she arose.

Both young women became pregnant by their father Lot and their plan to preserve his seed was successful.

𝔊enesis 19:36–38 ³⁶Thus were both the daughters of Lot with child by their father. ³⁷And the firstborn bare a son, and called his name Moab: the same is the father of the Moabites unto this day. ³⁸And the younger, she also bare a son, and called his name Ben-am'mi: the same is the father of the children of Ammon unto this day.

The tale of Lot and his daughters is a favorite topic when I do talk shows, so let me now give you an idea of how a debate usually goes.

Baptist Minister: In your *The X-Rated Bible*, are you saying that the Word of God is as bad as pornographic magazines like *Playboy*, *Penthouse*, and *Forum?*
Akerley: I'm saying that *Playboy*, *Penthouse*, and *Forum* do not claim to be inspired.

Baptist Minister: Oh sure, there's a lot of immorality mentioned in the Scriptures, but God always uses those examples to teach us a moral lesson about what we should *not* do.

Akerley: What about Lot's two daughters getting their father intoxicated and then becoming pregnant by him?

Baptist Minister: They did that because they were the only survivors after God destroyed Sodom and Gomorrah for their perversion and terrible sinfulness.

Akerley: But the account says that they hid in a cave near Zoar because Lot was fearful of the people nearby.

Baptist Minister: Well then his daughters thought they were the only ones left on earth.

Akerley: So why did they have to get Lot drunk? Wouldn't he have understood the wisdom of their plan to repopulate a devastated world?

Baptist Minister: God moves in mysterious ways, his wonders to perform!

Apologists insist that even tales of sexual impropriety in the Good Book serve as a moral lesson. I must confess that I have searched long and hard (very *hard*) for one in this narrative and the only moral imperative that I can detect is that if two daughters want to commit incest with their own father, the older one should get her chance to fuck daddy first!

ABSALOM'S DEFIANT ACT OF MULTIPLE INCEST

 BSALOM HAD JOINED WITH ALL THE MEN OF ISRAEL IN A conspiracy against his father David. When David fled Jerusalem before Absalom's arrival there, he left ten of his concubines (mistresses) to keep the house.

II Samuel 15:16   And the king went forth, and all his household after him. And the king left ten women, which were concubines, to keep the house.

When Absalom arrived in Jerusalem, he fornicated with the ten concubines in a special tent constructed on the roof of the palace so that all Israel would be aware of what he was doing. His act of multiple incest was the ultimate symbol of his utter disdain for David's authority.

Of course, this had all been predicted by the prophet Nathan and Absalom was merely fulfilling the prophetic vision which Nathan had already shared with David prior to Absalom's birth (see Chapter 18).

Absalom's fulfillment of the prophecy provided all Israel with an opportunity to become voyeurs while watching the royal philanderer "hard" at work.

II Samuel 16:15–23   [15]And Ab'salom, and all the people the men of Israel, came to Jerusalem, and Ahith'ophel with him. [16]And it came to pass, when Hu'shai the Archite, David's friend, was come unto Ab'salom that Hu'shai said unto Ab'salom, God save the king, God save the king. [17]And Ab'salom said to Hu'shai, Is this thy kindness to thy friend? why wentest thou not with thy friend? [18]And Hu'shai said unto Ab'salom, Nay; but whom the Lord, and this people, and all the men of Israel, choose, his will I be, and with him will I abide. [19]And again, whom should I serve? should I not serve in the presence of his son? as I have served in thy father's presence, so will I be in thy presence. [20]Then said Ab'salom to Ahith'ophel, Give counsel among you what we shall do. [21]And Ahith'ophel said unto Ab'salom, Go in unto thy father's concubines, which he hath left to keep the house; and all Israel shall hear that thou art abhorred of thy father: then shall the hands of all that are with thee be strong. [22]So they spread Ab'salom a tent upon the top of the house; and Ab'salom went in unto his father's concubines in the sight of all Israel. [23]And the counsel of Ahith'ophel, which he counseled in those days, was as if a man had inquired at the oracle of God: so was all the counsel of Ahith'ophel both with David and with Ab'salom.

After David's return to Jerusalem, he virtually disowned these ten concubines who had slept with Absalom. He made them prisoners in their own house and never had sexual relations with them again. They remained prisoners of David until their deaths, for by imposing this sexual quarantine, the king regained some of the honor he had lost through Absalom's shameful actions.

II Samuel 20:3   And David came to his house at Jerusalem; and the king took the ten women his concubines, whom, he had left to keep the house, and put them in ward, and fed them, but went not in unto them. So they were shut up unto the day of their death, living in widowhood.

Despite Absalom's rebellion and estrangement from his father, David still loved him deeply. Absalom met his demise when he caught his head in a tree branch as he was riding along on a mule and was murdered by Joab who plunged three daggers into Absalom's heart while he dangled from the tree. To make sure that the job was complete, the ten armor-bearers who accompanied Absalom also stabbed him (II Samuel 18:9–15). Upon learning of Absalom's death, David was overcome with uncontrollable grief and mourned greatly for his slain son.

Part II
SEXUAL POLLUTION

Onan's Fatal Orgasm

R. Ruth Westheimer, the sex therapist and TV and radio personality, reports that one of her patients named his pet bird Onan because he was always spilling his seed. The inspiration for that amusing anecdote is the subject of this chapter.

Genesis 38:1–10 ¹And it came to pass at that time, that Judah went down from his brethren, and turned in to a certain Adul'lamite, whose name was Hirah. ²And Judah saw there a daughter of a certain Canaanite, whose name was Shu'ah; and he took her, and went in unto her. ³And she conceived, and bare a son; and he called his name Er. ⁴And she conceived again, and bare a son; and she called his name Onan. ⁵And she yet again conceived, and bare a son; and called his name Shelah: and he was at Chezib, when she bare him. ⁶And Judah took a wife for Er his firstborn, whose name was Tamar. ⁷And Er, Judah's firstborn, was wicked in the sight of the Lord; and the Lord slew him. ⁸And Judah said unto Onan, Go in unto thy brother's wife and marry her, and raise up seed to thy brother. ⁹And Onan knew that the seed should not be his; and it came to pass, when he went in unto his brother's wife, that he spilled it on the ground, lest that he should give seed to his brother. ¹⁰And the thing which he did displeased the Lord: wherefore he slew him also.

One of the most familiar of erotic Scriptural stories is that of Onan. The term "onanism" has suffered a fate similar to that of the term "sodomy" in the sense that it has evolved to have a meaning far different from its original usage (see Chapter 11). Although there is no contextual justification whatever to interpret Onan's deed as being one of sexual self-gratification, the term "onanism" is universally used as a synonym for masturbation.

I will recap the facts of the story just to set the record straight: Judah and his wife had a son, Er, who found disfavor in Jehovah's sight and was killed by Jehovah for his wickedness. Er had two younger brothers, Onan and Shelah. According to the levirate law, it was Onan's obligation as the next older brother to sire a child with Er's widow Tamar for Er had died leaving her childless.

The term "levirate" derives from the Latin word *levir* which means "husband's brother." The law reads as follows:

Deuteronomy 25:5–10 ⁵If brethren dwell together, and one of them die, and have no child, the wife of the dead shall not marry without unto a stranger: her husband's brother shall go in unto her, and take her to him to wife, and perform the duty of a husband's brother unto her. ⁶And it shall be that the firstborn which she beareth shall succeed in the name of his brother which is dead that his name be not put out of Israel. ⁷And if the man like not to take his brother's wife, then let his brother's wife go up to the gate unto the elders, and say, My husband's brother refuseth to raise up unto his brother a name in Israel, he will not perform the duty of my husband's brother. ⁸Then the elders of his city shall call him, and speak unto him: and if he stand to it, and say, I like not to take her; ⁹then shall his brother's wife come unto him in the presence of the elders, and loose his shoe from off his foot, and spit in his face, and shall answer and say, So shall it be done unto that man that will not build up his brother's house. ¹⁰And his name shall be called in Israel, The house of him that hath his shoe loosed.

Since Onan apparently didn't like the idea of being a surrogate for his recently slain brother or of fathering a child that would never be his, when he was engaging in coitus with Tamar, he withdrew from her vagina and ejaculated his semen on the ground. For this act of defiance, Jehovah slew Onan as well. But the divine execution was because of disobedience, not because of any sexual impropriety.

This tale represents the only example of birth control that one can unearth in the Bible and it significantly represents one of the least reliable methods known, next to the rhythm method. With modern knowledge of sexual anatomy and physiology, it is evident that Tamar's failure to conceive was more probably due to it having been the wrong time of month than to Onan's pulling out in time.

In an average ejaculation, there are hundreds of millions of sperm cells. On the head of a straight pin, it is possible to collect 3,000 or more sperm. Obviously, if it takes only one sperm to fertilize the female ovum, the simple act of withdrawal or *coitus interruptus* does not always accomplish avoidance of pregnancy.

First of all, the male secretes a lubricant prior to ejaculation and this pre-ejaculate may and often does contain some sperm so that by the time he withdraws, it is already too late. Secondly, it is a common practice to withdraw just as ejaculation begins so that only the entire emission is not deposited inside the vagina. The greatest concentration of sperm is in the very first drops of semen to be discharged and simply withdrawing before the completion of ejaculation is inadequate to prevent thousands of sperm from starting on their very rapid journey toward the uterus. Viewed in this light, Tamar's failure to get pregnant probably was due much more to pure luck than to Onan's technical prowess.

Just think of the trauma poor Tamar must have suffered! As Onan was about to climax, she noticed his eyes rolling around and naturally thought that he was coming, but alas he was going!

Why fundamentalists insist that this passage indicates that Onan withdrew and then masturbated himself to the point of ejaculation is difficult to explain except on the basis of there being no other definite reference to withdrawal or to masturbation in all of the Holy Writ. Literalists hold that any sex act which deliberately frustrates the procreative urge must be a sin. Since both *coitus interruptus* and masturbation are non-procreative sex techniques, they must be sinful indeed—so much so that Onan paid for his sin with his very life.

St. Thomas Aquinas went so far as to consider masturbation as more evil than forcible rape. His reasoning was that even though forcible rape might cause injury to another person, it could still result in procreation and therefore could not be *peccatum contra naturam* (a crime against nature) whereas masturbation was definitely against nature since it could never result in procreation. Aquinas no doubt had this text in mind when he wrote in the thirteenth century that "right reason declares the appointed end of sexual acts in procreation."

In all fairness, it should be pointed out that at least one Roman Catholic scholar does not take this extreme view and distort the meaning of the Onan incident. Canon A. de Smet, writing in his book *Betrothment and Marriage* had this comment about Onan:

> From the text and context, however, it would seem that the blame of the sacred writer applies directly to the wrongful frustration of the law of the levirate, intended by Onan, rather than the spilling of the seed.

In the New Testament, Christ was queried about the levirate and it is noteworthy that he in no way indicated that it had been abrogated or superseded—he merely used the occasion to assert that there would be no marriage or sex in heaven. Upon first learning of this celestial state of sexlessness, I for one lost absolutely all interest in the hereafter and life eternal.

Matthew 22:23–30 [23]The same day came to him the Sadducees, which say that there is no resurrection, and asked him, [24]saying, Master, Moses said, If a man die, having no children, his brother shall marry his wife, and raise up seed unto his brother. [25]Now there were with us seven brethren; and the first, when he had married a wife, deceased, and, having no issue, left his wife unto his brother: [26]likewise the second also, and the third, unto the seventh. [27]And last of all the woman died also. [28]Therefore in the resurrection, whose wife shall she be of the seven? for they all had her. [29]Jesus answered and said unto them, Ye do err, not knowing the Scriptures, nor the power of God. [30]For in the resurrection they neither marry, nor are given in marriage, but are as the angels of God in heaven.

The levirate was highly specific with respect to a brother's obligation to raise up seed to his dead brother. Just as specific was the law forbidding a brother from impregnating his brother's wife if her husband was still living. The punishment was sterility for all such liaisons.

Leviticus 20:21   And if a man shall take his brother's wife, it is an unclean thing: he hath uncovered his brother's nakedness; they shall be childless.

But with sterility guaranteed any man who impregnated his sister-in-law, this might be interpreted as an inducement to take advantage of the situation since without the risk of pregnancy, no one would ever know unless the couple was actually caught *in flagrante delicto!*

As a recurring theme in the Bible, the primitive Hebrew mind was convinced that Jehovah offered or withheld fertility according to the mood of the day. This superstition made the Israelites easy prey for the fertility religions which surrounded them with their alluring enticements of wild orgies, temple prostitution and phallic imagery and idols glorifying both the male and female reproductive organs.

Wearing the Rag

HE HEBREWS WERE AS PRIMITIVE AS THE TRIBES WHICH surrounded them when it came to a belief in animism—that is, that blood is the very source of life. This was the basis for the prohibition of eating any flesh which still contained the blood of the dead animal.

> **Leviticus 17:14**   For it is the life of all flesh; the blood of it is for the life thereof: therefore I said unto the children of Israel, Ye shall eat the blood of no manner of flesh; for the life of all flesh is the blood thereof: whosoever eateth it shall be cut off.

After Cain's fratricide of Abel, Jehovah spoke to Cain and remarked that Abel's blood was crying from the ground to accuse him of his brother's murder.

> **Genesis 4:9–11**   ⁹And the Lord said unto Cain, Where is Abel thy brother? And he said, I know not: Am I my brother's keeper? ¹⁰And he said, What hast thou done? the voice of thy brother's blood crieth unto me from the ground. ¹¹And now art thou cursed from the earth, which hath opened her mouth to receive thy brother's blood from thy hand.

Jehovah's direct revelations to Israel as his chosen people did not seem to diminish in the slightest their naive animistic beliefs. To them, the blood had special, magical powers since it literally contained the life force.

It was inevitable, then, that the ceremonial purification for a menstruating woman would be a most elaborate one. It was precisely for this reason that it would have been unthinkable for a woman to be a priest—her monthly uncleanness precluded that she even worship regularly, for it was impossible for her to enter the sanctuary during her monthly menstrual period.

> **Leviticus 15:19–23**   ¹⁹And if a woman have an issue, and her issue in her flesh be blood, she shall be put apart seven days: and whosoever toucheth her shall be unclean until the even. ²⁰And every thing that she lieth upon in her separation shall be unclean: every thing also that she sitteth upon shall be unclean. ²¹And whosoever toucheth her bed shall wash his clothes, and bathe himself in water, and be unclean until the even. ²²And whosoever toucheth any thing that she sat upon shall wash his clothes, and bathe

himself in water, and be unclean until the even. ²³And if it be on her bed, or on any thing whereon she sitteth, when he toucheth it, he shall be unclean until the even.

Leviticus 15:25–28 ²⁵And if a woman have an issue of her blood many days out of the time of her separation, or if it run beyond the time of her separation; all the days of the issue of her uncleanness shall be as the days of her separation: she shall be unclean. ²⁶Every bed whereon she lieth all the days of her issue shall be unto her as the bed of her separation: and whatsoever she sitteth upon shall be unclean, as the uncleanness of her separation. ²⁷And whosoever toucheth those things shall be unclean, and shall wash his clothes, and bathe himself in water, and be unclean until the even. ²⁸But if she be cleansed of her issue, then she shall number to herself seven days, and after that she shall be clean.

A man having intercourse with a menstruating woman would, of course, be contaminated according to the primitive Hebrew view. He was to avoid this defilement at all costs.

Leviticus 18:19 Also thou shalt not approach unto a woman to uncover her nakedness, as long as she is put apart for her uncleanness.

This prohibition demanded the death penalty for any couple engaging in coitus during the monthly menstrual flow.

Leviticus 20:18 And if a man shall lie with a woman having her sickness, and shall uncover her nakedness; he hath discovered her fountain, and she hath uncovered the fountain of her blood: and both of them shall be cut off from among their people.

Since the death penalty was demanded for adultery, bestiality, fornication, loss of virginity and homosexuality, it should come as no surprise that it was also exacted for intercourse during menstruation.

Some apologists argue that the penalty of being "cut off from among their people" was nothing stronger than excommunication. A leading Biblical commentator has this to say: "Exile or death was the punishment decreed for sexual relations during menstruation." (Rev. William Graham Cole in *Sex and Love in the Bible*, p. 280.) Another authority who states that the "Levitical law imposes capital punishment on both the man and the woman who commit this sin" is Raphael Patai in *Sex and Family in the Bible and the Middle East*, p. 153.

In another verse, the only penalty for sex during menstruation was a week's ceremonial defilement which of course was easily removed by ritual purification rites.

The Tabooed Woman
(She's having her period!)

Leviticus 15:24

And if any man lie with her at all, and her flowers be upon him, he shall be unclean seven days; and all the bed whereon he lieth shall be unclean.

Since Bible chronology almost never corresponds to the order of the Scriptural account, it is uncertain whether capital punishment came first and was softened later on or whether the ceremonial defilement eventually evolved into a capital offense.

In the book of Ezekiel, a passage suggests that not all Israelites abstained from intercourse during menstruation. The prophet delineates the characteristics of a just man and among them (Ezekiel 18:6) is his praise for anyone who has not "come near to a menstruous woman." It can also be deduced from the passage that by this much later time in Israel's history, the taboo had weakened to the point that sex during a woman's period was quite commonplace. This statement would fortify the position that capital punishment for menstrual sex preceded the mere observance of ceremonial purging.

When the menstruating woman finished her week's purification rites subsequent to the end of her period, she was to come to the priest with both a burnt offering and a sin offering as atonement for her uncleanness. Since the requirements for a woman in childbirth were similar, I shall explore the "sin" aspect of both menstruation and childbirth in Chapter 10.

Leviticus 15:29–30   [29]And on the eighth day she shall take

unto her two turtles, or two young pigeons, and bring them unto the priest, to the door of the tabernacle of the congregation. [30]And the priest shall offer the one for a sin offering and the other for a burnt offering; and the priest shall make an atonement for her before the Lord for the issue of her uncleanness.

Even the Talmud refers to the taboo associated with a menstruating woman and the dread in which she is held while in that condition. It relates that when a woman meets a snake on the road, it is enough for her to say, "I am menstruating," and the reptile will glide hastily away. According to the Talmud, if a woman at the beginning of her period passes between two men, she will cause one of them to die; if she passes between them near the end of her period, she only causes them to quarrel violently.

Another text reveals that the Israelites had the equivalent of Kotex and tampons and that "wearing the rag" was associated with real filth.

> Isaiah 30:22   Ye shall defile also the covering of thy graven images of silver, and the ornament of thy molten images of gold: thou shalt cast them away as a menstruous cloth; thou shalt say unto it, Get thee hence.

That we have not really come a very long way since the time of the Israelites and that we are still inclined to view menstruation as a period of contagion and contamination is evidenced in a revealing article from the September, 1973, issue of *Psychology Today*. The article is entitled "Women Learn to Sing the Menstrual Blues" and in it, author Karen E. Paige analyzes the feelings women experience during menstruation according to the profile of our three major religious groups: Protestants, Catholics and Jews.

She found that Jewish women who think that sex during menstruation is unenjoyable and embarrassing and who follow a variety of social and hygienic rituals during their periods are those most likely to have severe menstrual problems, both physical and emotional.

Catholic women were more likely to consider menstrual distress as an integral part of their traditional female role and this meant that those women who believe most strongly that a woman's place is in the home and who have no personal career ambitions are the most likely to have severe menstrual difficulties.

Protestants were more difficult to categorize since they represent more heterogeneous backgrounds, but in general, they shared with Jewish and Catholic women the tendency to suffer from menstrual problems in direct ratio to their religiosity, and to their view of traditional femininity. What Protestant women didn't share with their Jewish and Catholic sisters was the strong taboo against sexual relations during menstruation.

In the case of Catholic women, the Church merely urges abstinence during a woman's period, but among Orthodox Jews, women are supposed to abstain from sex during their entire period as well as during seven full days thereafter. They must enter the *mikvah*, a ritual purification bath, which certifies that they are "clean" again and able to return to their regular duties and to engage in intercourse with their husbands once more.

The author summarizes her excellent article by stating: "The United States does not relegate menstruating women to special huts, but we have our share of superstitions, and the implicit belief lingers that the menstruating woman is unclean."

She could have added that the death penalty is no longer exacted for any couple engaging in intercourse during the menstrual period and that this does represent a degree of progress.

DOING THE NASTY

Leviticus 15:18   The woman also with whom man shall lie with seed of copulation, they shall both bathe themselves in water, and be unclean until the even.

There is no mention in the Hebrew law that a conjugal sex act rendered a married couple unclean. Therefore, the above text is highly enigmatic and controversial, for it is not clear whether it refers to extra-conjugal acts or to the conjugal act as well as to any pre-marital or extra-marital intercourse.

At any rate, the important point here is that it was not the sex act in itself which caused the defilement, but rather the seminal discharge which naturally involved both partners.

We will see in other quotations that any object which was touched by a seminal discharge became unclean. It logically followed that the female partner in the sex act became corrupted by virtue of contact with semen.

It is but a step, however, from thinking of the seminal discharge as being unclean to thinking of the sex act itself as being contaminating and this view has undoubtedly had a disastrous impact resulting in the baleful anti-sexual bias of the Judeo-Christian tradition with its legacy of shame and guilt.

Another text which supports the view of Leviticus 15:18 as being an indication that all sex acts were defiling, even those between spouses, is the text in which Moses enjoined the Israelites not to engage in sexual intercourse for three days since Jehovah was going to make a personal appearance in their midst and this was a condition of their preparing themselves for this manifestation. Moses had just rendezvoused with Jehovah on Mount Sinai and these words were his first injunction to the Israelites upon descending from his personal confrontation with the mountaintop tribal deity.

> **Exodus 19:14–15**   ¹⁴And Moses went down from the mount unto the people, and sanctified the people; and they washed their clothes. ¹⁵And he said unto the people, Be ready against the third day: come not at *your* wives.

At least in this instance, there was a modicum of sexual equality among the Israelites, for if they indulged in sex during menstruation, it was the woman who contaminated the man. Conversely, in the above exhortation, it was now the man who contaminated the woman by polluting her with his semen.

WET DREAMS AND WANKING (SPANKING THE MONKEY)

ECAUSE OF ISRAEL'S SUPERSTITIOUS BELIEF IN BOTH ANIMISM and in blood pollution, it naturally followed that they viewed menstruation in a negative and unfavorable light. This does not satisfactorily explain, however, why they also viewed semen itself as being contaminating except that, like menstrual blood, it was a bodily discharge that defiled everything with which it came in contact. But in the case of semen, the defilement lasted only one day. In the following quote, "a man whose seed goeth from him" could refer either to semen discharged during masturbation or during a nocturnal emission.

> **Leviticus 22:4–7**   ⁴And whoso toucheth any thing that is unclean by the dead, or a man whose seed goeth from him; ⁵or whosoever toucheth any creeping thing, whereby he may be made unclean, or a man of whom he may take uncleanness, whatsoever uncleanness he hath; ⁶the soul which hath touched any such shall be unclean until even, and shall not eat of the holy things, unless he wash his flesh with water. ⁷And when the sun is down, he shall be clean, and shall afterward eat of the holy things; because it is his food.

The most conclusive text on masturbation is the following, for when it speaks of garments being contaminated by semen, it is clear that the author is not referring to intercourse. Once again, of course, it could be a reference to a nocturnal emission, provided that the sleeping male had his clothes on!

> ℒeviticus 15:16–17   ¹⁶And if any man's seed of copulation go out from him then he shall wash all his flesh in water, and be unclean until the even. ¹⁷And every garment, and every skin, whereon is the seed of copulation, shall be washed with water, and be unclean until the even.

Still another possible reference to masturbation is found in II Samuel 3:29 where David pronounced a curse on Joab because he was infuriated at his unruly commander. The Revised Standard Version translates the verse: "May the house of Joab never be without one who has a discharge, or who is leprous, or who holds a spindle." A major Biblical scholar and translator, R. H. Pfeiffer, translates the latter phrase in *The Hebrew Iliad* as "masturbator." Current British slang would say "wanker."

The following reference could only refer to a "wet dream" because of the quaint wording that the seminal loss of the man "chanceth him by night."

> Deuteronomy 23:10–11   ¹⁰If there be among you any man, that is not clean by reason of uncleanness that chanceth him by night, then shall he go abroad out of the camp, he shall not come within the camp: ¹¹but it shall be, when evening cometh on, he shall wash himself with water: and when the sun is down, he shall come into the camp again.

There are really only two ways to view the fact that a seminal discharge, whether voluntary or involuntary, caused pollution for only one day vis-à-vis a menstrual discharge which caused pollution for seven days beyond its termination: (1) The Hebrews viewed menstrual blood as being more taboo than semen or (2) The Hebrews were practical people above all and from a purely economic vantage point, men simply could not spend as much time engaging in purification rites as did women.

In either instance, they were ill-prepared to deal with the secretions of nature and had to concoct elaborate rites to decontaminate themselves from what they viewed as a defiling substance although it is the very source of life itself.

We should not overlook the possibility that all of the foregoing texts could also refer to premature ejaculation. Psychotherapists contend that it is the most frequent sexual disorder which they treat in the male and it is not unlikely that it was a frequent sexual dysfunction among Hebrew men also.

The Clap and Other STDs

HE TERM "VENEREAL" DERIVES FROM VENUS, THE GODDESS OF love. Popular misconception holds that venereal disease was virtually unknown until Columbus discovered America, at which time he also discovered VD. But there are sufficient references to VD in the Bible to dispel that myth.

I have previously mentioned the curse which David pronounced upon Joab (see Chapter 8). The first part of the curse declares: "Let there not fail from the house of Joab one that hath an issue." (II Samuel 3:29) R. H. Pfeiffer translates this in *The Hebrew Iliad* as "one ill with gonorrhea." It is impossible to conjecture what else it would be.

Two probable references to gonorrhea are found in Leviticus where the ceremony is virtually identical to the ritual for menstruation.

> *Leviticus* 15:1–15 ¹And the Lord spake unto Moses and to Aaron, saying, ²Speak unto the children of Israel, and say unto them, When any man hath a running issue out of his flesh, because of his issue he is unclean. ³And this shall be his uncleanness in his issue: whether his flesh run with his issue, or his flesh be stopped from his issue, it is his uncleanness. ⁴Every bed, whereon he lieth that hath the issue, is unclean: and every thing, whereon he sitteth shall be unclean. ⁵And whosoever toucheth his bed shall wash his clothes, and bathe himself in water, and be unclean until the even. ⁶And he that sitteth on any thing whereon he sat that hath the issue shall wash his clothes, and bathe himself in water, and be unclean until the even. ⁷And he that toucheth the flesh of him that hath the issue shall wash his clothes, and bathe himself in water, and be unclean until the even. ⁸And if he that hath the issue spit upon him that is clean: then he shall wash his clothes, and bathe himself in water, and be unclean until the even. ⁹And what saddle soever he rideth upon that hath the issue shall be unclean. ¹⁰And whosoever toucheth any thing that was under him shall be unclean until the even: and he that beareth any of those things shall wash his clothes,

and bathe himself in water, and be unclean until the even. [11]And whomsoever he toucheth that hath the issue, and hath not rinsed his hands in water, he shall wash his clothes, and bathe himself in water, and be unclean until the even. [12]And the vessel of earth, that he toucheth which hath the issue, shall be broken: and every vessel of wood shall be rinsed in water. [13]And when he that hath an issue is cleansed of his issue, then he shall number to himself seven days for his cleansing, and wash his clothes, and bathe his flesh in running water, and shall be clean. [14]And on the eighth day he shall take to him two turtledoves, or two young pigeons, and come before the Lord unto the door of the tabernacle of the congregation, and give them unto the priest: [15]and the priest shall offer them, the one for a sin offering, and the other for a burnt offering; and the priest shall make an atonement for him before the Lord for his issue.

Leviticus 22:4   What man soever of the seed of Aaron is a leper, or hath a running issue; he shall not eat of the holy things, until he be clean.

A fairly certain reference to syphilis can be found in the story of Miriam, the sister of Moses and Aaron. Jehovah was angry with Miriam and struck her with a curse of leprosy. Aaron implored Moses to intercede on her behalf: "Let her not be as one dead, of whom the flesh is half consumed when he cometh out of his mother's womb." (Numbers 12:12) R. R. Willcox wrote an article for the *British Journal of Venereal Diseases* and interpreted this verse to refer to a case of a stillbirth due to macerated syphilis.

Some Bible exegetes interpret a stanza from the Psalms as indicative that David suffered from a venereal infection which was probably syphilis. It must be borne in mind that "loins" is a euphemism for "genitals" and that this choice of words makes a strong case for venereal disease.

Psalms 38:3–8   [3]There is no soundness in my flesh because of thine anger; neither is there any rest in my bones because of my sin. [4]For mine iniquities are gone over mine head: as a heavy burden they are too heavy for me. [5]My wounds stink and are corrupt because of my foolishness. [6]I am troubled; I am bowed down greatly; I go mourning all the day long. [7]For my loins are filled with a loathsome disease: and there is no soundness in my flesh. [8]I am feeble and sore broken: I have roared by reason of the disquietness of my heart.

In the New Testament, Matthew 9:20, Luke 8:43 and Mark 5:26 all refer to Christ healing a woman "who had had a flow of blood for twelve years." Although this could refer to an abnormal menstrual flow, it could also have been a venereal infection which had not been diagnosed and treated properly since Mark reveals that she "had suffered much under many physicians." The legend is retold with emphasis on Christ not turning her away or objecting to her touching him to effect her "miraculous" cure.

EVE'S CURSE FULFILLED

EHOVAH HAD PROMISED THAT MOTHERHOOD WOULD BE A trying experience because of the curse pronounced on Eve.

Genesis 3:16   Unto the woman he said, I will greatly multiply thy sorrow and thy conception; in sorrow thou shalt bring forth children; and thy desire shall be to thy husband, and he shall rule over thee.

The Psalmist adopted the view that all are conceived and born in sin.

Psalms 51:3–5   ³For I acknowledge my transgressions: and my sin is ever before me. ⁴Against thee, thee only, have I sinned, and done this evil in thy sight: that thou mightest be justified when thou speakest, and be clear when thou judgest. ⁵Behold, I was shapen in iniquity; and in sin did my mother conceive me.

It is not unusual, therefore, to learn that maternity constituted a form of contamination with specific instructions for ceremonial purification.

Leviticus 12:1–8   ¹And the Lord spake unto Moses, saying, ²Speak unto the children of Israel, saying, If a woman have conceived seed, and borne a man child, then she shall be unclean seven days; according to the days of the separation for her infirmity shall she be unclean. ³And in the eighth day the flesh of his foreskin shall be circumcised. ⁴And she shall then continue in the blood of her purifying three and thirty days; she shall touch no hallowed thing, nor come into the sanctuary, until the days of her purifying be fulfilled. ⁵But if she bear a maid child, then she shall be unclean two weeks, as in her separation: and she shall continue in the blood of her purifying threescore and six days. ⁶And when the days of her purifying are fulfilled, for a son, or for a daughter, she shall bring a lamb of the first year for a burnt offering, and a young pigeon, or a turtledove, for a sin offering, unto the door of the tabernacle of the congregation unto the priest: ⁷who shall offer it before the Lord, and make an atonement for her; and she shall be cleansed from the issue of her blood. This is the law for her that hath borne a male or a female. ⁸And if she be not able to bring a lamb, then she shall bring two turtles, or two young pigeons: the one for the burnt offering, and the other for a sin offering: and the priest shall make an atonement for her, and she shall be clean.

What is unusual about this Hebrew law is the marked difference between the contamination produced by female and male babies. If a Hebrew mother gave birth to a female child, her period of defilement was exactly double that of giving birth to a male. Some Bible commentators interpret this as merely a prejudice of a patriarchal society where males were always more important.

At least one writer, Joseph Lewis, has a different opinion. In his book, *In the Name of Humanity*, Lewis expounds the novel view that because a male Hebrew infant was circumcised on the eighth day after his birth, this sacrificial act of circumcision automatically reduced the time required for the mother's ceremonial purification and cut in half her obligations under the law.

In summary then, if a Hebrew mother produced a female child, she was unclean for eighty days; if she produced a male child, she was only unclean for forty days. Intercourse during this period would have been unthinkable so that a father was left in the anomalous position of being happier to have a son than a daughter, but having to abstain from sex with his wife twice as long each time a daughter was born!

While it is relatively easy to comprehend the primitive conception of the contaminating aspect of menstrual blood and even of semen, it is not so easy to understand why giving birth, in itself, should contaminate.

Some Bible students have suggested that the contaminating aspect of birth was not the parturition per se, but rather the defilement caused by fluid from the amniotic sac which ruptures during the childbirth process. This flow then, like the menstrual or seminal flow, was another bodily discharge which the Hebrew saw as polluting both the mother and the infant.

Notwithstanding the corrupting nature of the afterbirth, at least one Biblical admonition says that in time of great famine, it is permissible for the mother to eat both the afterbirth and the newborn child.

>𝔇euteronomy 28:56–57 ⁵⁶The tender and delicate woman among you, which would not adventure to set the sole of her foot upon the ground for delicateness and tenderness, her eye shall be evil toward the husband of her bosom, and toward her son, and toward her daughter, ⁵⁷And toward her young one that cometh out from between her feet, and toward her children which she shall bear: for she shall eat them for want of all things secretly in the siege and straitness, wherewith thine enemy shall distress thee in thy gates.

At this point, we must consider the "sin" aspect of both menstruation and of motherhood, since Hebrew women were adjured to make a sin offering unto Jehovah for both "offenses." This harkens back to the curse pronounced on Eve and the whole concept of original sin. It is difficult to accept the fundamentalist dogma that Jehovah would create woman with a menstrual cycle and give her the responsibility of childbearing only to condemn both acts as sinful. The result of this teaching, of course, has been to regard sex as a necessary evil, which concept culminated in outrageous *pronunciamentos* by theologians who either should have known better or simply shut up about the matter.

Jerome, who translated the Latin version of the Bible known as the Vulgate, would not permit couples to partake of the Eucharist in Holy Communion unless they had refrained from the "beastly" act of intercourse for several days. He even went so far as to declare that "he who too ardently loves his own wife is an adulterer." So obsessed was he with sex as evil that he fled to the desert to be closer to God, yet unable to escape from sexual fantasies, he wrote:

> I fancied myself amongst bevies of dancing maidens. My face was pale and my frame chilled with fasting; yet my mind was burning with the cravings of desire, and the fires of lust that flared up from my flesh was as that of a corpse. So helpless, I used to lie at the feet of Christ, watering them with my tears, wiping them with my hair, struggling to subdue my rebellious flesh with seven days' fasting.

Like other church fathers, Jerome was convinced that Jehovah had originally intended for humans to propagate the planet in "angelic fashion," but they never clarified just what this angelic technique would have been like. They speculated that Jehovah had foreseen the Fall and had given Adam and Eve their genitals because they would eventually become "animals."

St. Augustine saw sex as sordid even when it was for procreation. He lamented that we have to come into this world "between the urine and the feces." He also conjectured that if Adam and Eve had not fallen into disfavor with Jehovah, the human race would probably have reproduced itself by some "clean" method similar to plant pollination.

The nadir of this negative view of sex was reached by the early church fathers who advised conti-

Blood Atonement

nence on Thursday in remembrance of Christ's arrest; on Friday out of respect for the crucifixion; on Saturday to honor the Virgin Mother; on Sunday in regard for the resurrection and on Monday out of deference to souls who have departed. Although this left Tuesday and Wednesday for marriage partners to satisfy their "base instincts," some of the church fathers even forbade sex during all holy days and holy seasons. With such a myriad of prohibitions and regulations, we can see just how powerful was the legacy of the Judeo-Christian sexual, or more accurately, anti-sexual tradition.

The Italian theologian Peter Lombard pontificated with a straight face that the Holy Spirit left the bedroom of a couple engaging in sex even if their purpose was the "legitimate" one of producing offspring. Subsequently, the idea gained currency that any type of sexual enjoyment "causes sorrow to the Holy Virgin."

Even Martin Luther succumbed to this extreme anti-sexual bias and stated characteristically: "It is impossible to pray upon the marriage bed. It is impossible to have spiritual feelings about what you do with your wife in bed." Although he was never able to escape from the feeling that sex was basically a "brute-like" quality, he assured his followers that God "winks" at marital intercourse. When asked how often he felt spouses could legitimately copulate, Luther replied that about twice a week would be permissible. Thus we have the great reformer to thank for the too-long-held concept that intercourse twice a week is "normal" for everyone.

In order to couch his twice-a-week prescription for sexual indulgence in more memorable terms, reformer Martin Luther composed a brief poem:

A week two
Is the woman's due.
Harms neither me nor you.
Make in a year, twice fifty-two.

And while to some such a declaration by Luther might seem perfectly innocuous, the degree to which the "normalcy" factor has been incorporated into our sexual mores can be most dramatically demonstrated by an actual legal case discovered by sex researcher Alfred Kinsey in his background work on sexual behavior in the human female. The usually staid and undemonstrative Kinsey had to stifle the tears when he came across a situation in which the Minnesota Supreme Court in 1943 upheld the commitment as a sexual psychopath of a 42-year-old father of six who "was mentally bright, capable, and a good worker," because of his uncontrollable craving for sexual intercourse with his wife, amounting in the year before his commitment to approximately three or four times a week!

Part III
HOMOSEXUALITY

Lot Thwarts a Gay Mob Assault in Sodom

I T IS A CURIOUS FACT OF ETYMOLOGY THAT THE TERM "SODOMY," which originated as a highly specific description of homosexual anal intercourse, has evolved to mean so many other different things. Our archaic statute books throughout the United States repeatedly refer to homosexual oral sodomy, sodomy with animals, and to both heterosexual oral and anal sodomy.

This is how it all began: Abraham's nephew Lot went to live in Sodom. Because of the great wickedness of the inhabitants of Sodom, Jehovah revealed to Abraham that he was going to destroy this city of the plain together with her sister city of Gomorrah. Abraham entreated Jehovah to spare Sodom, but to no avail. Jehovah was willing to spare the life of Lot and his family, however, and as our story opens, two angel messengers have just arrived in Sodom and Lot has invited them to stay at his home.

> **Genesis 19:1–3** ¹And there came two angels to Sodom at even; and Lot sat in the gate of Sodom: and Lot seeing them rose up to meet them; and he bowed himself with his face toward the ground; ²and he said, Behold now, my lords, turn in, I pray you, into your servant's house, and tarry all night, and wash your feet, and ye shall rise up early, and go on your ways. And they said Nay; but we will abide in the street all night. ³And he pressed upon them greatly; and they turned in unto him, and entered into his house; and he made them a feast, and did bake unleavened bread, and they did eat.

The lustful men of the city had noticed the two strangers in their midst and they went to Lot's home to seek them out so that they could use them for their own sexual gratification. In verse 5, we encounter the Hebrew verb *yada* once again, but here the best translation would be: "Bring them out unto us so that we may rape them."

> **Genesis 19:4–5** ⁴But before they lay down, the men of the city, even the men of Sodom, compassed the house round, both old and young, all the people from every quarter: ⁵and they called unto Lot, and said unto him, Where are the men which came in to thee this night? bring them out unto us, that we may know them.

Lot was horrified at the suggestion of sexual liberties being taken with men who were guests under his roof and he forthright offered to give his two virgin daughters to the mob to do with what they wanted. He was obviously much more concerned about his male guests' rear ends than his own daughters' front ends.

I HAVE TWO DAUGHTERS WHICH HAVE NOT KNOWN MEN

Genesis 19:6–8

⁶And Lot went out at the door unto them, and shut the door after him, ⁷and said, I pray you, brethren, do not so wickedly. ⁸Behold now, I have two daughters which have not known man; let me, I pray you, bring them out unto you, and do ye to them as is good in your eyes: only unto these men do nothing; for therefore came they under the shadow of my roof.

The Sodomites were resentful of Lot, a relative newcomer to the area, setting himself up as their judge and they lunged at him and attempted to break down the door of his house.

Genesis 19:9

And they said, Stand back. And they said again, This one fellow came in to sojourn, and he will needs be a judge: now will we deal worse with thee, than with them. And they pressed sore upon the man, even Lot, and came near to break the door.

The angel guests pulled Lot inside, bolted the door and struck all of the Sodomite mob with blindness.

Genesis 19:10–11

¹⁰But the men put forth their hand, and pulled Lot into the house to them, and shut to the door. ¹¹And they smote the men that were at the door of the house with

blindness, both small and great: so that they wearied themselves to find the door.

The angels then warned Lot of the impending doom of the city and instructed him to flee with all his family.

Genesis 19:12–14   [12]And the men said unto Lot, Hast thou here any besides? son-in-law, and thy sons, and thy daughters, and whatsoever thou hast in the city, bring them out of this place: [13]for we will destroy this place, because the cry of them is waxen great before the face of the Lord; and the Lord hath sent us to destroy it. [14]And Lot went out, and spake unto his sons-in-law, which married his daughters, and said, Up, get you out of this place; for the Lord will destroy this city. But he seemed as one that mocked unto his sons-in-law.

The next morning, Lot and his family fled from Sodom and headed for Zoar.

Genesis 19:18–22   [18]And Lot said unto them, O, not so, my Lord: [19]behold now, thy servant hath found grace in thy sight, and thou hast magnified thy mercy, which thou hast showed unto me in saving my life; and I cannot escape to the mountain, lest some evil take me, and I die: [20]behold now, this city is near to flee unto, and it is a little one: O, let me escape thither, (is it not a little one?) and my soul shall live. [21]And he said unto him, See, I have accepted thee concerning this thing also, that I will not overthrow this city, for the which thou hast spoken. [22]Haste thee, escape thither; for I cannot do any thing till thou be come thither. Therefore the name of the city was called Zo'ar.

As soon as Lot and his family entered Zoar, Jehovah obliterated both Sodom and Gomorrah.

Genesis 19:23–25   [23]The sun was risen upon the earth when Lot entered into Zo'ar. [24]Then the Lord rained upon Sodom and upon Gomorrah brimstone and fire from the Lord out of heaven; [25]and he overthrew those cities, and all the plain, and all the inhabitants of the cities, and that which grew upon the ground.

Somewhat in defense of what appears as a heinous act on the part of Lot in offering both his virgin daughters to this sensual mob, it should be noted that Lot must have taken his responsibilities of Near Eastern hospitality so seriously that he did not hesitate to do anything to protect his guests. That he undoubtedly would have done the same thing for ordinary human visitors is borne out by the similar account in Judges 19 (see Chapter 16), but he surely felt his obligation to be even greater with divine house guests who were personal emissaries of Jehovah. And, of course, as *paterfamilias*, he was able to exercise unlimited and unquestioned authority over the life and death of his progeny.

When the two angel-messengers at first declined Lot's invitation to spend the night under his roof, they no doubt were following the same Near Eastern protocol which demanded polite refusal of an offer of hospitality, compelling the host to insist on acceptance of his offer.

Some interpreters have declared that the real sin of the Sodom story was simple inhospitality and that like the story of Onan, reading anything more into it is pure speculation. This issue is settled at least partially by a New Testament writer named Jude. In his epistle, the writer indicates that the annihilation of Sodom and Gomorrah was due to their general and not just to their deviant sexual practices. However, if Jehovah obliterated the two cities of the plain strictly for their gay indulgences, it strikes me as more than a bit sadistic that any god would create male humans with an anus that is an exquisitely sensitive and extremely responsive erogenous zone (another design defect?) and then turn around and cremate them for butt fucking.

Jude 6–7 ⁶And the angels which kept not their first estate, but left their own habitation, he hath reserved in everlasting chains under darkness unto the judgment of the great day. ⁷Even as Sodom and Gomorrah, and the cities about them in like manner, giving themselves over to fornication, and going after strange flesh, are set forth for an example, suffering the vengeance of eternal fire.

Nonetheless, the literalness with which all fundamentalists and many others interpret this story of Lot is evidenced by an incident at a California legislative session as recent as 1973. When a law was being considered that would legalize all consensual sex acts between adults, an elderly Pasadena solon who happened also to be a devout fundamentalist arose to address the floor and proudly proclaimed in the climax to his appeal to reject the proposed law: "Our capital is Sacramento—not Sodom and Gomorrah!"

Much to the chagrin of this legislator and others of his ilk, California finally passed the consensual sex law in 1975 and to this day, both San Francisco and Los Angeles, the contemporary equivalents of Sodom and Gomorrah, are thriving without divine interference.

DAVID'S QUESTIONABLE LOVE AFFAIR WITH JONATHAN

UCH HAS BEEN MADE OF THE INNUENDO OF HOMOSEXUALITY in the love felt between David and Jonathan. One theologian who refuses to see any basis for suspecting a gay love affair between the two also condemns any interpretation to the contrary. William Graham Cole writes in *Sex and Love in the Bible:* "Some have seen . . . a suggestion of homosexual relations between David and Jonathan. . . . They buttress their arguments by citing [several verses]. These few verses, however, are very flimsy hooks on which to hang such a theory. The suspicion is strong that this interpretation comes from those whose own angle of vision finds homosexuality in every possible area." (pp. 383–384.)

Well, so much for the theological argument. Let us examine the verses which are the most implicating and let you, the reader, arrive at your own conclusion.

The first quote indicates an unusually strong bond between the two men and relates an infatuation which we today would probably call "love at first sight." If in real life David even remotely resembled the magnificent statue of him sculpted by Michelangelo, we who ardently admire the male physique can readily empathize with Jonathan's infatuation.

> **I Samuel 18:1–5** ¹And it came to pass, when he had made an end of speaking unto Saul, that the soul of Jonathan was knit with the soul of David, and Jonathan loved him as his own soul. ²And Saul took him that day, and would let him go no more home to his father's house. ³Then Jonathan and David made a covenant, because he loved him as his own soul. ⁴And Jonathan stripped himself of the robe that was upon him and gave it to David, and his garments, even to his sword, and to his bow, and to his girdle. ⁵And David went out whithersoever Saul sent him, and behaved himself wisely: and Saul set him over the men of war, and he was accepted in the sight of all the people, and also in the sight of Saul's servants.

The second passage divulges that Jonathan so loved David that he jeopardized his own standing with his father Saul in order to save the life of his "lover."

I **Samuel** 19:1–7   ¹And Saul spake to Jonathan his son, and to all his servants, that they should kill David. ²But Jonathan Saul's son delighted much in David: and Jonathan told David, saying, Saul my father seeketh to kill thee: now therefore, I pray thee, take heed to thyself until the morning, and abide in a secret place, and hide thyself: ³And I will go out and stand beside my father in the field where thou art, and I will commune with my father of thee; and what I see, that I will tell thee. ⁴And Jonathan spake good of David unto Saul his father, and said unto him, Let not the king sin against his servant, against David; because he hath not sinned against thee, and because his works have been to thee-ward very good: ⁵For he did put his life in his hand, and slew the Philistine, and the Lord wrought a great salvation for all Israel: thou sawest it, and didst rejoice: wherefore then wilt thou sin against innocent blood, to slay David without a cause? ⁶And Saul hearkened unto the voice of Jonathan: and Saul sware, As the Lord liveth, he shall not be slain. ⁷And Jonathan called David, and Jonathan shewed him all those things. And Jonathan brought David to Saul, and he was in his presence, as in times past.

The third excerpt recounts that Jonathan could not eat because of his distress over Saul's plan to kill his beloved David—he was lovesick. And it retells a scene in which they kissed and cried together until David ran out of tears in the arms of his idolized companion.

I **Samuel** 20:31–42   ³¹For as long as the son of Jesse liveth upon the ground, thou shalt not be established, nor thy kingdom. Wherefore now send and fetch him unto me, for he shall surely die. ³²And Jonathan answered Saul his father, and said unto him, Wherefore shall he be slain? what hath he done? ³³And Saul cast a javelin at him to smite him: whereby Jonathan knew that it was determined of his father to slay David. ³⁴So Jonathan arose from the table in fierce anger, and did eat no meat the second day of the month: for he was grieved for David, because his father had done him shame. ³⁵And it came to pass in the morning, that Jonathan went out into the field at the time appointed with

David, and a little lad with him. ³⁶And he said unto his lad, Run, find out now the arrows which I shoot. And as the lad ran, he shot an arrow beyond him. ³⁷And when the lad was come to the place of the arrow which Jonathan had shot, Jonathan cried after the lad, and said, Is not the arrow beyond thee? ³⁸And Jonathan cried after the lad, Make speed, haste, stay not. And Jonathan's lad gathered up the arrows, and came to his master. ³⁹But the lad knew not any thing: only Jonathan and David knew the matter. ⁴⁰And Jonathan gave his artillery unto his lad, and said unto him, Go, carry them to the City. ⁴¹And as soon as the lad was gone, David arose out of a place toward the south, and fell on his face to the ground, and bowed himself three times: and they kissed one another, and wept one with another, until David exceeded. ⁴²And Jonathan said to David, Go in peace, forasmuch as we have sworn both of us in the name of the Lord, saying, The Lord be between me and thee, and between my seed and thy seed for ever. And he arose and departed: and Jonathan went into the city.

Probably the most revealing statement about the true nature of this passionate relationship is in the reaction of Saul when he learned of Jonathan's attraction for David, for when Saul cursed Jonathan by saying that he had shamed his mother by his actions, he was making as strong an accusation as he could make under the circumstances.

> **I Samuel 20:30**   Then Saul's anger was kindled against Jonathan, and he said unto him, Thou son of the perverse rebellious woman, do not I know that thou hast chosen the son of Jesse to thine own confusion, and unto the confusion of thy mother's nakedness?

Perhaps David's own comment about this affair will shed the most light on the subject. These are David's own words lamenting the death of his dearest comrade:

> **II Samuel 1:25–26**   ²⁵How are the mighty fallen in the midst of the battle! O Jonathan, thou wast slain in thine high places. ²⁶I am distressed for thee, my brother Jonathan: very pleasant hast thou been unto me: thy love to me was wonderful, passing the love of women.

In his *Sex in the Bible*, Rev. Tom Horner says of David and Jonathan's affair: "They were essentially bisexual men." Maybe that's all that needs to be said.

THE LOVE THAT DARES NOT SPEAK ITS NAME

HAT MUST UNDOUBTEDLY BE THE LONGEST EUPHEMISM IN THE English language is the Victorian paraphrase used to refer to homosexuality: "the love that dares not speak its name." Ever since the Stonewall Riot of 1969 and the advent of Gay Lib, some cynics now call it "the love that won't shut up!"

The Bible was much more direct in speaking of this universally practiced sexual variation. Paul had the most lengthy comment to make about it in his letter to the Church at Rome.

> ℜomans 1:18–27 [18]For the wrath of God is revealed from heaven against all ungodliness and unrighteousness of men, who hold the truth in unrighteousness; [19]Because that which may be known of God is manifest in them; for God hath shewed it unto them. [20]For the invisible things of him from the creation of the world are clearly seen, being understood by the things that are made, even his eternal power and Godhead; so that they are without excuse: [21]Because that, when they knew God, they glorified him not as God, neither were thankful; but became vain in their imaginations, and their foolish heart was darkened. [22]Professing themselves to be wise, they became fools. [23]And changed the glory of the uncorruptible God into an image made like to corruptible man, and to birds, and fourfooted beasts, and creeping things. [24]Wherefore God also gave them up to uncleanness, through the lusts of their own hearts, to dishonor their own bodies between themselves: [25]Who changed the truth of God into a lie, and worshipped and served the creature more than the Creator, who is blessed for ever. Amen. [26]For this cause God gave them up unto vile affections: for even their women did change the natural use into that which is against nature: [27]And likewise also the men, leaving the natural use of the woman, burned in their just one toward another; men with men working that which is unseemly, and receiving in themselves that recompense of their error which was meet.

Paul wrote again, this time to the Church at Corinth, and expressed his conviction that homosexuals were among those whose perversity in following a hedonistic life made their salvation quite hopeless.

I Corinthians 6:9–11 ⁹Know ye not that the unrighteous shall not inherit the kingdom of God? Be not deceived: neither fornicators, nor idolaters, nor adulterers, nor effeminate, nor abusers of themselves with mankind, ¹⁰Nor thieves, nor covetous, nor drunkards, nor revilers, nor extortioners, shall inherit the kingdom of God. ¹¹And such were some of you: but ye are washed, but ye are sanctified, but ye are justified in the name of the Lord Jesus, and by the Spirit of our God.

And in a letter to Timothy, Paul made it quite clear that homosexuals were lawbreakers in the same class with thieves and murderers.

I Timothy 1:8–11 ⁸But we know that the law is good, if a man use it lawfully; ⁹Knowing this, that the law is not made for a righteous man, but for the lawless and disobedient, for the ungodly and for sinners, for unholy and profane, for murderers of father and murderers of mothers, for manslayers, ¹⁰For whoremongers, for them that defile themselves with mankind, for menstealers, for liars, for perjured persons, and if there be any other thing that is contrary to sound doctrine; ¹¹According to the glorious gospel of the blessed God, which was committed to my trust.

Paul, of course, was simply carrying on the anti-gay tradition which had been his legacy from the Old Testament writings and the Hebrew law.

Leviticus 18:22 Thou shalt not lie with mankind, as with womankind: it is abomination.

Leviticus 20:13 If a man also lie with mankind, as he lieth with a woman, both of them have committed an abomination: they shall surely be put to death; their blood shall be upon them.

The primitive Hebrew mind saw male and female as such clear-cut, disparate entities that it was unthinkable that either sex should even don the apparel of the opposite sex.

Deuteronomy 22:5 The woman shall not wear that which pertaineth unto a man, neither shall a man put on a woman's garment: for all that do so are abomination unto the Lord thy God.

As we shall see in Chapter 28, many texts quoted to indicate a strong anti-gay bias in the Hebrew psyche really do not refer to homosexuality per se, but rather the omnipresent cult prostitution which abounded in the Fertile Crescent.

Some have suggested that the male cult prostitute served female clients only, but since the reference to them is constantly as "dogs," which is a synonym for "sodomites," we can be sure that if they did service the female worshippers, they serviced the males as well. In the last book of the Bible, John includes among those "excluded" from the Heavenly City the "dogs," which is to say "sodomites."

Revelation 22:14–15 [14]Blessed are they that do his commandments, that they may have right to the tree of life, and may enter in through the gates into the city. [15]For without are dogs, and sorcerers, and whoremongers, and murderers, and idolaters, and whosoever loveth and maketh a lie.

That there was a demand for both sacred and secular male prostitutes is further evidenced by a remarkable passage from one of the prophets in which we have a case of a harlot being exchanged for a boy prostitute.

Joel 3:1–3 [1]For, behold, in those days, and in that time, when I shall bring again the captivity of Judah and Jerusalem, [2]I will also gather all nations, and will bring them down into the valley of Jehosh'-a-phat, and will plead with them there for my people and for my heritage Israel, whom they have scattered among the nations, and parted my land. [3]And they have cast lots for my people; and have given a boy for an harlot, and sold a girl for wine, that they might drink.

A serious question which begs an answer is just what the Bible means by "homosexual" since there is really no equivalent in Hebrew or Greek for our English term. In *The Church and the Homosexual*, Jesuit author Father John J. McNeill puts it this way:

> It can . . . be argued (1) that what is referred to, especially in the
> New Testament, under the rubric of homosexuality is not the
> same reality at all or (2) that the Biblical authors do not manifest
> the same understanding of that reality as we have today. Further,
> it can be seriously questioned whether what is understood today as
> the true homosexual and his or her activity is ever the object of
> explicit moral condemnation in Scripture.

To be sure, it can reasonably be argued that there were no prohibitions against female homosexuality in the Old Testament and that this very omission indicates that the Hebrew aversion to homosexuality was based on their fierce, competitive struggle with other nomadic tribes and that this struggle required all sexual activity to be directed toward procreation.

However, when we arrive at Paul's New Testament pronouncements, he classified male and female homosexuality under the same rubric of "unnatural affection" and in his reference in Romans to female homosexuality, calls it "that which is against nature," an epithet which was to find its way into our many American law statute books as a generic term for all homosexual acts as being "the crime against nature." We did not really have a clear understanding of unnatural sex until sex researcher Alfred Kinsey provided the ultimate scientific definition: "An unnatural sex act is a sex act which would be impossible to perform."

With all of this as background, then, it is of compelling interest to examine a recent work which suggests that Christ was very possibly inclined toward homosexuality. The book would not have received much notice except that it was written by an eminent Biblical scholar, Dr. Morton Smith, an Episcopalian priest and professor of history at Columbia University.

Smith spent fourteen arduous years in painstaking, soul-searching background research. He unearthed a copy of a letter attributed to Clement of Alexandria, a Greek theologian who died about 215 A.D. The document quotes two passages from a supposedly secret gospel composed by Mark in Alexandria after the death of Peter and intended only for the eyes of those being initiated into the inner mysteries of Christianity as a fledgling religion.

Smith's book is entitled *The Secret Gospel: The Discovery and Interpretation of The Secret Gospel According to Mark* and its publication in 1973 touched off an immediate ecclesiastical storm of controversy.

The passage which leads Smith to his conclusions of Christ's homophile proclivities is the following:

And they come in Bethany, and a certain woman, whose brother had died, was there. And, coming, she prostrated herself before Jesus and says to him, "Son of David have mercy on me." But the disciples rebuked her. And Jesus being angered, went off with her into the garden where the tomb was, and straightaway a great cry was heard from the tomb. And going near Jesus rolled away the stone from the door of the tomb.

And straightway going in where the youth was, he stretched forth his hand and raised him seizing his hand. But the youth, looking upon him, loved him and began to beseech him that he might be with him.

And going out of the tomb they came into the house of the youth, for he was rich. And after six days Jesus told him what to do and in the evening the youth comes to Him, wearing a linen cloth over [his] naked [body]. And he remained with Him that night, for Jesus taught him the mystery of the kingdom of God. And thence, arising, he returned to the other side of the Jordan.

In the secret gospel, Christ emerges as a teacher and practitioner of forbidden occult practices with strong erotic overtones. It would, of course, be the bitterest of ironies if Smith is correct in suggesting that Christ himself indulged in sexual practices which have been condemned in his name for nearly 2,000 years.

Part IV
RAPE: SOLO AND GROUP

Reuben Rapes His Father's Mistress

Genesis 35:22 And it came to pass, when Israel dwelt in that land, that Reuben went and lay with Bilhah his father's concubine: and Israel heard it.

It is somewhat difficult to comprehend why Reuben was so severely condemned for having sex with Bilhah. In the miasma that is Bible morality, perhaps the denouncement came because Reuben chose to lie with Bilhah, who was Rachel's servant, rather than with Zilpah, who was the servant of his own real mother Leah!

At any rate, Jacob was greatly affronted by Reuben's incestuous action and openly reproached him before all of his brothers. Reuben was the firstborn son, and Jacob's disenchantment was especially poignant in view of it having been his eldest son who betrayed him.

Genesis 49:1–4 ¹And Jacob called unto his sons, and said, Gather yourselves together, that I may tell you that which shall befall you in the last days. ²Gather yourselves together, and hear, ye sons of Jacob; and hearken unto Israel your father. ³Reuben, thou art my firstborn, my might, and the beginning of my strength, the excellency of dignity, and the excellency of power: ⁴unstable as water, thou shalt not excel; because thou wentest up to thy father's bed; then defiledst thou it: he went up to my couch.

Reuben was fortunate indeed to get off with nothing more than a public reprimand from Jacob. According to the Hebrew law, he was liable for the death penalty for his rebellion against his father.

Exodus 21:15–17 ¹⁵And he that smiteth his father, or his mother, shall be surely put to death. ¹⁶And he that stealeth a man, and selleth him, or if he be found in his hand, he shall surely be put to death. And he that curseth his father, or his mother, shall surely be put to death.

Leviticus 20:9 For every one that curseth his father or his mother shall be surely put to death: he hath cursed his father or his mother; his blood shall be upon him.

Deuteronomy 21:18–21   ¹⁸If a man have a stubborn and rebellious son, which will not obey the voice of his father, or the voice of his mother, and that, when they have chastened him, will not hearken unto them: ¹⁹then shall his father and his mother lay hold on him, and bring him out unto the elders of his city, and unto the gate of his place; ²⁰and they shall say unto the elders of his city, This our son is stubborn and rebellious, he will not obey our voice; he is a glutton, and a drunkard. ²¹And all the men of his city shall stone him with stones, that he die: so shalt thou put evil away from among you; and all Israel shall hear, and fear.

That the death penalty was even extended to a rebellious son reflects the deeply superstitious belief of the Hebrews in the inherent power of words. Consequently, they believed that neither a blessing nor a curse, once stated, could ever be retracted and it therefore became an eternal pronouncement.

Quite apart from the filial irreverence and disobedience which Reuben's act of incest constituted, he was also guilty of breaking the Hebrew law and he could hardly have been unaware of it. The law was specific and enunciated frequently in the Old Testament canon.

Leviticus 20:11   And the man that lieth with his father's wife hath uncovered his father's nakedness: both of them shall surely be put to death; their blood shall be upon them.

Deuteronomy 22:30   A man shall not take his father's wife, nor discover his father's skirt.

Deuteronomy 27:20   Cursed be he that lieth with his father's wife; because he uncovereth his father's skirt: and all the people shall say, Amen.

SHECHEM, THE RAPIST, LOSES HIS FORESKIN AND HIS LIFE

INAH WAS JACOB'S ONLY DAUGHTER. SHECHEM, A MEMBER OF the heathen tribe of the Hivites, desired Dinah for a bed partner and raped her. He fell madly in love with her after raping her and asked his father Hamor to get Dinah for him as his wife.

Genesis 34:1–4   ¹And Dinah the daughter of Le'ah, which she bare unto Jacob, went out to see the daughters of the land. ²And when Shechem the son of Hamor the Hivite, prince of the country, saw her, he took her, and lay with her, and defiled her. ³And his soul clave unto Dinah the daughter of Jacob, and he loved the damsel, and spake kindly unto the damsel. ⁴And Shechem spake unto his father Hamor, saying, Get me this damsel to wife.

Shechem's father Hamor conferred with Jacob and asked him for Dinah's hand in marriage to his son, hoping thereby to effect a union between the two families.

Genesis 34:5–12   ⁵And Jacob heard that he had defiled Dinah his daughter: now his sons were with his cattle in the field: and Jacob held his peace until they were come. ⁶And Hamor the father of Shechem went out unto Jacob to commune with him. ⁷And the sons of Jacob came out of the field when they heard it: and the men were grieved, and they were very wroth, because he had wrought folly in Israel in lying with Jacob's daughter; which thing ought not to be done. ⁸And Hamor communed with them, saying, The soul of my son Shechem longeth for your daughter: I pray you give her him to wife. ⁹And make ye marriages with us, and give your daughters unto us, and take our daughters unto you. ¹⁰And ye shall dwell with us: and the land shall be before you; dwell and trade ye therein, and get you possessions therein. ¹¹And Shechem said unto her father and unto her brethren, Let me find grace in your eyes, and what ye shall say unto me I will give. ¹²Ask me never so much dowry and gift, and I will give according as ye shall say unto me: but give me the damsel to wife.

Jacob's sons were resentful of their sister's rape and they lied to the Hivites by telling them that the marriage was out of the question unless the Hivites would agree to be circumcised, thus making possible a bond of free intermarriage between the two families.

Genesis 34:13–17   ¹³And the sons of Jacob answered Shechem and Hamor his father deceitfully, and said, because he had defiled Dinah their sister: ¹⁴And they said unto them, We cannot do this thing, to give our sister to one that is uncircumcised; for that were a reproach unto us: ¹⁵but in this will we consent unto you: If ye will be as we be, that every male of you be circumcised; ¹⁶Then will we give our daughters unto you, and we will take your daughters to us, and we will dwell with you, and we will become one people. ¹⁷But if ye will not hearken unto us, to be circumcised; then will we take our daughter, and we will be gone.

Hamor and Shechem were pleased with the offer and they persuaded all of their fellow Hivites to submit to the operation in order to cement the bond between the two groups.

Genesis 34:18–24

¹⁸And their words pleased Hamor and Shechem Hamor's son. ¹⁹And the young man deferred not to do the thing, because he had delight in Jacob's daughter: and he was more honorable than all the house of his father. ²⁰And Hamor and Shechem his son came unto the gate of their city, and communed with the men of their city, saying, ²¹These men are peaceable with us; therefore let them dwell in the land, and trade therein; for the land, behold, it is large enough for them; let us take their daughters to us for wives, and let us give them our daughters. ²²Only herein will the men consent unto us for to dwell with us, to be one people, if every male among us be circumcised, as they are circumcised. ²³Shall not their cattle and their substance and every beast of theirs be ours? only let us consent unto them, and they will dwell with us. ²⁴And unto Hamor and unto Shechem his son hearkened all that went out of the gate of his city; and every male was circumcised, all that went out of the gate of his city.

The Israelites knew full well that three days after adult males were circumcised, they would be suffering with a high fever and a very inflamed penis. As a result, on the third day after the circumcision had been performed on all the Hivites, Simeon and Levi entered the Hivite camp, and taking advantage of their severely infirm condition, slew all of the men including Hamor and Shechem. True to Hebrew tradition, they captured all of the women and children and appropriated the cattle and wealth of the Hivites declaring that they were thus avenging the rape of their sister Dinah.

Genesis 34:25–31

²⁵And it came to pass on the third day, when they were sore, that two of the sons of Jacob, Simeon and Levi, Dinah's brethren, took each man his sword, and came upon the city boldly, and slew all the males. ²⁶And they slew Hamor and Shechem

his son with the edge of the sword, and took Dinah out of Shechem's house, and went out. ²⁷The sons of Jacob came upon the slain, and spoiled the city, because they had defiled their sister. ²⁸They took their sheep, and their oxen, and their asses, and that which was in the city, and that which was in the field, ²⁹And all their

AND THEIR WIVES TOOK THEM CAPTIVE

wealth, and all their little ones, and their wives took they captive, and spoiled even all that was in the house. ³⁰And Jacob said to Simeon and Levi, Ye have troubled me to make me to stink among the inhabitants of the land, among the Canaanites, and the Per'izzites: and I being few in number, they shall gather themselves together against me, and slay me; and I shall be destroyed, I and my house. ³¹And they said, Should he deal with our sister as with a harlot?

Shechem had made a sincere offer to marry Dinah and thus demonstrated his willingness to comply with the Israelite law. The law declared that if a man violated a young woman who was already betrothed, he then merited death. If, however, the young woman whom he had violated was not already betrothed at the time of her deflowering, he could escape any punishment by paying fifty shekels of silver and marrying her.

Exodus 22:16–17 ¹⁶And if a man entice a maid that is not betrothed, and lie with her, he shall surely endow her to be his wife. ¹⁷If her father utterly refuse to give her unto him, he shall pay money according to the dowry of virgins.

Deuteronomy 22:28–29 ²⁸If a man find a damsel that is a virgin, which is not betrothed, and lay hold on her, and lie with her, and they be found; ²⁹Then the man that lay with her shall give unto the damsel's father fifty shekels of silver, and she shall be his wife; because he hath humbled her, he may not put her away all his days.

According to this law, the only thing Shechem would have been forfeiting besides his money was his right ever to divorce Dinah.

The whole tale takes on even more sadistic overtones if one stops to reflect that <u>circumcision for an adult male is extremely painful, especially so when it</u> <u>is performed without the benefit of anesthesia and with nothing comparable</u> <u>to our efficient scalpel</u>. The usual instruments referred to in the Bible are <u>sharp knives or sharp stones and it was truly an unconscionable act for Jacob's</u> sons to make the Shechemites submit to this ordeal when they knew that they were going to slay all of them anyway.

THE ALL NIGHT GANG BANG

 CERTAIN LEVITE ACQUIRED A CONCUBINE WHO LATER PROVED to be unfaithful. She returned to her father's house in Bethlehem and after she had been gone four months, the Levite went after her in order to try to win her back. The woman's father kept the Levite there for three days. But on the fourth day, the Levite attempted to leave with his concubine-wife.

Judges 19:1–4 ¹And it came to pass in those days, when there *was* no king in Israel, that there was a certain Levite sojourning on the side of mount Ephraim, who took to him a concubine out of Bethlehem-judah, ²And his concubine played the whore against him, and went away from him unto her father's house to Bethlehem-judah, and was there four whole months. ³And her husband arose, and went after her, to speak friendly unto her, and to bring her again, having his servant with him, and a couple of asses: and she brought him into her father's house; and when the father of the damsel saw him, he rejoiced to meet him. ⁴And his father-in-law, the damsel's father, retained him; and he abode with him three days: so they did eat and drink, and lodged there.

The father-in-law persuaded the Levite to remain still another day.

Judges 19:5–7 ⁵And it came to pass on the fourth day, when they arose early in the morning, that he rose up to depart: and the damsel's father said unto his son-in-law, Comfort thine heart with a morsel of bread, and afterward go your way. ⁶And they sat down and did eat and drink both of them together: for the damsel's father had said unto the man, Be content, I pray thee, and tarry all night, and let thine heart be merry. ⁷And when the man rose up to depart, his father-in-law urged him: therefore he lodged there again.

On the fifth day, the father-in-law again attempted to induce the Levite to stay still another night, but this time he went on his way with his concubine-wife and his servant. They journeyed as far as Jebus but decided against spending the night there since it was not a city of Israel. They therefore continued on to Gibeah, a city of the tribe of Benjamin.

Upon their arrival in Gibeah, they were without lodging since no one invited them to spend the night in the comfort of a home.

Judges 19:8–15 ⁸And he arose early in the morning on the fifth day to depart: and the damsel's father said, Comfort thine heart, I pray thee. And they tarried until afternoon, and they did eat both of them. ⁹And when the man rose up to depart, he, and his concubine, and his servant, his father-in-law, the damsel's father, said unto him, Behold, now the day draweth toward evening, I pray you tarry all night: behold, the day groweth to an end, lodge here, that thine heart may be merry; and tomorrow get you early on your way, that thou mayest go home. ¹⁰But the man would not tarry that night, but he rose up and departed, and came over against Jebus, which is Jerusalem; and there were with him two asses saddled, his concubine also was with him. ¹¹And when they were by Jebus, the day was far spent: and the servant said unto his master, Come, I pray thee, and let us turn in into this city of the Jebusites, and lodge in it. ¹²And his master said unto him, We will not turn aside hither into the city of a stranger, that is not of the children of Israel; we will pass over to Gib'e-ah. ¹³And he said unto his servant, Come, and let us draw near to one of these places to lodge all night, in Gib'e-ah, or in Ramah. ¹⁴And they passed on and went their way; and the sun went down upon them when they were by Gib'e-ah, which belongeth to Benjamin. ¹⁵And they turned aside thither, to go in and to lodge in Gib'e-ah: and when he went in, he sat him down in a street of the city: for there was no man that took them into his house to lodging.

Finally, an old man came along and offered them lodging for the night at his home.

> **Judges 19:16–21** ¹⁶And, behold, there came an old man from his work out of the field at even, which *was* also of mount Ephraim; and he sojourned in Gib'e-ah: but the men of the place were Benjamites. ¹⁷And when he had lifted up his eyes, he saw a wayfaring man in the street of the city: and the old man said, Whither goest thou? and whence comest thou? ¹⁸And he said unto him, We are passing from Bethlehem-judah toward the side of mount Ephraim; from thence am I: and I went to Bethlehem-judah, but I am now going to the house of the Lord; and there is no man that receiveth me to house. ¹⁹Yet there is both straw and provender for our asses; and there is bread and wine also for me, and for thy handmaid, and for the young man which is with thy servants: there is no want of any thing. ²⁰And the old man said, Peace be with thee; howsoever, let all thy wants lie upon me; only lodge not in the street. ²¹So he brought him into his house, and gave provender unto the asses: and they washed their feet, and did eat and drink.

As the guests were enjoying themselves at the home of their host, <u>some of the men of the city surrounded the house and beat on the door of the house demanding that the host give them his male guest so that they could rape him.</u>

> **Judges 19:22** Now as they were making their hearts merry, behold, the men of the city, certain sons of Be'li-al, beset the house round about, and beat at the door, and spake to the master of the house, the old man, saying, Bring forth the man that came into thine house, that we may know him.

<u>The master of the house attempted to dissuade them from their lustful assault by offering them his virgin daughter and also the man's concubine-wife</u> for their sexual gratification.

> **Judges 19:23–24** ²³And the man, the master of the house, went out unto them, and said unto them, Nay, my brethren, nay, I pray you, do not so wickedly; seeing that this man is come into mine house, do not this folly. ²⁴Behold, here is my daughter a maiden, and his concubine; them I will bring out now, and humble ye them, and do with them what seemeth good unto you: but unto this man do not so vile a thing.

The men of the city rejected the old man's offer, but when the Levite gave them his concubine-wife in a genuine display of Biblical chivalry, they took her and raped her, abusing her all night. They finally released her at dawn.

TOOK HIS CONCUBINE AND BROUGHT HER FORTH UNTO THEM

Judges 19:25 But the men would not hearken to him: so the man took his concubine, and brought her forth unto them; and they knew her, and abused her all the night until the morning: and when the day began to spring, they let her go.

At daybreak, the concubine fell down at the door of the house. When the Levite discovered her lying there at the door, he commanded her to get up to prepare to leave. She did not respond, however, since she was already dead. He then loaded her body onto his jackass and departed for his home.

Judges 19:26–27 ²⁶Then came the woman in the dawning of the day, and fell down at the door of the man's house where her lord *was,* till it was light. ²⁷And her lord rose up in the morning, and opened the doors of the house, and went out to go his way: and, behold, the woman his concubine was fallen down at the door of the house, and her hands were upon the threshold.

Upon arriving home, the Levite dismembered his wife's body into twelve parts and then sent one part to each of the twelve tribes of Israel to apprise them of what had happened to her at the hands of the Benjaminites of Gibeah.

Judges 19:28–30 ²⁸And he said unto her, Up, and let us be going. But none answered. Then the man took her up upon an ass, and the man rose up, and gat him unto his place. ²⁹And when he was come into his house, he took a knife, and laid hold on his concubine, and divided her, together with her bones, into twelve pieces, and sent her into all the coasts of Israel. [30]And it was so, that all that saw it said, There was no such deed done nor seen from the day that the children of Israel came up out of the land of Egypt unto this day: consider of it, take advice, and speak your minds.

The similarities between this narrative and the story of Lot in Sodom are so great that even some Biblical commentators have been unable to resist the temptation to declare that they are merely two versions of the same event.

This viewpoint overlooks some important considerations, namely the fact that there are significant differences of detail between the two accounts:

1. In the Sodom story, Lot entertained two angels disguised as men who had been sent by Jehovah to warn of the impending doom of the depraved city, whereas in the Gibeah account, the host entertained a Levite, an ordinary human, and his mistress, both of whom happened to be traveling and sought lodging for the night.

2. In the Sodom story, Lot offered both his virgin daughters to the raucous mob to dissuade them from raping his two male guests, whereas in the Gibeah account, the host had only one virgin daughter whom he also offered in place of his male guest.

3. In the Sodom story, the mob of Sodomites showed no interest in Lot's offer of his two daughters, whereas in the Gibeah account, although the mob rejected the offer of the host's single virgin daughter to do with what they pleased, they did accept the offer of the male guest's concubine and proceeded anon to abuse her all night.

4. In the Sodom story, the punishment of the Sodomites was the immediate execration of blindness imposed by the two angels and the eventual annihilation of the entire city by Jehovah, whereas in the Gibeah account, the retaliation was purely human in the form of a bloody battle with Jehovah as overseer. This unbelievably cruel carnage was precipitated by the Levite who cut the corpse of his mistress into twelve pieces and sent each piece to one of the twelve tribes of Israel as evidence of the murderous rape she had suffered at the hands of the Benjaminites (see Chapter 40).

art V
ADULTERY: ATTEMPTED, REAL AND FORGIVEN

Potiphar's Wife Hits on Teen Hunk Joseph

ccording to Genesis 37:2, Joseph was a 17-year-old late adolescent at the time of his being sold into slavery. The Ishmaelites sold Joseph in Egypt to Potiphar, the captain of Pharaoh's guard. Jehovah so favored Joseph in his position that he prospered and found much favor in Potiphar's sight.

> **Genesis 39:1–3**   ¹And Joseph was brought down to Egypt; and Pot'iphar, an officer of Pharaoh, captain of the guard, an Egyptian, bought him of the hands of the Ish'-maelites, which had brought him down thither. ²And the Lord was with Joseph, and he was a prosperous man; and he was in the house of his master the Egyptian. ³And his master saw that the Lord was with him, and that the Lord made all that he did to prosper in his hand.

Potiphar soon promoted Joseph to the position of overseer of his household and Potiphar shared in the blessings which Jehovah rained on Joseph. Verse 6 reveals that Joseph was "well-favored" which means in today's parlance that he was a strikingly handsome young man.

> **Genesis 39:4–6**   ⁴And Joseph found grace in his sight, and he served him: and he made him overseer over his house, and all that he had he put into his hand. ⁵And it came to pass from the time that he had made him overseer in his house, and over all that he had, that the Lord blessed the Egyptian's house for Joseph's sake; and the blessing of the Lord was upon all that he had in the house, and in the field. ⁶And he left all that he had in Joseph's hand: and he knew not ought he had, save the bread which he did eat. And Joseph was a goodly person and well-favored.

Potiphar's wife found the comely lad's youthful charm and innocence irresistible, but she was hardly prepared for Joseph's rejection of her advances.

> **Genesis 39:7–9**   ⁷And it came to pass after these things, that his master's wife cast her eyes upon Joseph; and she said, Lie with me. ⁸But he refused, and said unto his master's wife, Behold, my master wotteth not what is with me in the house, and he hath committed all that he hath to my hand; ⁹there is none greater in this house than I; neither hath he kept back any thing from me but

thee, because thou art his wife: how then can I do this great wickedness, and sin against God?

HE LEFT HIS GARMENT IN HER HAND AND FLED

She was persistent in her attempts to seduce the youth, but Joseph was just as steadfast in refusing to comply.

Genesis 39:10

And it came to pass, as she spake to Joseph day by day, that he hearkened not unto her, to lie by her, or to be with her.

One day Potiphar's wife could restrain herself no longer and she grabbed Joseph by the sleeve of his garment and begged him to fornicate with her. As the attractive youth fled from her presence, his garment tore and Potiphar's wife was left with it in her hand.

Genesis 39:11–12

[11]And it came to pass about this time, that Joseph went into the house to do his business; and there was none of the men of the house there within. [12]And she caught him by his garment, saying, Lie with me: and he left his garment in her hand, and fled, and got him out.

She then called the other men of the household and contrived the story that Joseph had tried to rape her.

Genesis 39:13–15

[13]And it came to pass, when she saw that he had left his garment in her hand, and was fled forth, [14]That she called unto the men of her house, and spake unto them, saying, See, he hath brought in an Hebrew unto us to mock us; he came in unto me to lie with me, and I cried with a loud voice: [15]And it came to pass, when he heard that I lifted up my voice and cried, that he left his garment with me, and fled, and got him out.

She kept Joseph's rent garment so that when Potiphar returned, she was able to relate the story to him and to dramatize her accusation by showing him the torn garment as evidence of Joseph's intended assault.

> **Genesis 39:16–18** [16]And she laid up his garment by her, until his lord came home. [17]And she spake unto him according to these words, saying, The Hebrew servant, which thou hast brought unto us, came in unto me to mock me: [18]And it came to pass, as I lifted up my voice and cried, that he left his garment with me, and fled out.

Potiphar was predictably enraged over Joseph's alleged rape of his wife and he consigned him to Pharaoh's prison for his supposed misconduct.

> **Genesis 39:19–20** [19]And it came to pass, when his master heard the words of his wife, which she spake unto him, saying, After this manner did thy servant to me; that his wrath was kindled. [20]And Joseph's master took him, and put him into the prison, a place where the king's prisoners were bound: and he was there in the prison.

The story has a happy ending since, despite the malevolent scheme of Potiphar's wife, Joseph eventually rose to a position of prominence in Egypt that made him second-in-command to Pharaoh and enabled him to help his family during a period of great famine. For a change, the story of Joseph relates the tale of someone who respected what he considered to be the property of another person!

KING DAVID COMMITS
BOTH ADULTERY AND MURDER

HEN DAVID FIRST SPOTTED BATHSHEBA FROM HIS ROOF AS SHE was taking a bath, he wasted no time in finding out who she was and in having her brought to him so that he could fornicate with her. He was willing to obey the Hebrew law in part— before committing adultery with Bathsheba, he made sure that she had finished her post-menstrual ceremonial purification rites. Only then did he freely engage in the adulterous act with her.

AND FROM THE ROOF HE SAW A WOMAN WASHING HERSELF

II Samuel 11:2–4   [2]And it came to pass in an eveningtide, that David arose from off his bed, and walked upon the roof of the king's house: and from the roof he saw a woman washing herself; and the woman was very beautiful to look upon. [3]And David sent and inquired after the woman. And one said, Is not this Bath-she'ba, the daughter of Eli'am, the wife of Uri'ah the Hittite? [4]And David sent messengers, and took her; and she came in unto him, and he lay with her; for she was purified from her uncleanness: and she returned unto her house.

Bathsheba became pregnant by David and upon hearing this, he arranged for the return from the front lines of Bathsheba's husband Uriah. David inquired of Uriah how the war was progressing and he told him that he was free to spend the night at home. Uriah, however, as a faithful warrior, spent the night instead at the gate of David's palace and therefore foiled David's plan to cover up Bathsheba's pregnancy.

II Samuel 11:5–9   ⁵And the woman conceived, and sent and told David, and said, I am with child. ⁶And David sent to Jo'ab, saying, send me Uri'ah the Hittite. And Joab sent Uri'ah to David. ⁷And when Uri'ah was come unto him, David demanded of him how Jo'ab did, and how the people did, and how the war prospered. ⁸And David said to Uri'ah, Go down to thy house, and wash thy feet. And Uri'ah departed out of the king's house, and there followed him a mess of meat from the king. ⁹But Uri'ah slept at the door of the king's house with all the servants of his lord, and went not down to his house.

When David learned that Uriah had not gone home, he queried him and he explained that he could not in a time of war put his own comfort and pleasure first.

II Samuel 11:10–11   ¹⁰And when they had told David, saying, Uri'ah went not down unto his house, David said unto Uri'ah, Camest thou not from thy journey? Why then didst thou not go down unto thine house? ¹¹And Uri'ah said unto David, The ark, and Israel, and Judah, abide in tents; and my lord Jo'ab, and the servants of my lord, are encamped in the open fields; shall I then go into mine house, to eat and to drink, and to lie with my wife? As thou livest, and as thy soul liveth, I will not do this thing.

David urged Uriah to spend one more day with him and even though David got Uriah plastered that night, he once again stayed at the palace rather than take advantage of the opportunity to spend the night with his wife Bathsheba.

II Samuel 11:12–13   ¹²And David said to Uri'ah, Tarry here today also, and tomorrow I will let thee depart. So Uri'ah abode in Jerusalem that day, and the morrow. ¹³And when David had called him, he did eat and drink before him; and he made him drunk: and at even he went out to lie on his bed with the servants of his lord, but went not down to his house.

The next day, David sent a message to his commander Joab for Uriah to be put in the front lines of battle and Joab executed his command. Uriah then died in battle and the message of his death was immediately transmitted to David so that the monarch knew that his plot had succeeded.

II Samuel 11:14–25   [14]And it came to pass in the morning, that David wrote a letter to Jo'ab, and sent it by the hand of Uri'ah. [15]And he wrote in the letter, saying, Set ye Uri'ah in the forefront of the hottest battle, and retire ye from him, that he may be smitten, and die. [16]And it came to pass, when Jo'ab observed the city, that he assigned Uri'ah unto a place where he knew that valiant men were. [17]And the men of the city went out, and fought with Jo'ab: and there fell some of the people of the servants of David; and Uri'ah the Hittite died also. [18]Then Jo'ab sent and told David all the things concerning the war; [19]and charged the messenger, saying, When thou hast made an end of telling the matters of the war unto the king, [20]and if so be that the king's wrath arise, and he say unto thee, Wherefore approached ye so nigh unto the city when ye did fight? knew ye not that they would shoot from the wall? [21]Who smote Abim'elech the, son of Jerub'besheth? did not a woman cast a piece of a millstone upon him from the wall, that he died in Thebez? why went ye nigh the wall? then say thou, Thy servant Uri'ah the Hittite is dead also.

[22]So the messenger went, and came and showed David all that Jo'ab had sent him for. [23]And the messenger said unto David, Surely the men prevailed against us, and came out unto us into the field, and we were upon them even unto the entering of the gate. [24]And the shooters shot from off the wall upon thy servants; and some of the king's servants be dead, and thy servant Uri'ah the Hittite is dead also. [25]Then David said unto the messenger, Thus shalt thou say unto Jo'ab, Let not this thing displease thee, for the sword devoureth one as well as another: make thy battle more strong against the city, and overthrow it: and encourage thou him.

Upon learning of her husband's demise, Bathsheba observed a suitable period of mourning and then married David and bore him a son.

II Samuel 11:26–27   [26]And when the wife of Uri'ah heard that Uri'ah her husband was dead, she mourned for her husband. [27]And when the mourning was past, David sent and fetched her to his house, and she became his wife, and bare him a son. But the thing that David had done displeased the Lord.

David was unquestionably familiar with the Seventh Commandment of the Decalogue and its prohibition against adultery. It would have been advisable for him to follow the advice that his son, Solomon, was to write far in the future in the Book of Proverbs.

Proverbs 6:20–29   20My son, keep thy father's commandment, and forsake not the law of thy mother: 21bind them continually upon thine heart, and tie them about thy neck. 22When thou goest, it shall lead thee; when thou sleepest, it shall keep thee; and when thou awakest, it shall talk with thee. 23For the commandment is a lamp; and the law is light; and reproofs of instruction are the way of life: 24to keep thee from the evil woman, from the flattery of the tongue of a strange woman. 25Lust not after her beauty in thine heart; neither let her take thee with her eyelids. 26For by means of a whorish woman a man is brought to a piece of bread: and the adulteress will hunt for the precious life. 27Can a man take fire in his bosom, and his clothes not be burned? 28Can one go upon hot coals, and his feet not be burned? 29So he that goeth in to his neighbor's wife; whosoever toucheth her shall not be innocent.

The prophet Nathan severely denounced David for his deplorable act of murder and for his illicit liaison with Bathsheba and he prophesied that Jehovah would punish David for his transgressions by allowing the child he would have by Bathsheba to die.

The child did die, despite David's fasting and prayers of entreaty to Jehovah to spare the child's life. Undaunted, David sired another child by Bathsheba. This son, Solomon, was allowed to live.

But Nathan also promised David that his wives would one day be given to another man who would go to bed with them in public view to shame David before all Israel. David's concupiscence for Bathsheba had been in secret, but the violation of David's wives would be in public. Little could David have guessed that the "man" who would do this ignominious act to him would be his own son, Absalom (see Chapter 4).

II Samuel 12:11–18   11Thus saith the Lord, Behold, I will raise up evil against thee out of thine own house, and I will take thy wives before thine eyes, and give them unto thy neighbor, and he shall lie with thy wives in the sight of this sun. 12For thou didst it secretly: but I will do this thing before all Israel, and before the sun. 13And David said unto Nathan, I have sinned against the Lord. And Nathan said unto David, The Lord also hath put away thy sin; thou shalt not die. 14Howbeit, because by this deed thou hast given great occasion to the enemies of the Lord to blaspheme, the child also that is born unto thee shall surely die. [15]And Nathan departed unto his house. And the Lord struck the child that Uri'ah's wife bare unto David, and it was very sick. [16]David therefore besought God for the child; and David fasted, and went in, and lay all night upon the earth. [17]And the elders of his house arose, and went to him, to raise him up from the earth: but he would not, neither did he eat bread with them. [18]And it came to pass on the seventh day, that the child died.

II Samuel 12:24   And David comforted Bath-she'ba his wife, and went in unto her, and lay with her; and she bare a son, and he called his name Solomon: and the Lord loved him.

One other important point needs clarification here with respect to the story of David's adultery with Bathsheba and murder of Uriah. When David urged Uriah to go in to his wife and spend the night with her, Uriah's reply indicated that it was customary for soldiers of war to refrain from sexual relations when they were involved with fulfilling their military responsibilities.

II Samuel 11:11   And Uri'ah said unto David, The ark, and Israel, and Judah, abide in tents; and my lord Jo'ab, and the servants of my lord, are encamped in the open fields; shall I then go into mine house, to eat and to drink, and to lie with my wife? as thou livest, and as thy soul liveth, I will not do this thing.

Another account which stresses this point even more effectively is that of David's getting holy bread from Ahimelech the priest and being told by Ahimelech that he could not have the bread for his men unless they had been continent. David's reply indicates that it was always the practice to abstain sexually when on military expeditions. Unfortunately, this particular quote is extremely obscure in the King James Version and the quote used here is from the Revised Standard Version of 1952.

I Samuel 21:1–6   [1]Then came David to Nob to Ahimelech the priest; and Ahimelech came to meet David trembling, and said to him, "Why are you alone, and no one with you?" [2]And David said to Ahimelech the priest, "The king has charged me with a matter, and said to me, 'Let no one know anything of the matter about which I send you, and with which I have charged you.' I have made an appointment with the young men for such and such a place. ³Now then, what have you at hand? Give me five loaves of bread, or whatever is here." ⁴And the priest answered David, "I have no common bread at hand, but there is holy bread; if only the young men have kept themselves from women." ⁵And David answered the priest, "Of a truth women have been kept from us as always when I go on an expedition; the vessels of the young men are holy, even when it is a common journey; how much more today will their vessels be holy?" ⁶So the priest gave him the holy bread; for there was no bread there but the bread of the Presence, which is removed from before the Lord, to be replaced by hot bread on the day it is taken away.

Poor Uriah would have been well-advised to follow the advice given earlier about leaving a wife in time of war.

𝔇euteronomy 20:7   And what man is there that hath betrothed a wife, and hath not taken her? let him go and return unto his house, lest he die in the battle, and another man take her.

In their sexual naivete, the Israelites no doubt thought that by refraining from sexual indulgence, they would have more strength to devote to their duties. This myth dies hard, for even today, in both college and professional athletics, coaches frequently insist that team members be continent before a game. The myth seemingly continues because of a belief that a seminal discharge weakens, and conversely, avoidance of ejaculation will allow the semen to be reabsorbed into the system and provide increased strength and endurance.

There is also room for conjecture that among the Hebrews, abstinence from sex was looked upon as a sacrifice made "in the line of duty."

CAST THE FIRST STONE

𝔍o𝔥n 8:1–11   ¹Jesus went unto the mount of Olives. ²And early in the morning he came again into the temple, and all the people came unto him; and he sat down, and taught them. ³And the scribes and Pharisees brought unto him a woman taken in adultery; and when they had set her in the midst, ⁴they say unto him, Master, this woman was taken in adultery, in the very act. ⁵Now Moses in the law commanded us, that such should be stoned: but what sayest thou? [6]This they said, tempting him, that they might have to accuse him. But Jesus stooped down, and with his finger wrote on the ground, as though he heard them not. [7]So when they continued asking him, he lifted up himself, and said unto them, He that is without sin among you, let him first cast a stone at her. [8]And again he stooped down, and wrote on the ground. [9]And they which heard it, being convicted by their own conscience, went out one by one, beginning at the eldest, even unto the last: and Jesus was left alone, and the woman standing in the midst. [10]When Jesus had lifted up himself, and saw none but the woman, he said unto her, Woman, where are those thine accusers? hath no man condemned thee? [11]She said, No man, Lord. And Jesus said unto her, Neither do I condemn thee: go, and sin no more.

It is frequently pointed out that Christ did not insulate himself from the common people and that he often consorted with thieves, prostitutes and, in this case, an adulteress. True enough, but the significance of this familiar incident is that Christ had a perfect opportunity to condemn the severity of the Hebrew law which required death for adultery.

> *Leviticus* 20:10   And the man that committeth adultery with another man's wife, even he that committeth adultery with his neighbor's wife, the adulterer and the adulteress shall surely be put to death.

Instead of denouncing the monstrous and barbaric law, all the King of Kings, the Prince of Peace and the Lord of Lords did was to make a pronouncement about hypocrisy by scribbling some incriminating evidence in the sand. Although the would-be executioners disbanded and the adulteress' life was saved, the alleged son of God gave his implicit approval of the cruel and inhumane prohibition against adultery and his hesitation to speak out serves as a stinging indictment of his own moral code. Can death ever be considered just punishment for a mere sexual infraction? By virtue of his silence, Jesus Christ condoned and upheld the horrendous Mosaic statute and considered it to be fair and just punishment which made him a willing accomplice and accessory to murder in the first degree.

I've had a lot of fun sparring with fundamentalists about my book and I recall in particular a debate with a Baptist preacher in which I took the position that the moral code of the Bible is cruel, unjust and inhumane. Then I asked him point blank:

Akerley: Reverend, if a woman is taken in adultery today, should she be stoned to death according to the Biblical injunction?

Baptist Preacher: (after hesitating a few moments) Well, she should be punished according to the full extent of the law.

Akerley: Reverend, once again, if a woman is taken in adultery today, should she be executed according to the Biblical injunction? I want a straight yes or no answer, please.

Baptist Preacher: (after hesitating even longer than before) Well, I repeat, she should be punished according to the full extent of the law.

He knew, of course, that I had him by the pastoral balls and he wasn't about to incriminate himself. Ah, the workings of the mystical mind never cease to amaze and confound me!

Christ's own view of adultery was narrow in the extreme and he gave a command which indicates that even to look on a woman and to desire her is to be guilty of committing adultery in one's heart. This commandment makes a distressingly large portion of the world's male population into adulterers.

> **Matthew 5:27–28** ²⁷Ye have heard that it was said by them of old time, Thou shalt not commit adultery: ²⁸but I say unto you, That whosoever looketh on a woman to lust after her hath committed adultery with her already in his heart.

Even many born-again Christians admit that this decree constitutes a standard which is virtually impossible to obey. And why not indulge in real-life sins of the flesh if their mere contemplation equals the actual act?

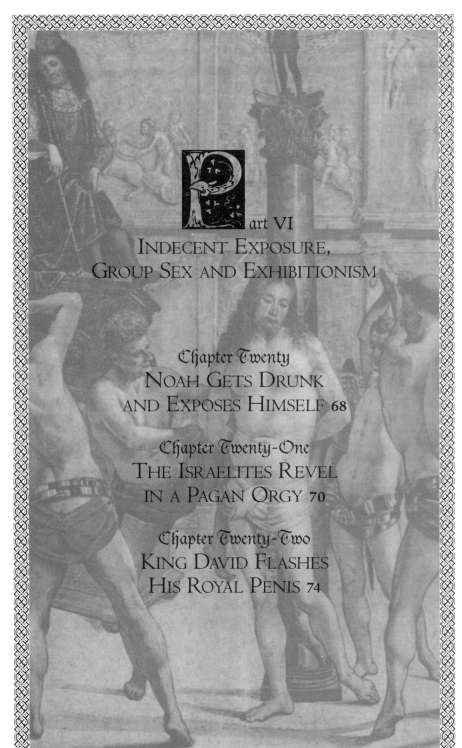

Part VI
INDECENT EXPOSURE, GROUP SEX AND EXHIBITIONISM

Noah Gets Drunk and Exposes Himself

Genesis 9:18–29   ¹⁸And the sons of Noah, that went forth of the ark, were Shem, and Ham, and Japheth: and Ham is the father of Canaan. ¹⁹These are the three sons of Noah: and of them was the whole earth overspread. ²⁰And Noah began to be a husbandman, and he planted a vineyard: ²¹and he drank of the wine, and was drunken; and he was uncovered within his tent. ²²And Ham, the father of Canaan, saw the nakedness of his father, and told his two brethren without. ²³And Shem and Japheth took a garment, and laid it upon both their shoulders, and went backward, and covered the nakedness of their father; and their faces were backward, and they saw not their father's nakedness. ²⁴And Noah awoke from his wine, and knew what his younger son had done unto him. ²⁵and he said, Cursed be Canaan; a servant of servants shall he be unto his brethren. ²⁶And he said, Blessed be the Lord God of Shem; and Canaan shall be his servant. ²⁷God shall enlarge Japheth, and he shall dwell in the tents of Shem; and Canaan shall be his servant. ²⁸And Noah lived after the flood three hundred and fifty years. ²⁹And all the days of Noah were nine hundred and fifty years: and he died.

There is much more to this curious tale than meets the eye. First of all, Noah's inebriation is made to look like the inevitable result of his having planted a vineyard. This anti-horticultural stance had already been posited earlier in the story of Cain and Abel. Cain was a farmer and Abel a shepherd and Jehovah summarily rejected Cain's offering of fruit from his orchard but readily accepted Abel's offering of a slain lamb from his flock, the outcome of which was Cain's fratricide of Abel.

The propensity to favor a nomadic economy over an agrarian one runs as a continuous theme through all the Scriptures. The explanation is a simple one: surrounding Israel in the Fertile Crescent were other tribes that were both agrarian and heathen. Since they were all idolaters, they worshiped the pagan fertility gods so stringently forbidden by Jehovah, and agriculture therefore came to represent the pursuit of strange gods and the worship of the fertility god Baal. Jehovah was determined that Israel would learn to eschew these tribes, their gods and their economy.

Secondly, the filial embarrassment over their father Noah lying naked in his own tent reveals a people who were prudish in the extreme about nudity, a predictable result of Adam and Eve's being ashamed of their own nakedness after the Fall. This prudery was so evident that Shem and Japheth walked into Noah's tent carrying a robe to cover his naked body and as they did so, they walked backwards with their heads facing the front portal so that they would not accidentally see their father's naked body. As seen through the nomadic eye, Noah's intoxication and peculiar behavior demonstrated his loss of self-control and modesty, something no good shepherd would ever think of doing.

Thirdly, there is a suggestion from Noah's overreaction to the predicament after sobering up that Ham did more than merely observe his father's nakedness. *The Interpreter's Bible* says of this excerpt: "In the primary, popular form of the story there probably occurred here—as shown by the reference in verse 24 to what his younger son had done to him—an account of an indecent attack."

Lastly, Ham was guilty of observing his father's nakedness, and putting aside the possible occurrence of sexual assault on the part of Ham, this act was tantamount to "uncovering his father's nakedness," an act severely condemned in the Hebrew law, for it was equated with incest.

> *Leviticus 18:6–7* ⁶None of you shall approach to any that is near of kin to him, to uncover their nakedness: I am the Lord. ⁷The nakedness of thy father, or the nakedness of thy mother, shalt thou not uncover: she is thy mother; thou shalt not uncover her nakedness.

Ham's act of filial indignity earned him Noah's unmitigated curse and all the descendants of Ham's son Canaan were relegated to a position of perpetual servitude to the descendants of Noah's two other sons, Japheth and Shem. According to tradition, Ham was black and this represented the beginning of the subjection of the Negro race, but this view is now widely disputed.

Jehovah seemed to have made a poor choice in singling out Noah to survive the Deluge and to become a paragon of moral rectitude for all future humankind, for although he lived to the ripe old age of 950 years, he was given to indulgence in strong drink and to immodesty, two unforgivable traits for a good shepherd!

THE ISRAELITES REVEL IN A PAGAN ORGY

WHILE THE HEBREW TRIBES DWELT IN SHITTIM, THEY READILY succumbed to the allurement of the heathen Canaanites whom they had conquered. These pagans who performed the sexual act in honor of their deity as a religious practice became an irresistible enticement to the all-too-willing Israelites and Jehovah's wrath was fiercely kindled over the wholesale orgy with Baal. He instructed Moses that the leaders responsible for the defiant debauchery were to be slain and their bodies hung up in open display to discourage any further apostasy.

Numbers 25:1–5 ¹And Israel abode in Shittim, and the people began to commit whoredom with the daughters of Moab. ²And they called the people unto the sacrifices of their gods: and the people did eat, and bowed down to their gods. ³And Israel joined himself unto Ba'al-pe'or: and the anger of the Lord was kindled against Israel. ⁴And the Lord said unto Moses, Take all the heads of the people, and hang them up before the Lord against the sun, that the fierce anger of the Lord may be turned away from Israel. ⁵And Moses said unto the judges of Israel, Slay ye every one his men that were joined unto Ba'al-pe'or.

One of the bolder Hebrews whom tradition identifies as Zimri actually married Cozbi, a Midianite woman. So outraged was the priest Phinehas by this mixed marriage that he entered their bridal tent and impaled both the bride and the groom with a javelin driven right through their guts.

Phinehas' ritual murder of Zimri and Cozbi must have temporarily appeased Jehovah's vengeful spirit, for a plague, which he had visited upon his followers as his favorite punishment, ended immediately. But not before 24,000 of the rebellious Israelites had perished.

Numbers 25:6–9 ⁶And, behold, one of the children of Israel came and brought unto his brethren a Mid'ianitish woman in the sight of Moses, and in the sight of all the congregation of the children of Israel, who were weeping before the door of the tabernacle of the congregation. ⁷And when Phin'e-has, the son of Ele-a'zar, the son of Aaron the priest, saw it, he rose up from among the congregation, and took a javelin in his hand; ⁸and he went after the man of Israel into the tent, and thrust both of them through, the man of Israel, and the woman through her belly. So the plague was stayed from the children of Israel. ⁹And those that died in the plague were twenty and four thousand.

But Jehovah's hard and vindictive heart was still not satisfied, for the death of 24,000 Israelites seemed only to have whetted his bloodthirsty appetite toward the real culprits for Israel's apostasy—the Midianites (see Chapter 41).

Jehovah's objection to the Israelites joining in any type of orgy was not really an objection to the sexual indulgence as such—it was the fact that the sexual practices of these heathen tribes were part and parcel of their religion, and he wanted Israel to avoid any contact with these competing creeds.

In particular, Jehovah objected to the frequent nudity which accompanied the pagan ceremonies. He wanted to be sure that his priests were always properly attired and that no exposure of the genitals would be possible as it was with the pagan priests. Since a short skirt was the usual attire for a priest, he was instructed to approach the altar so that his genitals would not be visible from the steps of the sanctuary.

Exodus 20:26   Neither shalt thou go up by steps unto mine altar, that thy nakedness be not discovered thereon.

When the Israelites later worshiped in a tent where there were no steps at the entrance, specific instructions were given for the priests to properly cover themselves.

Exodus 28:40–43   ⁴⁰And for Aaron's sons thou shalt make coats, and thou shalt make for them girdles, and bonnets shalt thou make for them, for glory and for beauty. ⁴¹And thou shalt put them upon Aaron thy brother, and his sons with him; and shalt anoint them, and consecrate them, and sanctify them, that they may minister unto me in the priest's office. ⁴²And thou shalt make them linen breeches to cover their nakedness; from the loins even unto the thighs they shall reach: ⁴³and they shall be upon Aaron, and upon his sons, when they come in unto the tabernacle of the congregation, or when they come near unto the altar to minister in the holy place; that they bear not iniquity, and die: it shall be a statute for ever unto him and his seed after him.

While Moses was on Mount Sinai receiving the Ten Commandments from Jehovah, the Israelites were fornicating freely in the nude, and three thousand of them paid with their lives for this orgiastic indulgence.

Ⓔxodus 32:25–29   ²⁵And when Moses saw that the people were naked, (for Aaron had made them naked unto their shame among their enemies,) ²⁶then Moses stood in the gate of the camp, and said, Who is on the Lord's side? let him come unto me. And all the sons of Levi gathered themselves together unto him. ²⁷And he said unto them, Thus saith the Lord God of Israel, Put every man his sword by his side, and go in and out from gate to gate throughout the camp, and slay every man his brother, and every man his companion, and every man his neighbor. ²⁸And the children of Levi did according to the word of Moses: and there fell of the people that day about three thousand men. ²⁹For Moses had said, Consecrate yourselves today to the Lord, even every man upon his son, and upon his brother; that he may bestow upon you a blessing this day.

Yes, Jehovah was determined that the Israelites would not rub shoulders (or other parts) with the myriad heathen tribes of the Fertile Crescent whose religion was purely phallic. With all of the frequently-stated objections to the Israelites joining their pagan neighbors in any type of religio-sexual orgy, it is no wonder that Jehovah killed 27,000 of them after their mass involvement with the Midianites.

These pagans also engaged in other sexual practices which Jehovah had strictly forbidden to the Hebrews. The familiar story of Elijah competing with the prophets of Baal to prove that the god of Israel was the only true god contains elements of masochism. During the ceremony, while waiting for fire from heaven to consume the animal sacrifice which they had placed on the altar, the priests of Baal began to lacerate themselves and to gush blood all over the altar.

I Ⓚings 18:20–29   ²⁰So Ahab sent unto all the children of Israel, and gathered the prophets together unto mount Carmel. ²¹And Elijah came unto all the people, and said, How long halt ye between two opinions? if the Lord be God, follow him; but if Ba'al, then follow him. And the people answered him not a word. ²²Then said Elijah unto the people, I, even I only, remain a prophet of the Lord; but Ba'al's prophets are four hundred and fifty men. ²³Let them therefore give us two bullocks; and let them choose one bullock for themselves, and cut it in pieces, and lay it on wood, and put no fire under: and I will dress the other bullock, and lay it on wood, and put no fire under: ²⁴and call ye on the name of your gods, and I will call on the name of the Lord: and the God that answereth by fire, let him be God. And all the people answered and said, It is well spoken. ²⁵And Elijah said unto the prophets of Ba'al, Choose you one bullock for yourselves, and dress it first; for ye are many; and call on the name of your gods, but put no fire under. ²⁶And they took the bullock which was given them, and they dressed it, and called on the name of Ba'al from morning even until noon, saying, O Ba'al, hear us. But there was no voice, nor any that answered. And they leaped upon the altar which was made. ²⁷And it came to pass at noon, that Elijah mocked them, and said, Cry aloud: for he is a god; either he is talking, or he is pursuing, or he is in a journey, or peradventure he sleepeth, and must be awaked. ²⁸And they cried aloud, and cut themselves after their manner with knives and lancets, till the blood gushed out upon them. ²⁹And it came to pass, when midday was past, and they prophesied until the time of the offering of the evening sacrifice, that there was neither voice, nor any to answer, nor any that regarded.

It was absolutely forbidden to the Israelites to cut their flesh in any way that would cause the letting of blood. They were even enjoined never to tattoo themselves.

Leviticus 19:28   Ye shall not make any cuttings in your flesh for the dead, nor print any marks upon you. I am the Lord.

Deuteronomy 14:1–2   ¹Ye are the children of the Lord your God: ye shall not cut yourselves, nor make any baldness between your eyes for the dead. ²For thou art a holy people unto the Lord thy God, and the Lord hath chosen thee to be a peculiar people unto himself, above all the nations that are upon the earth.

The above prohibitions would explicitly rule out any type of masochistic or sadistic sexual behavior in Israel. Such behavior was to be Jehovah's exclusive prerogative.

King David Flashes His Royal Penis

PON SAUL'S DEATH, DAVID BECAME KING OVER ALL ISRAEL AND much later on, he wanted to bring back home the Ark of the Covenant, the sacred, portable wooden box in which Jehovah's presence presumably dwelt. He and his men set the ark on a new cart in order to transport it safely. The drivers of the cart were Uzzah and Ahio and as the cart wended its homeward way with the ark perched safely on it, the accompanying procession sang and played musical instruments.

> **II Samuel 6:1–5** ¹Again, David gathered together all the chosen men of Israel, thirty thousand. ²And David arose, and went with all the people that were with him from Baale of Judah, to bring up from thence the ark of God, whose name is called by the name of the Lord of hosts that dwelleth between the cherubim. ³And they set the ark of God upon a new cart, and brought it out of the house of Abinadab that was in Gib'e-ah: and Uzzah and Ahi'o, the sons of Abinadab, drave the new cart. ⁴And they brought it out of the house of Abinadab which was at Gib'e-ah, accompanying the ark of God: and Ahi'o went before the ark. ⁵And David and all the house of Israel played before the Lord on all manner of instruments made of fir wood, even on harps, and on psalteries, and on timbrels, and on cornets, and on cymbals.

When they arrived at the threshing floor of Nachon, Uzzah put his hand out to steady the ark and to keep it from falling from its perch. Jehovah was displeased with his "error" and struck him dead on the spot for having touched the ark. David then became angry with Jehovah for having killed Uzzah and named the spot in Uzzah's honor.

> **II Samuel 6:6–8** ⁶And when they came to Nachon's threshingfloor, Uzzah put forth his hand to the ark of God, and took hold of it; for the oxen shook it. ⁷And the anger of the Lord was kindled against Uzzah, and God smote him there for his error; and there he died by the ark of God. ⁸And David was displeased, because the Lord had made a breach upon Uzzah: and he called the name of the place Pe'-rez-'uz'zah to this day.

Since at this point David was afraid to take the ark home with him, he left it at the home of Obededom for three months.

II Samuel 6:9–11   ⁹And David was afraid of the Lord that day, and said, How shall the ark of the Lord come to me? ¹⁰So David would not remove the ark of the Lord unto him into the city of David; but David carried it aside into the house of O'bed-edom the Gittite. ¹¹And the ark of the Lord continued in the house of O'bed-e'dom the Gittite three months: and the Lord blessed O'bed-e'dom, and all his household.

When David realized that Jehovah prospered and blessed Obededom for having the ark at his home, he decided to get it and to bring it home with him.

On that festive occasion, David was wearing a linen ephod, a very short garment usually worn by priests. The sacerdotal vestment was so scanty that when priests approached the altar during religious ceremonies in the temple, they were warned not to ascend the steps of the altar since it was never their practice to wear underwear and their privates would not have been private for very long. So during the triumphal entry into the city, David, clad only in his ephod, leaped and danced so wildly that Michal, who was watching from her window, despised him in her heart for his blatant exhibitionism.

II Samuel 6:12–16   ¹²And it was told king David, saying, the Lord hath blessed the house of O'bed-e'dom, and all that pertaineth unto him, because of the ark of God. So David went and brought up the ark of God from the house of O'bed-e'dom into the city of David with gladness. ¹³And it was so, that when they that bare the ark of the Lord had gone six paces, he sacrificed oxen and fatlings. ¹⁴And David danced before the Lord with all his might; and David was girded with a linen ephod. ¹⁵So David and all the house of Israel brought up the ark of the Lord with shouting, and with the sound of the trumpet. ¹⁶And as the ark of the Lord came into the city of David, Michal Saul's daughter looked through a window, and saw king David leaping and dancing before the Lord; and she despised him in her heart.

The ark was then placed in the tabernacle with appropriate peace offerings to Jehovah. David then blessed the people and dismissed them.

II Samuel 6:17–19   ¹⁷And they brought in the ark of the Lord, and set it in his place, in the midst of the tabernacle that David had pitched for it: and David offered burnt offerings and peace offerings before the Lord. ¹⁸And as soon as David had made an end of offering burnt offerings and peace offerings, he blessed the people in the name of the Lord of hosts. [19]And he dealt among all the people, even among the whole multitude of Israel, as well as to the women as men, to every one a cake of bread, and a good piece of flesh, and a flagon of wine. So all the people departed every one to his home.

As soon as he arrived home, Michal accused him of exposing himself like a common pervert or flasher, for as the maidens of the city lined the road of the royal procession that day, they were treated to the sight of their monarch quite literally letting it all hang out.

II Samuel 6:20   Then David returned to bless his household. And Michal the daughter of Saul came out to meet David, and said, How glorious was the king of Israel today, who uncovered himself today in the eyes of the handmaids of his servants, as one of the vain fellows shamelessly uncovereth himself!

David responded angrily to Michal by explaining that anything he did that afternoon was because of his joy in returning home with the ark. Seemingly as a result of this altercation, Michal remained childless all of her life either because David never had further sexual relations with her or because of a sterility curse meted out by Jehovah.

II Samuel 6:21–23   [21]And David said unto Michal, It was before the Lord, which chose me before thy father, and before all his house, to appoint me ruler over the people of the Lord, over Israel: therefore will I play before the Lord. [22]And I will yet be more vile than thus, and will be base in mine own sight: and of the maidservants which thou hast spoken of, of them shall I be had in honor. [23]Therefore Michal the daughter of Saul had no child unto the day of her death.

Michal was later taken from David and given to another husband, Phaltiel, because David had defected from the first king of Israel. When he became king of a united Israel, he stipulated that Michal would have to be taken from Phaltiel and returned to him once again. The distraught second husband followed Michal weeping, but to no avail, for she was now to be David's exclusive property.

II Samuel 3:13–16   ¹³And he said, Well; I will make a league with thee: but one thing I require of thee, that is, Thou shalt not see my face, except thou first bring Michal Saul's daughter, when thou comest to see my face. ¹⁴And David sent messengers to Ish-bo'sheth Saul's son, saying, Deliver me my wife Michal, which I espoused to me for an hundred foreskins of the Philistines. ¹⁵And Ish-bo'sheth sent, and took, her from her husband, even from Phaltiel the son of La'-ish. ¹⁶And her husband went with her along weeping behind her to Ba-hu'-rim. Then said Abner, unto him, Go, return. And he returned.

art VII
NUDITY AND STRIPTEASE

Prophesying in the Nude

> **I Samuel 19:20–24**   20And Saul sent messengers to take David:
> and when they saw the company of the prophets prophesying, and
> Samuel standing as appointed over them, the Spirit of God was upon
> the messengers of Saul, and they also prophesied. 21And when it was
> told Saul, he sent other messengers, and they prophesied likewise.
> And Saul sent messengers again the third time, and they prophesied
> also. 22Then went he also to Ramah, and came to a great well that is
> in Sechu: and he asked and said, Where are Samuel and David? And
> one said, Behold, they be at Nai'oth in Ramah. 23And he went thither
> to Nai'oth in Ramah: and the Spirit of God was upon him also, and
> he went on, and prophesied, until he came to Nai'oth in Ramah.
> 24And he stripped off his clothes also, and prophesied before Samuel
> in like manner, and lay down naked all that day and all that night.
> Wherefore they say, Is Saul also among the prophets?

Despite the shame felt by Adam and Eve over their own nakedness in Eden
and the domestic tribulation caused by Noah's drunken bout of exposing
himself, Saul shared none of their humiliation, embarrassment or remorse.
With respect to the witnesses of this display of nudity, they only seemed
shocked to learn that Saul had prophesied for the first time and should now
be counted among Israel's prophets.

Although Saul acted on his own, Isaiah was given a direct injunction by Jehovah
to prophesy in the nude, and this was to continue for a period of three years.

> **Isaiah 20:1–5**   1In the year that Tartan came unto Ashdod, (when
> Sargon the king of Assyria sent him,) and fought against Ashdod, and
> took it; 2at the same time spake the Lord by Isaiah the son of Amoz,
> saying, Go and loose the sackcloth from off thy loins, and put off thy
> shoe from thy foot. And he did so, walking naked and barefoot. 3And
> the Lord said, Like as my servant Isaiah hath walked naked and bare-
> foot three years for a sign and wonder upon Egypt and upon Ethiopia;
> 4So shall the king of Assyria lead away the Egyptians prisoners, and the
> Ethiopians captives, young and old, naked and barefoot, even with their
> buttocks uncovered, to the shame of Egypt. 5And they shall be afraid
> and ashamed of Ethiopia their expectation, and of Egypt their glory.

Isaiah's influence was felt among the minor prophets and the words of Micah
indicate that he would imitate Isaiah's actions as an adjunct to his prophesying.

Micah 1:8   Therefore I will wail and howl, I will go stripped and naked: I will make a wailing like the dragons, and mourning as the owls.

Jehovah seemingly was not affronted by nakedness if it related to prophesying. Yet he was determined to imbue his followers with a sense of shame over nudity associated with sex, especially because of its direct link with heathen sex worship.

SALOME STRIPS FOR KING HEROD

HANKS TO OSCAR WILDE'S DRAMATIZATION OF THE SALOME legend, the Dance of the Seven Veils has become history's most famous striptease.

The Biblical account reveals that King Herod imprisoned John the Baptist to pacify his wife Herodias who was infuriated because John had denounced her marriage to Herod since she had formerly been married to Herod's brother Philip. A daughter, Salome, had resulted from her previous marriage.

Herod, nonetheless, respected John as a holy man and instead of executing him as Herodias wished him to do, he merely had him thrown into prison.

Mark 6:17–20   ¹⁷For Herod himself had sent forth and laid hold upon John, and bound him in prison for Hero'di-as' sake, his brother Philip's wife: for he had married her. ¹⁸For John had said unto Herod, It is not lawful for thee to have thy brother's wife. ¹⁹Therefore Hero'di-as had a quarrel against him, and would have killed him; but she could not: ²⁰for Herod feared John, knowing that he was a just man and a holy, and observed him; and when he heard him, he did many things, and heard him gladly.

Finally, an opportunity presented itself for Herodias to put her diabolical plan against John into effect. Salome was asked to dance at Herod's birthday party feast and Herod was so pleased with his lovely stepdaughter's performance that he offered to grant her any wish that she might make.

Mark 6:21–23   ²¹And when a convenient day was come, that Herod on his birthday made a supper to his lords, high captains, and chief estates of Galilee; ²²and when the daughter of the said Hero'dias came in, and danced, and pleased Herod and them that sat with him, the king said unto the damsel, Ask of me whatsoever thou wilt, and

I will give it thee. ²³And he sware unto her, Whatsoever thou shalt ask of me, I will give it thee, unto the half of my kingdom.

Before asking Herod for any favors, Salome consulted with her mother who immediately told Salome to ask for the head of John the Baptist. Salome consented, and Herod was sorry for having made such an extravagant offer of any wish that Salome wanted.

> 𝔐ark 6:24–26   ²⁴And she went forth, and said unto her mother, What shall I ask? And she said, The head of John the Baptist. ²⁵And she came in straightway with haste unto the king, and asked, saying, I will that thou give me by and by in a charger the head of John the Baptist. ²⁶And the king was exceeding sorry; yet for his oath's sake, and for their sakes which sat with him, he would not reject her.

Herod sent an executioner to the prison and had John beheaded. His head was brought to the king on a platter. When the head was presented to Salome, she in turn presented it to Herodias. John's disciples then took his decapitated body and buried it.

> 𝔐ark 6:27–29   ²⁷And immediately the king sent an executioner, and commanded his head to be brought: and he went and beheaded him in the prison, ²⁸and brought his head in a charger, and gave it to the damsel: and the damsel gave it to her mother. ²⁹And when his disciples heard of it, they came and took up his corpse, and laid it in a tomb.

It is hard to tell who is the more sadistic and depraved of the two—Herodias for wanting John decapitated or Salome for agreeing to carry out her mother's orders. At any rate, Salome's dance before Herod must have been sufficiently erotic to arouse the king to a point of wishing to please Salome for possible future sexual favors.

All in all, the lustful Herod, the bloodthirsty Herodias and the conniving Salome form one of the Bible's most unseemly trios. And the additional horrifying scene of John's headless corpse being removed from the prison and being carried to a tomb for burial by his disciples adds a final gruesome touch to an already ghastly and sordid tale.

art VIII
PROSTITUTION
(SECULAR AND SACRED)
AND PHALLIC WORSHIP

Judah Patronizes a Disguised Hooker

FTER ONAN'S DEATH (SEE CHAPTER 5), JUDAH SENT TAMAR back to her family promising that when his youngest son Shelah was old enough, he would allow him to marry her. Judah probably had no intention of doing this, for both of his older sons had already died at Jehovah's hand and at this point in time, Tamar must have represented a curse to him. Not wanting to jeopardize the life of his only remaining son, therefore, he decided to send Tamar away from his home.

> **Genesis 38:11** Then said Judah to Tamar his daughter-in-law, Remain a widow at thy father's house, till Shelah my son be grown: for he said, Lest peradventure he die also, as his brethren did. And Tamar went and dwelt in her father's house.

Tamar probably sensed that Judah's promise of marriage to Shelah was spurious, and not wanting to remain forever barren, she decided to get her revenge on him by disguising herself as a harlot and offering herself to him as a desperate means of getting pregnant. Her opportunity came shortly after the death of Judah's wife when Judah made a journey through Timnath.

> **Genesis 38:12–14** ¹²And in process of time the daughter of Shu'ah Judah's wife died; and Judah was comforted, and went up unto his sheepshearers to Timnath, he and his friend Hirah the Adul'lamite. ¹³And it was told Tamar, saying, Behold, thy father-in-law goeth up to Timnath to shear his sheep. ¹⁴And she put her widow's garments off from her, and covered her with a veil, and wrapped herself, and sat in an open place, which is by the way to Timnath; for she saw that Shelah was grown, and she was not given unto him to wife.

Judah mistook Tamar for a hooker and propositioned her as soon as he saw her. Tamar immediately asked what her pay was to be and Judah offered her a young goat. As a security pledge for Tamar to hold until the arrival of the young goat, he gave her his ring, bracelets and staff. Then they fornicated. Convinced that she would now conceive, Tamar went away and removed her harlot's disguise and once again donned her garments of widowhood.

> **Genesis 38:15–19** ¹⁵When Judah saw her, he thought her to be a harlot; because she had covered her face. ¹⁶And he turned unto

AND SHE SAID WHAT WILT THOU GIVE ME?

her by the way, and said, Go to, I pray thee, let me come in unto thee; (for he knew not that she was his daughter-in-law.) and she said, What wilt thou give me, that thou mayest come in unto me? [17]And he said, I will send thee a kid from the flock. And she said, Wilt thou give me a pledge, till thou send it? [18]And he said, What pledge shall I give thee? And she said, Thy signet, and thy bracelets, and thy staff that is in thine hand. And he gave it her, and came in unto her, and she conceived by him. [19]And she arose, and went away, and laid by her veil from her, and put on the garments of her widowhood.

Judah sent his friend Hirah the Adullamite to search for the harlot and to give her the young goat which he had promised. Hirah was unable to find the prostitute to give her the goat or to recover Judah's ring, bracelets and staff. Upon hearing the news, Judah decided that it would be better to let the whore have his things than it would be to cause any embarrassment.

Genesis 38:20–23   [20]And Judah sent the kid by the hand of his friend the Adul'lamite, to receive his pledge from the woman's hand: but he found her not. [21]Then he asked the men of that place, saying, Where is the harlot, that was openly by the wayside? And they said, There was no harlot in this place. [22]And he returned to Judah, and said, I cannot find her; and also the men of the place said, that there was no harlot in this place. [23]And Judah said, Let her take it to her, lest we be shamed: behold, I sent this kid, and thou hast not found her.

Three months later, Judah discovered that his daughter-in-law Tamar was pregnant, and since he believed that she had been guilty of promiscuous and illicit sexual relations, he decreed that she should be burned to death, the severest penalty ever exacted for fornication under the Hebrew law.

Genesis 38:24   And it came to pass about three months after, that it was told Judah, saying, Tamar thy daughter-in-law hath played the harlot; and also, behold, she is with child by whoredom. And Judah said, Bring her forth, and let her be burnt.

When Tamar was brought before Judah, she declared that the man by whom she was pregnant was the man to whom belonged the ring, bracelets and the staff which she then produced. Judah recognized that Tamar was more honest than he because he had not honored his promise to her to send his youngest son Shelah to marry her, and he forgave her, but never again got it on with her.

Genesis 38:25–26   25When she was brought forth she sent to her father-in-law, saying, By the man, whose these are, am I with child: and she said, Discern, I pray thee, whose are these, the signet, and bracelets, and staff. 26And Judah acknowledged them, and said, She hath been more righteous than I; because that I gave her not to Shelah my son. And he knew her again no more.

Tamar finally gave birth to twin boys, Pharez and Zarah. A scarlet thread was tied to the hand of the twin whose hand first appeared in childbirth, but as the hand withdrew back into Tamar's womb, the midwife then declared that the child who came out first was in reality not the firstborn, for the son whose hand had the scarlet thread on it was technically the firstborn. Thus it was decided that Zarah was literally the firstborn and Pharez the second born.

Genesis 38:27–30   27And it came to pass in the time of her travail, that, behold, twins were in her womb. 28And it came to pass, when she travailed, that the one put out his hand: and the midwife took and bound upon his hand a scarlet thread, saying, This came out first. 29And it came to pass, as he drew back his hand, that, behold, his brother came out: and she said, How hast thou broken forth? this breach be upon thee: therefore his name was called Pharez. 30And afterward came out his brother, that had the scarlet thread upon his hand: and his name was called Zarah.

The distinction was an important one since the firstborn would be entitled to a double share of the father's inheritance. Needless to say, daughters did not count in this arrangement.

The story of Judah and the disguised harlot reveals that there was little or no prejudice in Israel against purely secular prostitution. This seems to be the case throughout the Old Testament and it is not until we arrive at the monomaniacal diatribes of Paul against sex in general that we have a really strong Biblical pronouncement against prostitution.

The strongest Old Testament admonition is that contained in Proverbs. It reads like the warnings fathers have given their sons throughout the ages in every generation. The careful reader will realize that the last verse which speaks of the way of the prostitute being the way to hell is, in reality, not so much an admonition against sexual permissiveness as it is a warning for the young not to squander their being and their possessions on trivial pursuits.

Proverbs 7:1–27   ¹My son, keep my words, and lay up my commandments with thee. ²Keep my commandments, and live; and my law as the apple of thine eye. ³Bind them upon thy fingers, write them upon the table of thine heart. ⁴Say unto wisdom, Thou art my sister; and call understanding thy kinswoman: ⁵that they may keep thee from the strange woman, from the stranger which flattereth with her words. ⁶For at the window of my house I looked through my casement, ⁷and beheld among the simple ones, I discerned among the youths, a young man void of understanding, ⁸passing through the street near her corner; and he went the way to her house, ⁹in the twilight, in the evening, in the black and dark night. ¹⁰And, behold, there met him a woman with the attire of a harlot, and subtile of heart. ¹¹(She is loud and stubborn; her feet abide not in her house: ¹²now is she without, now in the streets, and lieth in wait at every corner.) ¹³So she caught him, and kissed him, and with an impudent face said unto him, ¹⁴I have peace offering with me; this day have I paid my vows. ¹⁵Therefore came I forth to meet thee, diligently to seek thy face, and I have found thee. ¹⁶I have decked my bed with coverings of tapestry, with carved works, with fine linen of Egypt. ¹⁷I have perfumed my bed with myrrh, aloes, and cinnamon. ¹⁸Come, let us take our fill of love until the morning: let us solace ourselves with loves. ¹⁹For the goodman is not at home, he is gone a long journey: ²⁰he hath taken a bag of money with him, and will come home at the day appointed. ²¹With her much fair speech she caused him to yield, with the flattering of her lips she forced him. [22]He goeth after her straightway, as an ox goeth to the slaughter, or as a fool to the correction of the stocks: [23]till a dart strike through his liver; as a bird hasteth to the snare, and knoweth not that it is for his life. [24]Hearken unto me now therefore, O ye children, and attend to the words of my mouth. [25]Let not thine heart decline to her ways, go not astray in her paths. [26]For she hath cast down many wounded: yea, many strong men have been slain by her. [27]Her house is the way to hell, going down to the chambers of death.

These additional caveats against whores are to be found in the Scriptures of the Old Testament:

Leviticus 19:29–30   [29]Do not prostitute thy daughter, to cause her to be a whore: lest the land fall to whoredom, and the land become full of wickedness. [30]Ye shall keep my sabbaths, and reverence my sanctuary: I am the Lord.

Proverbs 5:1–14   [1]My son, attend unto my wisdom, and bow thine ear to my understanding; [2]that thou mayest regard discretion, and that thy lips may keep knowledge. [3]For the lips of a strange woman drop as a honeycomb, and her mouth is smoother than oil: [4]but her end is bitter as wormwood, sharp as a two-edged sword. [5]Her feet go down to death; her steps take hold on hell. [6]Lest thou shouldest ponder the path of life, her ways are movable, that thou canst not know them. [7]Hear me now therefore, O ye children, and depart not from the words of my mouth. [8]Remove thy way far from her, and come not nigh the door of her house: [9]lest thou give thine honor unto others, and thy years unto the cruel: [10]lest strangers be filled with thy wealth; and thy labors be in the house of a stranger; [11]and thou mourn at the last, when thy flesh and thy body are consumed, [12]and say, How have I hated instruction, and my heart despised reproof; [13]and have not obeyed the voice of my teachers, nor inclined mine ear to them that instructed me! [14]I was almost in all evil in the midst of the congregation and assembly.

Proverbs 6:23–26   [23]For the commandment is a lamp; and the law is light; and reproofs of instruction are the way of life: [24]to keep thee from the evil woman, from the flattery of the tongue of a strange woman. [25]Lust not after her beauty in thine heart; neither let her take thee with her eyelids. ²⁶For by means of a whorish woman a man is brought to a piece of bread: and the adulteress will hunt for the precious life.

Proverbs 23:27–28

²⁷For a whore is a deep ditch; and a strange woman is a narrow pit. ²⁸She also lieth in wait as for a prey, and increaseth the transgressors among men.

Proverbs 29:3

Whoso loveth wisdom rejoiceth his father: but he that keepeth company with harlots spendeth his substance.

RAHAB, THE FAVORED MADAM OF JERICHO

"Joshua fit the battle of Jericho, Jericho, Jericho,
Joshua fit the battle of Jericho, and the walls came tumblin' down."

The lyrics of this popular African-American spiritual memorialize the Bible's most renowned battle. But before Joshua launched his campaign against the doomed city, he sent two spies on a reconnaissance mission and they stayed in a brothel run by a madam named Rahab.

Joshua 2:1

And Joshua the son of Nun sent out of Shittim two men to spy secretly, saying, Go view the land, even Jericho. And they went, and came into a harlot's house, named Rahab, and lodged there.

The amazing part of this story is that Rahab was able to find the time to hide the two secret agents in her whorehouse. The administration of a cat-house is a very time-consuming occupation and like all sex entrepreneurs, Rahab surely must have followed the four cardinal rules for turning the most tricks and for making money on sheer volume. These four rules are: (1) get 'em in; (2) get 'em up; (3) get 'em off; (4) get 'em out.

Since they spent the entire night there, they most certainly must have done what any red-blooded heterosexual Israelite would have done in their shoes so that on their espionage assignment, they probably got more than just the lay of the land.

The king of Jericho heard rumors that there were two spies at Rahab's bordello, and he sent for the men. Rahab hid the spies on her roof and confessed to the king's envoys that the spies had been there, but she told them that they had already gone. The envoys pursued the spies as far as Jordan and the city gate was immediately shut behind them in case they were still at large in Jericho.

> **Joshua 2:2–7** ²And it was told the king of Jericho, saying, Behold, there came men in hither tonight of the children of Israel to search out the country. ³And the king of Jericho sent unto Rahab, saying, Bring forth the men that are come to thee, which are entered into thine house: for they be come to search out all the country. ⁴And the woman took the two men, and hid them, and said thus, There came men unto me, but I wist not whence they were: ⁵and it came to pass about the time of shutting of the gate, when it was dark, that the men went out; whither the men went, I wot not: pursue after them quickly; for ye shall overtake them. ⁶But she had brought them up to the roof of the house, and hid them with the stalks of flax, which she had laid in order upon the roof. ⁷And the men pursued after them the way to Jordan unto the fords: and as soon as they which pursued after them were gone out, they shut the gate.

Rahab next went to the spies and told them that she knew Jehovah was protecting them and that her land would soon be conquered by Israel.

> **Joshua 2:8–11** ⁸And before they were laid down, she came up unto them upon the roof; ⁹and she said unto the men, I know that the Lord hath given you the land, and that your terror is fallen upon us, and that all the inhabitants of the land faint because of you. ¹⁰For we have heard how the Lord dried up the water of the Red sea for you, when ye came out of Egypt; and what ye did unto the two kings of the Amorites, that were on the other side Jordan, Sihon and Og, whom ye utterly destroyed. ¹¹And as soon as we had heard these things, our hearts did melt, neither did there remain any more courage in any man, because of you: for the Lord your God, he is God in heaven above, and in earth beneath.

In return for her favor of hiding and protecting them, she asked that she and her family be spared when Israel came to conquer Jericho. The spies agreed to honor Rahab's request.

> **Joshua 2:12–14** ¹²Now therefore, I pray you, swear unto me by the Lord, since I have showed you kindness, that ye will also

show kindness unto my father's house, and give me a true token: [13]and that ye will save alive my father, and my mother, and my brethren, and my sisters, and all that they have, and deliver our lives from death. [14]And the men answered her, Our life for yours, if ye utter not this our business. And it shall be, when the Lord hath given us the land, that we will deal kindly and truly with thee.

She then let them down from her roof with a rope, and since her house was located on top of the town wall, the spies easily escaped from the city. She also warned them to hide in the mountains outside the city for at least three days so that the king's envoys who were still pursuing them would not find them.

Joshua 2:15–16 [15]Then she let them down by a cord through the window: for her house was upon the town wall, and she dwelt upon the wall. [16]And she said unto them, Get you to the mountain, lest the pursuers meet you: and hide yourselves there three days, until the pursuers be returned: and afterward may ye go your way.

The Israelite spies promised Rahab that both she and her family would be safe during the attack, but that they must remain inside the brothel and that the scarlet rope which they were going to use to escape should stay outside the window as an identifying sign for the attacking Israelite warriors. They also swore Rahab to secrecy.

Joshua 2:17–20 [17]And the men said unto her, We will be blameless of this thine oath which thou hast made us swear. [18]Behold, when we come into the land, thou shalt bind this line of scarlet thread in the window which thou didst let us down by: and thou shalt bring thy father, and thy mother, and thy brethren, and all thy father's household, home unto thee. [19]And it shall be, that whosoever shall go out of the doors of thy house into the street, his blood shall be upon his head, and we will be guiltless: and whosoever shall be with thee in the house, his blood shall be on our head, if any hand be upon him. [20]And if thou utter this our business, then we will be quit of thine oath which thou hast made us to swear.

Rahab agreed to abide by their terms and as soon as they departed, she fastened the scarlet cord to her window.

𝕵𝖔𝖘𝖍𝖚𝖆 2:21   And she said, According unto your word, so be it. And she sent them away, and they departed: and she bound the scarlet line in the window.

The spies spent three days in the mountains, later returning to Joshua and relating everything which had happened in Jericho to their leader.

𝕵𝖔𝖘𝖍𝖚𝖆 2:22–24   ²²And they went, and came unto the mountain, and abode there three days, until the pursuers were returned: and the pursuers sought them throughout all the way, but found them not. ²³So the two men returned, and descended from the mountain, and passed over, and came to Joshua the son of Nun, and told him all things that befell them: ²⁴and they said unto Joshua, Truly the Lord hath delivered into our hands all the land; for even all the inhabitants of the country do faint because of us.

Joshua did make good his promise and when the army arrived in Jericho, they had instructions to destroy the city except for Rahab and her house.

𝕵𝖔𝖘𝖍𝖚𝖆 6:15–21   ¹⁵And it came to pass on the seventh day, that they rose early about the dawning of the day, and compassed the city after the same manner seven times: only on that day they compassed the city seven times. ¹⁶And it came to pass at the seventh time, when the priests blew with the trumpets, Joshua said unto the people, Shout; for the Lord hath given you the city. ¹⁷And the city shall be accursed, even it, and all that are therein, to the Lord: only Rahab the harlot shall live, she and all that are with her in the house, because she hid the messengers that we sent. ¹⁸And ye, in any wise keep yourselves from the accursed thing, lest ye make yourselves accursed, when ye take of the accursed thing, and make the camp of Israel a curse, and trouble it. ¹⁹But all the silver, and gold, and vessels of brass and iron, are consecrated unto the Lord: they shall come into the treasury of the Lord. ²⁰So the people shouted when the priests blew with the trumpets: and it came to pass, when the people heard the sound of the trumpet, and the people shouted with a great shout, that the wall fell down flat, so that the people went up into the city, every man straight before him, and they took the city. ²¹And they utterly destroyed all that was in the city, both man and woman, young and old, and ox, and sheep, and ass, with the edge of the sword.

Not only did Joshua spare Rahab and all her household, but they were also allowed to continue living in Israel for her heroic act of assisting the two spies. The inquisitive reader cannot help wondering whether or not Rahab continued to ply her trade among the Israelites.

> **Joshua 6:22–25** ²²But Joshua had said unto the two men that had spied out the country, Go into the harlot's house, and bring out thence the woman, and all that she hath, as ye sware unto her. ²³And the young men that were spies went in, and brought out Rahab, and her father, and her mother, and her brethren, and all that she had; and they brought out all her kindred, and left them without the camp of Israel. ²⁴And they burnt the city with fire, and all that was therein: only the silver, and the gold, and the vessels of brass and of iron, they put into the treasury of the house of the Lord. ²⁵And Joshua saved Rahab the harlot alive, and her father's household, and all that she had; and she dwelleth in Israel even unto this day, because she hid the messengers, which Joshua sent to spy out Jericho.

In the New Testament, both Paul and James extol Rahab for her courageous help to Israel.

> **Hebrews 11:30–31** ³⁰By faith the walls of Jericho fell down, after they were compassed about seven days. ³¹By faith the harlot Rahab perished not with them that believed not, when she had received the spies with peace.

> **James 2:24–26** ²⁴Ye see then how that by works a man is justified, and not by faith only. ²⁵Likewise also was not Rahab the harlot justified by works, when she had received the messengers, and had sent them out another way? ²⁶For as the body without the spirit is dead, so faith without works is dead also.

These New Testament encomiums praising the cooperative prostitute awarded her the Biblical equivalent of a posthumous medal of honor.

Jehovah Commands Hosea to Marry a Whore

ERE IS STILL ANOTHER OLD TESTAMENT ACCOUNT OVER which Bible scholars have puzzled and ended up about equally divided as to whether it is, in fact, a genuine historical description or pure allegory once again employing the metaphor of Israel being nothing but a common whore.

Jehovah gave Hosea a direct command to marry the prostitute Gomer.

Ḣosea 1:1–3 ¹The word of the Lord that came unto Hose'a, the son of Be-e'ri, in the days of Uzzi'ah, Jotham, Ahaz, and Hezeki'ah, kings of Judah, and in the days of Jerobo'am the son of Jo'ash, king of Israel. ²The beginning of the word of the Lord by Hose'a. And the Lord said to Hose'a, Go, take unto thee a wife of whoredoms and children of whoredoms: for the land hath committed great whoredom, departing from the Lord. ³So he went and took Gomer the daughter of Dibla'im; which conceived, and bare him a son.

Although Gomer bore Hosea three children, she was patently unable to make a complete break with her past and continued to ply her trade and thus to commit adultery.

Ḣosea 2:1–5 ¹Say ye unto your brethren, Ammi, and to your sisters, Ruha'mah. ²Plead with your mother, plead; for she is not my wife, neither am I her husband: let her therefore put away her whoredoms out of her sight, and her adulteries from between her breasts; ³lest I strip her naked, and set her as in the day that she was born, and make her as a wilderness, and set her like a dry land, and slay her with thirst. ⁴And I will not have mercy upon her children; for they be the children of whoredoms. ⁵For their mother hath played the harlot: she that conceived them hath done shamefully; for she said, I will go after my lovers, that give me my bread and my water, my wool and my flax, mine oil and my drink.

He then moved with Gomer into the wilderness hoping that by isolating her from all temptation, she would be able to remain faithful to him and he could have her all to himself.

Hosea 2:14–15 [14]Therefore, behold, I will allure her, and bring her into the wilderness, and speak comfortably unto her. [15]And I will give her her vineyards from thence, and the valley of Achor for a door of hope: and she shall sing there, as in the days of her youth, and as in the day when she came up out of the land of Egypt.

Finally, in utter despair over Gomer's unfaithfulness, he sold her into slavery. But the prophet soon became aware that he himself was a slave to his love for her and repenting, he ransomed her and bought her back from her captors for fifteen pieces of silver.

Hosea 3:1–3 [1]Then said the Lord unto me, Go yet, love a woman beloved of her friend, yet an adulteress, according to the love of the Lord toward the children of Israel, who look to other gods, and love flagons of wine. [2]So I bought her to me for fifteen pieces of silver, and for a homer of barley, and a half homer of barley: [3]and I said unto her, Thou shalt abide for me many days; thou shalt not play the harlot, and thou shalt not be for another man: so will I also be for thee.

Despite the existing controversy about whether Hosea's marriage to a whore is symbolic or literal, there is no dispute about the later chapters referring once again to an apostate Israel freely consorting with temple prostitutes and sexually debauching themselves. Here, the condemnation applies equally to men and women for participating in the forbidden rites.

Hosea 4:12–14 [12]My people ask counsel at their stocks, and their staff declareth unto them: for the spirit of whoredoms hath caused them to err, and they have gone a whoring from under their God. [13]They sacrifice upon the tops of the mountains, and burn incense upon the hills, under oaks and poplars and elms, because the shadow thereof is good: therefore your daughters shall commit whoredom, and your spouses shall commit adultery. [14]I will not punish your daughters when they commit whoredom, nor your spouses when they commit adultery: for themselves are separated with whores, and they sacrifice with harlots: therefore the people that doth not understand shall fall.

We will explore this arcane subject of sacred prostitution in depth in Chapter 30.

CHRIST CONVERSES WITH TWO WOMEN OF ILL REPUTE

HILE IT IS NOTHING LESS THAN COMMENDABLE THAT CHRIST did not hesitate to mix freely with prostitutes, he did implicitly condemn their lifestyle by virtue of his pronouncements to them.

In the instance of the woman of Samaria, he chastised her for the common-law arrangement under which she was presently living.

John 4:1–30 ¹When therefore the Lord knew how the Pharisees had heard that Jesus made and baptized more disciples than John, ²(though Jesus himself baptized not, but his disciples,) ³he left Judea, and departed again into Galilee. ⁴And he must needs go through Samaria. ⁵Then cometh he to a city of Samaria, which is called Sychar, near to the parcel of ground that Jacob gave to his son Joseph. ⁶Now Jacob's well was there. Jesus therefore, being wearied with his journey, sat thus on the well: and it was about the sixth hour. ⁷There cometh a woman of Samaria to draw water: Jesus saith unto her, Give me to drink. ⁸(For his disciples were gone away unto the city to buy meat.) ⁹Then saith the woman of Samaria unto him, How is it that thou, being a Jew, askest drink of me, which am a woman of Samaria? for the Jews have no dealings with the Samaritans. ¹⁰Jesus answered and said unto her, If thou knewest the gift of God, and who it is that saith to thee, Give me to drink; thou wouldest have asked of him, and he would have given thee living water. ¹¹The woman saith unto him, Sir, thou hast nothing to draw with, and the well is deep: from whence then hast thou that living water? ¹²Art thou greater than our father Jacob, which gave us the well, and drank thereof himself, and his children, and his cattle? ¹³Jesus answered and said unto her, Whosoever drinketh of this water shall thirst again: ¹⁴but whosoever drinketh of the water that I shall give him shall never thirst; but the water that I shall give him shall be in him a well of water springing up into everlasting life. ¹⁵The woman saith unto him, Sir, give me this water, that I thirst not, neither come hither to draw. ¹⁶Jesus saith unto her, Go, call thy husband, and come hither. ¹⁷The woman answered and said, I have no husband. Jesus said unto her, Thou hast well said, I have no husband: ¹⁸for thou hast had five husbands; and he whom thou now hast is not thy husband: in that saidst thou truly. [19]The woman saith unto him, Sir, I perceive that thou art a prophet. [20]Our fathers worshipped in this mountain; and ye say, that in Jerusalem is the place where men ought to worship. [21]Jesus saith unto her, Woman, believe me, the hour cometh, when ye shall neither in this mountain, nor yet at Jerusalem, worship the Father. [22]Ye worship ye know not what: we know what we worship; for salvation is of the Jews. [23]But the hour cometh, and now is, when the true worshippers shall worship the Father in spirit and in truth: for the Father seeketh such to worship him. [24]God is a Spirit: and they that worship him must worship him in spirit and in truth. [25]The woman saith unto him, I know that Messiah cometh, which is called Christ: when he is come, he will tell us all things. [26]Jesus saith unto her, I that speak unto thee am he. [27]And upon this came his disciples, and marveled that he talked with the woman: yet no man said, What seekest thou? or, Why talkest thou with her? [28]The woman then left her waterpot, and went her way into the city, and saith to the men, [29]Come, see a man, which told me all things that ever I did: is not this the Christ? [30]Then they went out of the city, and came unto him.

In the instance of Mary of Bethany, who washed and anointed Christ's feet with her own hair as he sat to eat at the home of a Pharisee, he told her that her sins were forgiven.

Luke 7:36–50   [36]And one of the Pharisees desired him that he would eat with him. And he went into the Pharisee's house, and sat down to meat. [37]And, behold, a woman in the city, which was a sinner, when she knew that Jesus sat at meat in the Pharisee's house, brought an alabaster box of ointment, [38]and stood at his feet behind him weeping, and began to wash his feet with tears, and did wipe them with the hairs of her head, and kissed his feet, and anointed them with the ointment. [39]Now when the Pharisee which had bidden him saw it, he spake within himself, saying, This man, if he were a prophet, would have known who and what manner of woman this is that toucheth him; for she is a sinner. [40]And Jesus answering said unto him, Simon, I have somewhat to say unto thee. And he saith, Master, say on. [41]There was a certain creditor which had two debtors: the one owed five hundred pence, and the other fifty. [42]And when they had nothing to pay, he frankly forgave them both. Tell me therefore, which of them will love him most? [43]Simon answered and said, I suppose that he, to whom he forgave most. And he said unto him, Thou hast rightly judged. ⁴⁴And he turned to the woman, and said unto Simon, Seeth thou this woman? I entered into thine house, thou gavest me no water for my feet: but she hath washed my feet with tears, and wiped them with the hairs of her

THIS WOMAN HAS NOT CEASED TO KISS MY FEET

head. ⁴⁵Thou gavest me no kiss: but this woman, since the time I came in, hath not ceased to kiss my feet. ⁴⁶My head with oil thou didst not anoint: but this woman hath anointed my feet with ointment. ⁴⁷Wherefore I say unto thee, Her sins, which are many, are forgiven; for she loved much: but to whom little is forgiven, the same loveth little. ⁴⁸And he said unto her, Thy sins are forgiven. ⁴⁹And they that sat at meat with him began to say within themselves, Who is this that forgiveth sins also? ⁵⁰And he said to the woman, Thy faith hath saved thee; go in peace.

Mary of Bethany is associated by tradition with Mary Magdalene and the consensus of scholarly opinion is that they were one and the same person.

The other three Gospels give a similar account of Mary's anointing of Christ, but with some discrepancies.

John's Gospel has Mary anointing Christ's feet, but the event occurs at Mary's own home rather than at the house of Simon the leper as in Luke's account.

John 12:1–8 ¹Then Jesus six days before the passover came to Bethany, where Lazarus was which had been dead, whom he raised from the dead. ²There they made him a supper; and Martha served: but Lazarus was one of them that sat at the table with him. ³Then took Mary a pound of ointment of spikenard, very costly, and anointed the feet of Jesus, and wiped his feet with her hair: and the house was filled with the odor of the ointment. ⁴Then saith one of the disciples, Judas Iscar'iot, Simon's son, which should betray him, ⁵Why was not this ointment sold for three hundred pence, and given to the poor? ⁶This he said, not that he cared for the poor; but because he was a thief, and had the bag, and bare what was put therein. ⁷Then said Jesus, Let her alone: against the day of my burying hath she kept this. ⁸For the poor always ye have with you; but me ye have not always.

Matthew has Mary simply pouring the ointment on Christ's head.

𝕸𝖆𝖙𝖙𝖍𝖊𝖜 26:6–13   ⁶Now when Jesus was in Bethany, in the house of Simon the leper, ⁷there came unto him a woman having an alabaster box of very precious ointment, and poured it on his head, as he sat at meat. ⁸But when his disciples saw it, they had indignation, saying, To what purpose is this waste? ⁹For this ointment might have been sold for much, and given to the poor. ¹⁰When Jesus understood it, he said unto them, Why trouble ye the woman? for she hath wrought a good work upon me. ¹¹For ye have the poor always with you; but me ye have not always. ¹²For in that she hath poured this ointment on my body, she did it for my burial. ¹³Verily I say unto you, Wheresoever this gospel shall be preached in the whole world, there shall also this, that this woman hath done, be told for a memorial of her.

Mark, like Matthew, records the incident with Mary merely anointing Christ's head.

𝕸𝖆𝖗𝖐 14:3–9   ³And being in Bethany, in the house of Simon the leper, as he sat at meat, there came a woman having an alabaster box of ointment of spikenard very precious; and she brake the box, and poured it on his head. ⁴And there were some that had indignation within themselves, and said, Why was this waste of the ointment made? ⁵For it might have been sold for more than three hundred pence, and have been given to the poor. And they murmured against her. ⁶And Jesus said, Let her alone; why trouble ye her? she hath wrought a good work on me. ⁷For ye have the poor with you always, and whensoever ye will ye may do them good: but me ye have not always. ⁸She hath done what she could: she is come aforehand to anoint my body to the burying. Verily I say unto you, Wheresoever this gospel shall be preached throughout the whole world, this also that she hath done shall be spoken of for a memorial of her.

Christ broke even further with tradition when he announced that prostitutes weren't the worst sinners around.

Matthew 21:31   Verily I say unto you, That the publicans and the harlots go into the kingdom of God before you.

But he denounced anyone who consorted with a loose woman and considered it to be the worst form of dissipation and degradation as evidenced in his judgment on the prodigal son as retold in the famous parable.

Luke 15:30   But as soon as this thy son was come, which hath devoured thy living with harlots, thou hast killed for him the fatted calf.

The hitherto taboo subject of Christ's sexuality has been explored in great depth recently, with particular reference to Mary Magdalene. In *The Sexuality of Jesus*, William E. Phipps analyzes the statement made by Christ to Mary Magdalene subsequent to the resurrection.

John 20:17   Jesus saith unto her, Touch me not; for I am not yet ascended to my Father: but go to my brethren, and say unto them, I ascend unto my Father, and your Father; and to my God, and your God.

The verb *haptou*, used only here in the Fourth Gospel, ranges in meaning in the New Testament from making contact with a garment to having intercourse with a partner. The verbal tense here with the negative means to cease an action in which one has been engaged. This imperative graphically symbolizes the traumatic transformation to which Magdalene was adjusting as her tie with Jesus became exclusively intangible.

This same theology professor authored the book *Was Jesus Married?* in which he quotes the recently discovered Gospel of Philip as recording a tradition which referred to Magdalene as Christ's spouse.

All of this break with tradition gives an entirely new dimension of the true nature of Christ. Norman Pittenger, an Anglican specialist in Christology, has written recently in *Christology Reconsidered*, p. 61:

It is of first importance to stress that to speak of Jesus as being truly human is also to speak of him as a sexual being. Whatever ways he may have chosen to express or to rechannel his sexuality . . . it is clear that when his sinlessness is mentioned we do not, or should not, take this to imply asexuality.

ELI'S HORNY SONS

OR FORTY YEARS, ELI SERVED ISRAEL FAITHFULLY AS A PRIEST. His two sons, Hophni and Phinehas, became notorious whoremongers (womanizers). Because of Eli's sacerdotal position, the dishonor which they brought to their father's name was especially disgraceful.

> I Samuel 2:22–25 ²²Now Eli was very old, and heard all that his sons did unto all Israel; and how they lay with the women that assembled at the door of the tabernacle of the congregation. ²³And he said unto them, why do ye such things? for I hear of your evil dealings by all the people. ²⁴Nay, my sons; for it is no good report that I hear: ye make the Lord's people to transgress. ²⁵If one man sin against another, the judge shall judge him: but if a man sin against the Lord, who shall entreat for him? Notwithstanding, they hearkened not unto the voice of their father, because the Lord would slay them.

Through the mouth of a local prophet, Jehovah warned Eli of the impending death of both his sons.

> I Samuel 2:34 And this shall be a sign unto thee, that shall come upon thy two sons, on Hophni and Phin'e-has; in one day they shall die both of them.

True to the prediction, they were both killed on the same day in a battle with the Philistines. The truly arresting aspect of this narrative is the indication that Israel had begun to imitate her Canaanite neighbors by engaging in sacred sex acts, for there is every reason to suspect that in "lying" with the female worshippers, Hophni and Phinehas were serving as sex priests—a practice which was to become quite commonplace. So widespread, in fact, did this phallic worship become that the prophet Amos recounts a situation in which a father and son shared the same temple prostitute—proof that Israel at this point had thoroughly debauched themselves before Jehovah.

> *Amos* 2:6–8   ⁶Thus saith the Lord; For three transgressions of Israel, and for four, I will not turn away the punishment thereof; because they sold the righteous for silver, and the poor for a pair of shoes; ⁷that pant after the dust of the earth on the head of the poor, and turn aside the way of the meek: and a man and his father will go in unto the same maid, to profane my holy name: ⁸and they lay themselves down upon clothes laid to pledge by every altar, and they drink the wine of the condemned in the house of their god.

The subject of sacred prostitution is a difficult one at best, not only because we really do not know just how the system worked, but also because it is virtually impossible for the modern reader to comprehend such a practice. Gordon Rattray Taylor helps in conceptualizing this activity by his description in *Sex in History*, p. 227:

> The term prostitution, with its connotations of sordid commercialism and hole-and-corner lust, wholly misrepresents the sacred and uplifting character of the experience, as it was experienced by those who took part. It was nothing less than an act of communion with God and was as remote from sensuality as the Christian act of communion is remote from gluttony.

Nonetheless, Jehovah severely condemned these idolatrous practices, even when the money earned by the male or female in question was donated to the local temple.

> *Deuteronomy* 23:17–18   ¹⁷There shall be no whore of the daughters of Israel, nor a sodomite of the sons of Israel. ¹⁸Thou shalt not bring the hire of a whore, or the price of a dog, into the house of the Lord thy God for any vow: for even both these are abomination unto the Lord thy God.

Israel continuously vacillated between their devotion to Jehovah and their backsliding into the competing fertility religions. It must be borne in mind that Israel was a tiny nation living under the shadow of mighty states which were wholly devoted to phallic worship. There were heroic efforts to uproot any vestige of sex worship as revealed in the following extracts:

> **I Kings 22:45–46** ⁴⁵Now the rest of the acts of Jehosh'-a-phat, and his might that he showed, and how he warred, are they not written in the book of the Chronicles of the kings of Judah? ⁴⁶And the remnant of the sodomites, which remained in the days of his father Asa, he took out of the land.

> **Judges 2:16–17** ¹⁶Nevertheless the Lord raised up judges, which delivered them out of the hand of those that spoiled them. ¹⁷And yet they would not hearken unto their judges, but they went a whoring after other gods, and bowed themselves unto them: they turned quickly out of the way which their fathers walked in, obeying the commandments of the Lord: but they did not so.

Yet, despite these campaigns, a distinguished scholar of the period, Johannes Pedersen, has this to say in his book *Israel, III–IV:* "We receive the impression that sexual rites dominated the Israelite cultus throughout the monarchic period." (p. 470)

Another noted authority, L. M. Epstein, sums it up in *Sex Laws and Customs in Judaism:*

> The Bible reflected the native and higher Jewish ideal, while the routine of life fell a prey to the foreign influences which the people picked up from their neighbors. . . . All told, it presents the picture of a battle between the native Hebrew aversion to carnality in the name of religion, and the heathen groups, one after another, who made a religion of carnality. (p. 156)

Is it not plausible that Jehovah himself was largely responsible for Israel being so easily led astray and drifting so readily into these fertility cults and rites of sacred prostitution? After all, Jehovah had instituted the rite of circumcision in which the clipped penis became consecrated to him, and perhaps unwittingly, he had fostered a direct link to phallic worship and had created his own Frankenstein monster which was now very much out of control. Whereas in consorting with religious prostitutes Israel was occasionally forgetful of their mountaintop deity, through the use of sex idols and images, their attention was constantly riveted to the deification of the reproductive organs and the gods of fertility who ruled over both creation and procreation.

To this least understood, highly controversial and most important topic we must now turn our attention.

HUNG LIKE A JACKASS

ART AND PARCEL OF THE SACRED PROSTITUTION WHICH WAS now rampant in Israel was the worship of phallic images. A verse from Micah reveals that anyone consorting with these temple prostitutes had to pay a price for the privilege and that the income derived therefrom was used to erect (no pun intended) phallic images and idols.

> **Micah 1:7** And all the graven images thereof shall be beaten to pieces, and all the hires thereof shall be burned with the fire, and all the idols thereof will I lay desolate: for she gathered it of the hire of a harlot, and they shall return to the hire of a harlot.

Although these phallic idols were everywhere, it is difficult to realize how ubiquitous they really were because of the obfuscation of the texts by the translators. A keen student of the period, T. Clifton Longworth, says in *The Gods of Love: The Creative Process in Early Religion*:

> We must frankly admit that the translators of our Authorized Version of the Bible, acting with the best of motives, have deliberately camouflaged much of the phallic symbolism in the Old Testament by mistranslation.
> The two usual sex emblems are often mentioned; thus the pillar which was so often set up and anointed was, of course, the phallus, or male symbol; while the Hebrew word deliberately mistranslated "groves" was the *yoni*, or female organ. (pp. 64–65)

Even modern translations of the Bible do little to illuminate the obscurity surrounding the prevalence of phallic idols and images. In the famous story of Jacob's ladder, we have one of the earliest accounts of phallicism. After Jacob awakened from his dream, he set up a phallic image and named the place Bethel.

> **Genesis 28:18–19** [18]And Jacob rose up early in the morning, and took the stone that he had put for his pillows, and set it up

for a pillar, and poured oil upon the top of it. ¹⁹And he called the name of that place Bethel: but the name of the city was called Luz at the first.

If there is any doubt that the pillar was originally a sex symbol, during a later reform period, it was destroyed as a phallic idol.

II Kings 23:14–15 ¹⁴And he brake in pieces the images, and cut down the groves, and filled their places with the bones of men. ¹⁵Moreover the altar that was at Bethel, and the high place which Jerobo'am the son of Nebat, who made Israel to sin, had made, both that altar and the high place he brake down, and burned the high place, and stamped it small to powder, and burned the grove.

There seems to have been a hiatus in sex worship during the time of Saul, David and Solomon, but Solomon's son, Rehoboam, apparently through the influence of his Ammonite mother, introduced sex worship into the great temple at Jerusalem.

I Kings 14:22–24 ²²And Judah did evil in the sight of the Lord, and they provoked him to jealousy with their sins which they had committed, above all that their fathers had done. ²³For they also built them high places, and images, and groves, on every high hill, and under every green tree. ²⁴And there were also sodomites in the land: and they did according to all the abominations of the nations which the Lord cast out before the children of Israel.

Rehoboam's grandson, Asa, tried his best to eradicate this phallic worship.

I Kings 15:11–14 ¹¹And Asa did that which was right in the eyes of the Lord, as did David his father. ¹²And he took away the sodomites out of the land, and removed all the idols that his fathers had made. ¹³And also Ma'achah his mother, even her he removed from being queen, because she had made an idol in a grove; and Asa destroyed her idol, and burnt it by the brook Kidron. ¹⁴But the high places were not removed: nevertheless Asa's heart was perfect with the Lord all his days.

After some time, the saintly king Josiah brought all sex worship to an end through his assault on such idolatrous practices in the sanctuary of Solomon's great temple at Jerusalem. It is noteworthy here that a "grove" had actually been installed inside the sanctuary—this was no doubt a phallic representation of the vagina in honor of the goddess Ashtoreth, the wife of Baal.

> **II Kings 23:6–7** ⁶And he brought out the grove from the house of the Lord, without Jerusalem, unto the brook Kidron, and burned it at the brook Kidron, and stamped it small to powder, and cast the powder thereof upon the graves of the children of the people. ⁷And he brake down the houses of the sodomites, that were by the house of the Lord, where the women wove hangings for the grove.

The "pillars" and "groves" which we have been discussing were the phallic icons and images set up mostly in the great outdoors. Not content with these omnipresent effigies of the human sexual anatomy, the Isarelites also became addicted to smaller idols for use in the home or for worship inside the temples.

> **Judges 17:5** And the man Micah had an house of gods, and made an ephod, and teraphim, and consecrated one of his sons, who became his priest.

These smaller idols were called ephods and teraphim and in some cases were referred to simply as "household gods".

In the story of Jacob and his wives Leah and Rachel, we have an intriguing reference to these "household gods." Laban, the father of Leah and Rachel, was a pagan and when Jacob left without advance notice to Laban, Rachel stole her father's idols and hid them with her possessions.

When Laban finally overtook the group, he searched high and low for his idols but was unable to find them since Jacob was unaware of Rachel's theft.

As Laban entered Rachel's tent, Rachel feigned her monthly period so that Laban would not come near her, but all the while she was sitting on the idols.

> **Genesis 31:34–35** ³⁴Now Rachel had taken the images, and put them in the camel's furniture, and sat upon them. And Laban searched all the tent, but found them not. ³⁵And she said to her father, Let it not displease my lord that I cannot rise up before thee; for the custom of women is upon me. And he searched, but found not the images.

Since these household idols, like their larger counterparts, were shaped like an erect penis, the instance of Rachel sitting on the idols might be construed as an example of a female masturbating herself with a "sacred" dildo had it not been for the camel pouch intervening between her and her phallic "friends."

When Saul was intent on killing David, Michal took a "household idol" and put it in David's bed so that Saul's envoys would think that David himself was in the bed. For this idol to have been mistaken for a man, it must have been huge indeed!

> **I Samuel 19:12–16** ¹²So Michal let David down through a window: and he went, and fled, and escaped. ¹³And Michal took an image, and laid it in the bed, and put a pillow of goats' hair for his bolster, and covered it with a cloth. ¹⁴And when Saul sent messengers to take David, she said, He is sick. ¹⁵And Saul sent the messengers again to see David, saying, Bring him up to me in the bed, that I may slay him. ¹⁶And when the messengers were come in, behold, there was an image in the bed, with a pillow of goats' hair for his bolster.

Jezebel stands out as the most notorious practitioner of phallic worship in all of the Holy Writ. The vicious and vindictive queen idolized both Baal and Asherah, in all of their fertility-rite splendor, much to the consternation of her orthodox subjects and the rest of her court. Several of her eunuch attendants despised her apostasy so much that they hurled her out of a window to a violent death on the street below. Her blood was splattered against the palace wall, her corpse trampled by horses and what was left of her remains eaten by dogs. (see p. 172)

The canine cannibals did leave behind Jezebel's skull, feet and hands in fulfillment of Elijah's prophecy that her body would be scattered like shit on the field so that no one could tell who it was (II Kings 9). Still another pleasant Bible bedtime story!

The most convincing evidence that Israel constantly alternated between devotion to Jehovah and devotion to Baal and Ashtoreth is found in the history of Gideon's exploits. The warrior destroyed the phallic altar of Baal together with the vagina effigy which was next to it.

> **Judges 6:25–27** ²⁵And it came to pass the same night, that the Lord said unto him, Take thy father's young bullock, even the second bullock of seven years old, and throw down the altar of

Ba'al that thy father hath, and cut down the grove that is by it: [26]And build an altar unto the Lord thy God upon the top of this rock, in the ordered place, and take the second bullock, and offer a burnt sacrifice with the wood of the grove which thou shalt cut down. [27]Then Gideon took ten men of his servants, and did as the Lord had said unto him: and so it was, because he feared his father's household, and the men of the city, that he could not do it by day, that he did it by night.

Just a little later on, when Gideon had become a ruler in Israel, he set up a gold image which caused the people to revert once again to their phallic worship.

Judges 8:27   And Gideon made an ephod thereof, and put it in his city, even in Oph'-rah: and all Israel went thither a whoring after it: which thing became a snare unto Gideon and to his house.

Upon Gideon's death, there was still another campaign to supplant Jehovah worship with sex worship.

Judges 8:33–35   [33]And it came to pass, as soon as Gideon was dead, that the children of Israel turned again, and went a whoring after Ba'alim, and made Ba'al-be'rith their god. [34]And the children of Israel remembered not the Lord their God, who had delivered them out of the hands of all their enemies on every side: [35]neither showed they kindness to the house of Jerubba'al, namely, Gideon, according to all the goodness which he had showed unto Israel.

In the book of Hosea, a new element is introduced, for there now seems to be a cultic link between sex and alcohol in the prophet's pronouncement.

Hosea 4:11–16   [11]Whoredom and wine and new wine take away the heart. [12]My people ask counsel at their stocks, and their staff declareth unto them: for the spirit of whoredoms hath caused them to err, and they have gone a whoring from under their God. [13]They sacrifice upon the tops of the mountains, and burn incense upon the hills, under oaks and poplars and elms, because the shadow thereof is good. Therefore your daughters shall commit whoredom, and your spouses shall commit adultery. [14]I will not punish your daughters when they commit whoredom, nor your spouses when they commit adultery: for themselves are separated with whores, and they sacrifice with harlots: therefore the people that doth not understand shall fall. ¹⁵Though thou, Israel, play the harlot, yet let not Judah offend; and come not ye unto Gilgal, neither go ye up to Betha'ven, nor swear, The Lord liveth. ¹⁶For Israel slideth back as a backsliding heifer: now the Lord will feed them as a lamb in a large place.

Perhaps now it is easier to understand why a favorite metaphor used by the Bible chroniclers in general and the prophets in particular is that of Israel being a whore in pursuit of many lovers. This choice of metaphor was highly appropriate since Israel was quite literally prostituting itself by involvement with gods whose priests and priestesses offered sacramental sex to all comers (pun intended).

Exodus 34:12–16   ¹²Take heed to thyself, lest thou make a covenant with the inhabitants of the land whither thou goest, lest it be for a snare in the midst of thee: ¹³but ye shall destroy their altars, break their images, and cut down their groves: ¹⁴for thou shalt worship no other god: for the Lord, whose name is Jealous, is a jealous God. ¹⁵Lest thou make a covenant with the inhabitants of the land, and they go a whoring after their gods, and do sacrifice unto their gods, and one call thee, and thou eat of his sacrifice; ¹⁶and thou take of their daughters unto thy sons, and their daughters go a whoring after their gods, and make thy sons go a whoring after their gods.

Jeremiah went so far as to compare apostate Israel with a female ass in heat, and since both donkeys and asses were considered to be grossly sensual animals, that was saying a lot.

Jeremiah 2:24   A wild ass used to the wilderness, that snuffeth up the wind at her pleasure; in her occasion who can turn her away? all they that seek her will not weary themselves; in her month they shall find her.

Through the prophecies of Jeremiah and Ezekiel, Jehovah pulled all the stops, as it were, and condemned all of Israel as nothing more than a common whore for their pursuit of sensual worship. In this section, I would like to depart from my usual practice of quoting the King James Version and to provide, instead, a paraphrase of several divergent extracts which employ this metaphor most graphically. It is symbolic and allegorical prostitution, to be sure, but unbelievably explicit in detail.

I. Based on Jeremiah 3:1–6

There isn't any place in all the land that you haven't defiled by committing adultery against me. You sit like a whore alongside the road waiting for a customer to come along. You are like a faithless wife who gives herself freely to other men every time she gets the chance.

II. Based on Ezekiel 16:1–60

When I first saw you, you were still covered with blood and your umbilical cord had not as yet been cut. That same day of your birth, you were dumped into a field and left there to die until I came along and adopted you as my very own.

As you reached puberty, your breasts became well-rounded and your pubic hair began to grow fully, yet as far as I was concerned, you were still as naked as you were the day you were born.

I married you and you became mine legally, but then you began giving yourself freely as a prostitute to every Tom, Dick and Harry who walked by. All any man had to do to have you for his own was to ask you. And during all these many years of playing the whore against me, you never have stopped to think about that day of your birth when I first saw you still covered with the blood from your mother's womb.

You have gone ahead and built a spacious brothel and in that house you have offered to spread your legs for every man who came along. You have, in fact, been so eager to go to bed with every man available that you have not even charged for your services and for this reason, you are far worse than an ordinary prostitute who at least charges for her services and makes her living thereby.

But I will still have my revenge against you. I will personally knock down all your bordellos and strip you naked and embarrass you before all your lovers. You will be fully repaid for your unfaithfulness and then, although you don't deserve it, I will take you back as my wife and forgive you for everything that you have done.

III. Based on Ezekiel 23

(Israel had been divided into two kingdoms, and in this allegory, Ezekiel likens the two divided kingdoms to two sisters, Oholah and Oholibah, who have become prostitutes.)

Both of your sisters have become my wives. You, the older sister Oholah and you, Oholibah, the younger one, have become infatuated with the Assyrians, our neighbors.

You have found these attractive young men to be irresistible and you have gone to bed with captains, commanders and many other soldiers dashing about on their horses and wearing handsome blue uniforms.

Oholibah, you have become so thoroughly depraved that you have even fallen in love with painted pictures which you saw on a wall. They were pictures of Babylonian military officers and you were so sexually aroused by looking at these pictures, that in your imagination, you were already giving yourself freely to the men in the pictures.

You finally sent messengers to Chaldea to invite the officers whom the pictures represented to come to you in person, and you went to bed with them fornicating freely, although, after your brief affair was over, you hated them and broke off with them immediately.

Oholibah, like your older sister Oholah, you started your life of sexual promiscuity as a young girl when you were still in Egypt and the oversexed, gigolo lovers you had there were hung like a jackass and shot such a huge wad of sperm that it came out in floods like a load from a horse. And you let your bosom be caressed and your breasts fondled.

But I will soon stop both of you sisters from longing for Egypt and the many lovers you had to leave behind there. You will be fully repaid for whoring and then you will know who I really am.

If *Playboy* or *Penthouse* magazine describes a huge, jackass-size dick ejaculating gobs and gobs of come, fundamentalists label that pornography. But when the prophet Ezekiel portrays the very same thing, Bible thumpers call that divine inspiration! Every time I am asked what I consider the dirtiest verse in all the Bible, I point to Ezekiel 23:20 as the most hands-down obvious winner! And if Ezekiel was merely the ghost writer for the Almighty, then Jehovah indeed is just another dirty old man!

In the New Testament, John again employs the harlot metaphor in his book of Revelation, although here it no longer refers to an apostate Israel. The usual interpretation given to this passage is that the "Great Whore" and the "Mother of Harlots" who sits on seven hills is Rome because of its geographical site. The two most graphic quotes from Revelation are given in the King James Version.

Revelation 17:1–9 ¹And there came one of the seven angels which had the seven vials, and talked with me, saying unto me, Come hither; I will show unto thee the judgment of the great whore that sitteth upon many waters: ²with whom the kings of the earth have committed fornication, and the inhabitants of the earth have been made drunk with the wine of her fornication. ³So he carried me away in the spirit into the wilderness: and I saw a woman sit upon a scarlet-colored beast, full of names of blasphemy, having seven heads and ten horns. ⁴And the woman was arrayed in purple and scarlet color, and decked with gold and precious stones and pearls, having a golden cup in her hand full of abominations and filthiness of her fornication: ⁵and upon her forehead was a name written, MYSTERY, BABYLON THE GREAT, THE MOTHER OF HARLOTS AND ABOMINATIONS OF THE EARTH. ⁶And I saw the woman drunken with the blood of the saints, and with the blood of the martyrs of Jesus. And when I saw her, I wondered with great admiration. ⁷And the angel said unto me, Wherefore didst thou marvel? I will tell thee the mystery of the woman, and of the beast that carrieth her, which hath the seven heads and ten horns. ⁸The beast that thou sawest was, and is not; and shall ascend out of the bottomless pit, and go into perdition: and they that dwell on the earth shall wonder, whose names were not written in the book of life from the foundation of the world, when they behold the beast that was, and is not, and yet is. ⁹And here is the mind which hath wisdom. The seven heads are seven mountains, on which the woman sitteth.

Revelation 19:1–3 ¹And after these things I heard a great voice of much people in heaven, saying, Alleluia; Salvation, and glory, and honor, and power, unto the Lord our God: ²for true and righteous are his judgments; for he hath judged the great whore, which did corrupt the earth with her fornication, and hath avenged the blood of his servants at her hand. ³And again they said, Alleluia, And her smoke rose up for ever and ever.

Part IX
ABORTION, PREGNANCY BY PROXY, SEX DRUGS AND HUSBAND-SWAPPING

Jehovah's Penalty for Inducing An abortion

Exodus 21:22–25   ²²If men strive, and hurt a woman with child, so that her fruit depart from her, and yet no mischief follow: he shall be surely punished, according as the woman's husband will lay upon him; and he shall pay as the judges determine. ²³And if any mischief follow, then thou shalt give life for life, ²⁴eye for eye, tooth for tooth, hand for hand, foot for foot, ²⁵burning for burning, wound for wound, stripe for stripe.

This is the sole Biblical mention of abortion, and as one can decipher from the text, it really is an argument against a man injuring a pregnant woman and inducing a miscarriage, nothing more.

A fine was the only punishment meted out in the case of mere injury to the mother-to-be. The death penalty was exacted, however, if there was "mischief," which is to say if the pregnant woman died.

It is important to note that abortion was only considered to be a serious offense if it resulted in the death of the mother. This was the prevailing view for many centuries, even in the early Church.

It was Tertullian (A.D. 160–230) who first gave rise to the notion that the Bible specifically prohibits abortion, and his authority for his view of abortion being a crime was this very text quoted above. Tertullian then proceeded to expound his doctrine that the fetus became animated only after forty days if it was a male and after eighty days if it was a female. This was a moot point since there was no way to determine the sex of the fetus until after birth. And it should be noted that "animation" or "quickening" was not the same as viability. In the former case, it was when the soul entered the fetus; in the latter case, it was the point at which the fetus could survive outside the womb.

Jerome, who translated this text from Exodus into Latin from the original Hebrew, perpetuated this error although he should have known better. The subject was then bandied about among the early Church fathers who expressed many different points of view on when the fetus became animated, whether there was a difference between therapeutic abortion as opposed to abortion for convenience and whether it was the mother or the abortionist who was guilty of a crime.

The turning point came in 1869 with Pope Pius IX's pronouncement that abortion was always a grave moral offense and that anyone guilty of being associated with this crime was to be excommunicated. Since Pius IX had already enunciated the doctrine of papal infallibility, his fiat on abortion carried great weight.

Pius IX had also decreed in 1854 that Mary was free from original sin "in the first instant of her conception" and the idea soon gained currency that a soul was formed at the moment of conception and that while contraception merely prevented the formation of a new soul, abortion actually destroyed an already-formed soul, a belief held today not only by Roman Catholics, but also by many fundamentalists and orthodox Jews. This position views all abortions as murder and allows no exceptions.

HAGAR, THE BABY MAKER

ARAH WAS STERILE AND HER PRIMITIVE MIND ATTRIBUTED HER barrenness to Jehovah's having deliberately withheld from her the privilege of motherhood. She therefore urged Abraham to have intercourse with her maid Hagar in order to perpetuate his seed.

> *Genesis 16:1–3* ¹Now Sarai, Abram's wife, bare him no children: and she had a handmaid, an Egyptian, whose name was Hagar. ²And Sarai said unto Abram, Behold now, the Lord hath restrained me from bearing: I pray thee, go in unto my maid; it may be that I may obtain children by her. And Abram hearkened to the voice of Sarai. ³And Sarai, Abram's wife, took Hagar her maid the Egyptian, after Abram had dwelt ten years in the land of Canaan, and gave her to her husband Abram to be his wife.

Abraham acceded to Sarah's request, but enmity immediately developed between Sarah and Hagar with the result that Hagar ran away.

> *Genesis 16:4–6* ⁴And he went in unto Hagar, and she conceived: and when she saw that she had conceived, her mistress was despised in her eyes. ⁵And Sarai said unto Abram, My wrong be upon thee: I have given my maid into thy bosom; and when she saw that she had conceived, I was despised in her eyes: the Lord judge between me and thee. ⁶But Abram said unto Sarai, Behold, thy maid is in thy hand: do to her as it pleaseth thee. And when Sarai dealt hardly with her, she fled from her face.

Jehovah instructed Hagar to return to Abraham and Sarah, and Hagar obeyed the angel who delivered this solemn message. It was promised to

Hagar that her seed would be multiplied exceedingly.

I PRAY THEE, GO IN UNTO MY MAID

Genesis 16:7–16 ⁷And the angel of the Lord found her by a fountain of water in the wilderness, by the fountain in the way to Shur. ⁸And he said, Hagar, Sarai's maid, whence camest thou? and whither wilt thou go? And she said, I flee from the face of my mistress Sarai. ⁹And the angel of the Lord said unto her, Return to thy mistress, and submit thyself under her hands. ¹⁰And the angel of the Lord said unto her, I will multiply thy seed exceedingly, that it shall not be numbered for multitude. ¹¹And the angel of the Lord said unto her, Behold, thou art with child, and shalt bear a son, and shalt call his name Ish'ma-el: because the Lord hath heard thy affliction. ¹²And he will be a wild man; his hand will be against every man, and every man's hand against him: and he shall dwell in the presence of all his brethren. ¹³And she called the name of the Lord that spake unto her, Thou God seest me: for she said, have I also here looked after him that seeth me? ¹⁴Wherefore the well was called Beer-la'hai-roi: Behold, it is between Kadesh and Bered. ¹⁵And Hagar bare Abram a son: and Abram called his son's name, which Hagar bare, Ish'ma-el. ¹⁶And Abram was fourscore and six years old, when Hagar bare Ish'ma-el to Abram.

What is interesting about this entire incident of Hagar serving as a baby maker is that although Sarah had not conceived as yet, she was destined to conceive in her old age after her near-affair with King Abimelech (see Chapter 51). The lifting of the sterility curse on the king's household seemed to have had an effect on Sarah as well, and the once-barren wife of Abraham became fertile. The son of her old age was to be Isaac.

When three angel-messengers sent by Jehovah first announced to Sarah that she would bear a son in her old age, she was so incredulous of the possibility that she laughed to herself asking whether she was going to enjoy sex at her advanced age.

Genesis 18:9–12
⁹And they said unto him, Where is Sarah thy wife? And he said, Behold, in the tent. ¹⁰And he said, I will certainly return unto thee according to the time of life; and, lo, Sarah thy wife shall have a son. And Sarah heard it in the tent door, which was behind him. ¹¹Now Abraham and Sarah were old and well stricken in age; and it ceased to be with Sarah after the manner of women. ¹²Therefore Sarah laughed within herself, saying, After I am waxed old shall I have pleasure, my lord being old also?

She later lied to Jehovah and denied having laughed at the prospect of finally becoming a mother.

Genesis 18:13–15
¹³And the Lord said unto Abraham, Wherefore did Sarah laugh, saying, Shall I of a surety bear a child, which am old? ¹⁴Is any thing too hard for the Lord? At the time appointed I will return unto thee, according to the time of life, and Sarah shall have a son. ¹⁵Then Sarah denied, saying, I laughed not; for she was afraid. And he said, Nay; but thou didst laugh.

The precedent established by Sarah in conceiving a son after a lifetime of infertility was to be followed by other notable Bible personages. Manoah's wife was visited by an angel who announced that she would give birth to Samson (see Chapter 52).

Through the ministrations of the priest Eli, Elkanah's wife Hannah promised Jehovah that, if he would open up her womb, she would dedicate her son to him (I Samuel 1:1–28). She became the mother of Samuel whose very name in Hebrew means "asked of God." Samuel became one of Israel's most prominent judges and it was he who anointed David (I Samuel 16:13).

In the New Testament, the priest Zacharias was visited by the angel Gabriel who announced that his wife Elizabeth would conceive although she was well past menopause. Their son was to be John the Baptist (Luke 1:5–25). And of course, there followed the story of Elizabeth's cousin, Mary, who gave birth to Christ (see Chapter 49).

If Abraham had really been able to plug in to Jehovah's unfailing prescience, it would not have been necessary for him to turn Sarah's servant Hagar into a surrogate mother, especially in light of what happened after

Sarah gave birth to Isaac: there occurred <u>an incident with two diametrically opposite interpretations</u>.

Luke 1:20.

Zacharias, an aged priest, had a barren wife, Elizabeth. The angel Gabriel announced they would have a son, but because Zacharias doubted his word, he was struck dumb and unable to speak until the birth of the future John the Baptist.

Genesis 21:8–10 [8]And the child grew, and was weaned: and Abraham made a great feast the same day that Isaac was weaned. [9]And Sarah saw the son of Hagar the Egyptian, which she had borne unto Abraham, mocking. [10]Wherefore she said unto Abraham, <u>Cast out this bondwoman and her son: for the son of this bondwoman shall not be heir with my son, even with Isaac.</u>

<u>The more common explanation is that Ishmael merely taunted or made fun of the infant Isaac.</u> The other commentary is that the teenaged and sexually-capable Ishmael molested or sexually abused the baby.

Reading the text in the original Hebrew doesn't elucidate much, for just as the English verb "play with" can be a double entendre, the Hebrew verb *tzahak* also has the dual meaning of "verbally teasing" and of "sexually fondling."

Probably the best indication of what really transpired that day is the following account relating that the very next morning, Abraham expelled both Hagar and Ishmael from his household and sent them off into the wilderness.

Genesis 21:14 And Abraham rose up early in the morning, and took bread, and a bottle of water, and gave it unto Hagar, putting it on her shoulder, and the child, and sent her away: and she departed, and wandered in the wilderness of Be'er-she'ba.

JACOB'S FERTILITY CONTEST

FTER LABORING SEVEN YEARS TO WIN RACHEL'S HAND, JACOB understandably wanted to make up for lost time. Since Jacob favored Rachel over Leah, Jehovah inexplicably sided with Leah by allowing her to be fertile and making Rachel sterile.

Genesis 29:31   And when the Lord saw that Le'ah was hated, he opened her womb: but Rachel was barren.

Then began the fertility contest which resulted in the birth of the twelve sons who would later become the progenitors of the twelve tribes of Israel. (Jacob's name was subsequently changed to "Israel"—see Genesis 32:28.) First, Leah gave birth to four sons.

Genesis 29:32–35   ³²And Le'ah conceived, and bare a son; and she called his name Reuben: for she said, Surely the Lord hath looked upon my affliction; now therefore my husband will love me. ³³And she conceived again, and bare a son; and said, Because the Lord hath heard that I was hated, he hath therefore given me this son also: and she called his name Simeon. ³⁴And she conceived again, and bare a son; and said, Now this time will my husband be joined unto me, because I have borne him three sons: therefore was his name called Levi. ³⁵And she conceived again, and bare a son; and she said, Now will I praise the Lord: therefore she called his name Judah; and left bearing.

Rachel, in desperation over her own barrenness, offered her handmaid Bilhah to Jacob. Rachel's primitive mentality believed that fertility was contagious and she intended to sit underneath Bilhah when Bilhah gave birth so that a transfer of fertility might be effected.

Genesis 30:1–4   ¹And when Rachel saw that she bare Jacob no children, Rachel envied her sister; and said unto Jacob, Give me children, or else I die. ²And Jacob's anger was kindled against Rachel; and he said, Am I in God's stead, who hath withheld from thee the fruit of the womb? ³And she said, Behold my maid Bilhah, go in unto her; and she shall bear upon my knees, that I may also have children by her. ⁴And she gave him Bilhah her handmaid to wife: and Jacob went in unto her.

<u>Bilhah provided Jacob with two sons.</u>

Genesis 30:5–8   [5]And Bilhah conceived, and bare Jacob a son. [6]And Rachel said, God hath judged me, and hath also heard my voice, and hath given me a son: therefore called she his name Dan. [7]And Bilhah Rachel's maid conceived again, and bare Jacob a second son. [8]And Rachel said, With great wrestlings have I wrestled with my sister, and I have prevailed: and she called his name Naph'tali.

<u>Leah's productivity ebbed and she decided to offer her maidservant Zilpah to Jacob.</u>

Genesis 30:9   When Le'ah saw that she had left bearing, she took Zilpah her maid, and gave her Jacob to wife.

<u>Zilpah then bore Jacob two sons.</u>

Genesis 30:10–13   [10]And Zilpah Le'ah's maid bare Jacob a son. [11]And Le'ah said, A troop cometh: and she called his name Gad. [12]And Zilpah Le'ah's maid bare Jacob a second son. [13]And Le'ah said, Happy am I, for the daughters will call me blessed: and she called his name Asher.

<u>Leah's son Reuben, now a grown boy, went out into the fields and brought his mother some mandrakes. This Mediterranean herb is a member of the nightshade family of plants and to this day in the Middle East, it is believed to increase fertility in women, overcome impotence in men and to act as a powerful aphrodisiac. Even its roots have a decidedly phallic appearance.</u>
<u>Leah planned to keep the mandrakes for herself when Rachel asked that Leah give her some of the sex plants.</u>

Genesis 30:14   And Reuben went in the days of wheat harvest, and found mandrakes in the field, and brought them unto his mother Le'ah. Then Rachel said to Le'ah, Give me, I pray thee, of thy son's mandrakes.

<u>Leah became infuriated by the request from her sister who had already stolen her husband and she thought it presumptuous of Rachel to want the sex plants as well. Rachel then agreed, in exchange for the mandrakes, to allow</u>

FOR SURELY I HAVE HIRED THEE WITH THY SON'S MANDRAKES

Leah to sleep with Jacob that night in order to try out her fertility fruit. In polygamous marriages, the husband customarily alternated sleeping with his two wives. But one of the wives could always purchase from the other wife the privilege of sleeping with the husband on a given night. In the swingers' argot of today's society, this would doubtless be called "husband-swapping."

Genesis 30:15 And she said unto her, Is it a small matter that thou hast taken my husband? and wouldest thou take away my son's mandrakes also? And Rachel said, Therefore he shall lie with thee tonight for thy son's mandrakes.

When Jacob returned from working in the fields that day, Leah greeted him and advised him that she had purchased the privilege of sleeping with him that night through her love plants. Jacob acquiesced and slept with Leah that night.

Genesis 30:16 And Jacob came out of the field in the evening, and Le'ah went out to meet him, and said, Thou must come in unto me; for surely I have hired thee with my son's mandrakes. And he lay with her that night.

Jehovah restored Leah's fecundity (the account does not reveal whether or not the sex drug helped) and she bore Jacob two more sons as well as a daughter. Leah attributed her regained fruitfulness to the fact that she had offered her handmaid Zilpah to Jacob and she believed that Zilpah's productivity had now opened her own womb.

Genesis 30:17–21 [17]And God hearkened unto Le'ah and she conceived, and bare Jacob the fifth son. [18]And Le'ah said, God hath given me my hire, because I have given my maiden to my husband:

and she called his name Is'sachar. [19]And Le'ah conceived again, and bare Jacob the sixth son. [20]And Le'ah said, God hath endued me with a good dowry; now will my husband dwell with me, because I have borne him six sons; and she called his name Zeb'ulun. [21]And afterward she bare a daughter, and called her name Dinah.

Jehovah had a change of heart and finally allowed Rachel to conceive.

Genesis 30:22–24   [22]And God remembered Rachel, and God hearkened to her, and opened her womb. [23]And she conceived, and bare a son; and said, God hath taken away my reproach: [24]and she called his name Joseph; and said, The Lord shall add to me another son.

Rachel bore Jacob one more son but died in childbirth.

Genesis 35:16–20   [16]And they journeyed from Bethel; and there was but a little way to come to Ephrath: and Rachel travailed, and she had hard labor. [17]And it came to pass, when she was in hard labor, that the midwife said unto her, Fear not; thou shalt have this son also. [18]And it came to pass, as her soul was in departing, (for she died,) that she called his name Beno'ni: but his father called him Benjamin. [19]And Rachel died, and was buried in the way to Ephrath, which is Bethlehem. [20]And Jacob set a pillar upon her grave: that is the pillar of Rachel's grave unto this day.

In case you got lost in the complex narrative, the score card finally ends up reading like this:

Leah, seven children: Reuben, Simeon, Levi, Judah, Issachar, Zebulun, and Dinah.
Zilpah (Leah's maid), two children: Gad and Asher.
Rachel, two children: Joseph and Benjamin.
Bilhah (Rachel's maid), two children: Dan and Naphtali.

Except for the sole daughter, Dinah, the sons were destined to become the progenitors of the twelve tribes of Israel.

Part X
CIRCUMCISION OF THE LIVING AND THE DEAD

Jehovah's Foreskin Covenant

F I ASKED YOU WHAT YOU THOUGHT OF AN ORDINARY HUMAN father who subjected his helpless and defenseless infant son to a totally unnecessary and excruciatingly painful amputation operation, you would surely condemn that father as being sadistic, cruelly inhumane, and guilty of the grossest form of child abuse. Yet we are asked to believe that a kind, loving, and caring heavenly father, namely Yahweh or Jehovah, insisted on the amputation of the foreskin of all Hebrew male infants just eight days after their birth. I therefore submit that Jehovah, by virtue of his covenant with Abraham requiring permanent mutilation of the penis, qualifies as the number one child abuser of all time.

I also accuse Jehovah of creating Adam with a design defect. If this omniscient and omnipotent deity later decided that he wanted the foreskin removed, he shouldn't have put it there in the first place. Sad to say, the fate of all Hebrew males was to lose it before they ever had a chance to use it.

> **Genesis 17:1–13** ¹And when Abram was ninety years old and nine, the Lord appeared to Abram, and said unto him, I am the Almighty God; walk before me, and be thou perfect. ²And I will make my covenant between me and thee, and will multiply thee exceedingly. ³And Abram fell on his face: and God talked with him, saying, ⁴As for me, behold, my covenant is with thee, and thou shalt be a father of many nations. ⁵Neither shall thy name any more be called Abram, but thy name shall be Abraham; for a father of many nations have I made thee. ⁶And I will make thee exceeding fruitful, and I will make nations of thee, and kings shall come out of thee. ⁷And I will establish my covenant between me and thee and thy seed after thee in their generations, for an everlasting covenant, to be a God unto thee and to thy seed after thee. ⁸And I will give unto thee, and to thy seed after thee, the land wherein thou art a stranger, all the land of Canaan, for an everlasting possession; and I will be their God. ⁹And God said unto Abraham, Thou shalt keep my covenant therefore, thou, and thy seed after thee; in their generations. ¹⁰This is my covenant, which ye shall keep, between me and you and thy seed after thee; Every man child among you shall be circumcised. ¹¹And ye shall circumcise the flesh of your foreskin; and it shall be a token of the covenant betwixt me and you. ¹²And he that is eight days old shall be circumcised among you, every man child in your generations, he that is born in

the house, or bought with money of any stranger, which is not of thy seed. ¹³He that is born in thy house, and he that is bought with thy money, must needs be circumcised; and my covenant shall be in your flesh for an everlasting covenant.

Genesis 17:23–27   ²³And Abraham took Ish'ma-el his son, and all that were born in his house, and all that were bought with his money, every male among the men of Abraham's house; and circumcised the flesh of their foreskin in the selfsame day, as God had said unto him . ²⁴And Abraham was ninety years old and nine, when he was circumcised in the flesh of his foreskin. ²⁵And Ish'ma-el his son was thirteen years old, when he was circumcised in the flesh of his foreskin. ²⁶In the selfsame day was Abraham circumcised, and Ish'ma-el his son. ²⁷And all the men of his house, born in the house, and bought with money of the stranger, were circumcised with him.

From time immemorial, circumcision has been practiced as a tribal rite. The primitive mentality saw circumcision as a sacrificial offering to their tribal god, and what better sacrifice could they make than to offer a part of their very own anatomy?

Frequently, circumcision was practiced on both males and females, but in tribes where this evolved as a ritual, it did not usually occur until puberty at which time circumcision of both males and females is easily performed.

By Jehovah's insistence on having an infant circumcised on the eighth day after birth, female circumcision was precluded among the Israelites since it is virtually impossible to perform a clitoridectomy on a female infant.

Although most Biblical scholars and historians feel that the origin of circumcision has been lost in antiquity, none deny the importance it was given in Israel. The clearest indication of how solemnly the Israelites viewed this important rite is the fact that it was even allowed to be performed on the Sabbath if the eighth day after the birth of a male infant occurred then.

Death was decreed for any male whose foreskin was not sacrificed to Jehovah. Some interpreters insist that excommunication rather than death was the only penalty exacted.

Genesis 17:14   And the uncircumcised man child whose flesh of his foreskin is not circumcised, that soul shall be cut off from his people; he hath broken my covenant.

The Encyclopedia of the Jewish Religion indicates that an exception to the requirement of circumcision is permissible in cases of hereditary hemophilia, but only after two previous male children have hemorrhaged to death!

In his book, *In the Name of Humanity,* Joseph Lewis, who was quoted in Chapter 10, insists that circumcision was nothing more or less than a blood sacrifice and that it was made to preclude that the male child would be contaminated by his mother during her period of uncleanness. Since we already know that anything a woman touched during her period of uncleanness would be infected by virtue of contagion, this would hold true of her offspring as well. By circumcising her male child on the eighth day after his birth, this blood offering to Jehovah absolved the infant from being contaminated by his mother. For this reason, she would be unclean only forty days when giving birth to a son as opposed to eighty days when giving birth to a daughter.

In his very insightful book, *Jewish Magic and Superstition,* the Hebrew scholar, Joshua Trachtenberg, considers circumcision a magical rite and a protection against the forces of evil, much as magic wands and amulets are still widely used to bring good luck or to ward off harm (pp. 170–172).

During the eight days before the Hebrew child was ushered into the community with this operation, both the mother and child were in constant danger from evil spirits. But, once made, the blood sacrifice was considered sufficient to drive off evil spirits and to invoke the guardianship of the powers of good.

One method related by Trachtenberg for accomplishing this was to place the bloody foreskin in a bowl containing water and spices, and as members of the congregation left the ceremony, they would bathe their hands and faces in it. Another interesting method of producing a truly wonderful charm was that during the days preceding the rite, the foreskin of a child previously circumcised was put into the mouth of one who was to undergo the operation.

In *Sex Laws and Customs of Israel,* L. M. Epstein relates that according to Hebrew law, a stillborn child must be circumcised at the grave before burial. Also, any child who died before he was eight days old was supposed to be circumcised before burial in order to guarantee the salvation of his soul. These facts alone should convince the skeptical reader that the rite had nothing whatever to do with cleanliness as such.

In *The Christian Response to the Sexual Revolution,* the foremost Bible interpreter, David Mace, has this to say about circumcision:

> Every Hebrew man carried on his body the mark of his identity as a member of God's chosen race. And it was no accident that he carried this mark on his sex organ. Far from being disreputable,

this was the most sacred part of his whole body; therefore it was appropriate that it should be specially dedicated to God as the symbol that his whole body, his whole person, was dedicated to God. For it was with this organ that he became, in a special sense, a co-worker with God. (p. 20)

In both Hebrew and Arabic, the literal meaning of circumcision is "purifying" or "cleansing" in a religious sense and it must be viewed, therefore, in the light of being a blood sacrifice of purification. To impute to the rite a hygienic or sanitary factor is as fallacious as imputing these same qualities to the purpose behind the Hebrew custom of removing blood from meat so that it becomes kosher.

Throughout the Old Testament, circumcision is equated as being a sign of Jehovah's personal covenant with Israel and uncircumcision is a sign of belonging to the many heathen, idolatrous tribes which surrounded Israel.

Isaiah 52:1   Awake, awake, put on thy strength, O Zion; put on thy beautiful garments, O Jerusalem, the holy city: for henceforth there shall no more come into thee the uncircumcised and the unclean.

Jeremiah 9:25–26   [25]Behold, the days come, saith the Lord, that I punish all them which are circumcised with the uncircumcised; [26]Egypt, and Judah, and Edom, and the children of Ammon, and Moab, and all that are in the utmost corners, that dwell in the wilderness: for all these nations are uncircumcised, and all the house of Israel are uncircumcised in the heart.

Ezekiel 44:5–9   [5]And the Lord said unto me, Son of man, mark well, and behold with thine eyes, and hear with thine ears all that I say unto thee concerning all the ordinances of the house of the Lord, and all the laws thereof; and mark well the entertaining in of the house, with every going forth of the sanctuary. [6]And thou shalt say to the rebellious, even to the house of Israel, Thus saith the Lord God; O ye house of Israel, let it suffice you of all your abominations, [7]in that ye have brought into my sanctuary strangers, uncircumcised in heart, and uncircumcised in flesh, to be in my sanctuary, to pollute it, even my house, when ye offer my bread, the fat and the blood, and they have broken my covenant because of all your abominations. [8]And ye have not kept the charge of mine holy things: but ye have set keepers of my charge in my sanctuary for yourselves. ⁹Thus saith the Lord God; No stranger, uncircumcised in heart, nor uncircumcised in flesh, shall enter in my sanctuary, of any stranger that is among the children of Israel.

So deeply ingrained in the Hebrew psyche was the necessity of circumcision that Paul stirred a great controversy among the early Christians when he suggested that circumcision was not necessary for the Gentile converts to Christianity.

Mohel performing circumcision.

A genuine schism had developed over the matter and Paul felt he had resolved it once and for all when he pointed out that salvation was now obtainable through faith rather than merely by works or outward signs. For proof that Paul came to this conclusion quite late in his ministry, we have evidence that Paul himself performed the act on Timothy, a grown man, upon the latter's conversion.

Acts 16:1–3   ¹Then came he to Der'-be and Lys'-tra: and, behold, a certain disciple was there, named Timo'-the-us, the son of a certain woman, which was a Jewess, and believed; but his father was a Greek: ²Which was well reported of by the brethren that were at Lys'-tra and I-co'-nium. ³Him would Paul have to go forth with him; and took and circumcised him because of the Jews which were in those quarters: for they knew all that his father was a Greek.

Many historians view ritualistic circumcision as a form of symbolic castration. Seen in this light, it is unmistakably not a hygienic or sanitary measure, but rather a sacrificial act and ritualistic offering to appease Jehovah, and for that very reason, in Paul's view, it was no longer necessary under the new dispensation of grace which Christ had brought to the world on his kamikaze mission of salvation and vicarious atonement.

Acts 15:1–11   ¹And certain men which came down from Judea taught the brethren, and said, Except ye be circumcised after the manner of Moses, ye cannot be saved. ²When therefore Paul and Barnabas had no small dissension and disputation with them, they determined that Paul and Barnabas and certain other of them, should go up to Jerusalem unto the apostles and elders about this question. ³And being brought on their way by the church, they passed through Phoenicia and Samaria, declaring the conversion of the Gentiles: and they caused great joy unto all the brethren. ⁴And when they were come to Jerusalem, they were received of the church, and of the apostles and elders, and they declared all things that God had done with them. ⁵<u>But there rose up certain of the sect of the Pharisees which believed, saying, That it was needful to circumcise them, and to command them to keep the law of Moses.</u> ⁶And the apostles and elders came together for to consider of this matter. ⁷And when there had been much disputing, Peter rose up, and said unto them, Men and brethren, ye know how that a good while ago God made choice among us, that the Gentiles by my mouth should hear the word of the gospel, and believe. ⁸And God, which knoweth the hearts, bare them witness, giving them the Holy Ghost, even as he did unto us; ⁹and <u>put no difference between us and them, purifying their hearts by faith.</u> ¹⁰<u>Now therefore why tempt ye God, to put a yoke upon the neck of the disciples, which neither our fathers nor we were able to bear?</u> ¹¹<u>But we believe that through the grace of the Lord Jesus Christ we shall be saved,</u> even as they.

Galatians 5:6   For in Jesus Christ neither circumcision availeth any thing, nor uncircumcision; but faith which worketh by love.

Galatians 6:15   For in Christ Jesus neither circumcision availeth any thing, nor uncircumcision, but a new creature.

Colossians 2:8–15   ⁸Beware lest any man spoil you through philosophy and vain deceit, after the tradition of men, after the rudiments of the world, and not after Christ. ⁹For in him dwelleth all the fullness of the Godhead bodily. ¹⁰And ye are complete in him, which is the head of all principality and power: ¹¹in whom also ye are circumcised with the circumcision made without hands, in putting off the body of the sins of the flesh by the circumcision of

Christ: [12]buried with him in baptism, wherein also ye are risen with him through the faith of the operation of God, who hath raised him from the dead. [13]And you, being dead in your sins and the uncircumcision of your flesh, hath he quickened together with him, having forgiven you all trespasses; [14]blotting out the handwriting of ordinances that was against us, which was contrary to us, and took it out of the way, nailing it to his cross; [15]and having spoiled principalities and powers, he made a show of them openly, triumphing over them in it.

In summary, then, rather than considering circumcision to be a hygienic measure, the Israelites felt it was a religious act—a blood sacrifice. The removal of the foreskin marked a male as a member of the special covenant people. It was a token but permanent reminder that the male's reproductive powers belonged to Jehovah and that his penis was consecrated to Jehovah in order to fulfill the covenant promise.

In our somewhat more sophisticated and enlightened times, more and more doubt is being cast on the desirability of circumcision, even for hygienic purposes. We now know that cutting away the prepuce of the penis in circumcision causes the nerves under the foreskin to atrophy with a lessening of sensation. This raises the very legitimate question of whether or not the ulterior motive behind circumcision in Israel was that of reducing the potential in the male for sexual pleasure—consistent with other anti-sexual proclivities!

At least one eminent and respected Jewish scholar and historian argues convincingly that desexualization was an important aspect of penis pruning. Recognizing the sexual role of the foreskin, the great eleventh-century rabbi Moses Maimonides quite succinctly stated that the effect—indeed, a primary purpose—of circumcision was . . .

> . . . to limit sexual intercourse, and to weaken the organ of generation as far as possible, and thus cause man to be moderate . . . for there is no doubt that circumcision weakens the power of sexual excitement, and sometimes lessens the natural enjoyment; the organ necessarily becomes weak when . . . deprived of its covering from the beginning. Our sages say distinctly: It is hard for a woman, with whom an uncircumcised [man] had sexual intercourse, to separate from him.
>
> —*Guide for the Perplexed*, Part III, Chapter XLIX

One of the first physicians to challenge the practice of routine circumcision was Dr. G. S. Thompson who wrote this in a 1924 edition of the *British Medical Journal:*

> At one time, when I accepted what authorities and books told me, I was such a believer in the orthodox cult of circumcision that I performed the operation upon myself; but increasing experience has convinced me of the unsoundness of this operation. . . . I would strongly urge that this, amongst many other unnecessary and evil mutilations, be relegated to limbo.

Dr. Miles Atkinson, in his book *Behind the Mask of Medicine,* has even stronger words to say:

> My purpose was to discover why the religious rite of one people should have become the common practice of many others, and what justification there is for it when divorced from its religious implications.
>
> It seems impossible to avoid the conclusion that the large majority of circumcisions are done, not on any scientific principle, but rather as an automatic ritual . . . The operation has become a custom, an unthinking habit.
>
> The terminal part of the organ (glans penis) is covered by a delicate membrane and is highly sensitive. The function of the foreskin is to preserve this sensitiveness. Circumcision does away with this protection, the covering membrane becomes coarsened from exposure, and sensation is impaired. Worse still, the point of the maximum sensation is on the inner surface of the prepuce close to the frenum, and this point is bound to be removed. That the intensity of sexual sensation is impaired by circumcision is vouched for by men who have undergone the operation in adult life. This is surely an aesthetic tragedy that requires some justification, even if what you've never had you never miss.
>
> Very few babies actually require circumcision. To sum up the case, the weight of factual evidence is strongly against circumcision. . . . Aesthetically, it is undoubtedly bad—at best, a mutilation, at worst a tragedy.

Through a curious happenstance of fate, I still have my own foreskin only because Pittsburgh, PA, had a very active red light district in 1932, the year of my birth. The doctor who delivered me at home had quite a lucrative practice among the hookers there and really didn't care about the extra $5 normally charged to perform the operation, So I owe Pittsburgh's ladies of the night my everlasting gratitude for being intact and uncut!

The United States remains the only industrial country in the world where routine infant circumcision prevails as a medical procedure consistently ranked as the most common form of surgery. Cock clipping became entrenched in American medical practice in the late 1800s primarily to prevent, cure or at least minimize jacking off in the more lustful male segment of our population. America's foreskin folly!

Since our unique and unenviable stance on this issue is losing ground at a near-exponential rate, parents who still have difficulty making a decision about their own sons should contact this extremely helpful agency:

National Organization of Circumcision
Information Resource Centers (NOCIRC)
P.O. Box 2412, San Anselmo, CA 94960
Telephone: 415 488–9883

For the latest update on the pros and cons of circumcision, read two complete books on the subject: *Circumcision: An American Health Fallacy* by Edward Wallerstein (Springer Publishing Company, New York, NY, 1980) and *Circumcision: The Painful Dilemma* by Rosemary Romberg (Bergin & Garvey Publishers, Inc., South Hadley, MA, 1985).

The Holocaust serves as an historical footnote to any discussion of the tragic consequences of the Jews' slavish adherence to this mindless and unfortunate ritual. No self-respecting Aryan German would have sacrificed his prepuce for love, money or religion. Consequently, it was supremely easy for Hitler and his murderous Nazi henchmen to identify male Jews. Countless numbers of victims might otherwise have had their lives spared had they been able to pass as uncut Gentiles.

MOSES AND THE FLYING FORESKIN

𝕰𝖝𝖔𝖉𝖚𝖘 4:18–26　 [18]And Moses went and returned to Jethro his father-in-law, and said unto him, Let me go, I pray thee, and return unto my brethren which are in Egypt, and see whether they be yet alive. And Jethro said to Moses, Go in peace. [19]And the Lord said unto Moses in Mid'ian, Go, return into Egypt: for all the men are dead which sought thy life. [20]And Moses took his wife and his sons, and set them upon an ass, and he returned to the land of Egypt: and Moses took the rod of God in his hand. [21]And the Lord said unto Moses, When thou goest to return into Egypt, see that thou do all those wonders before Pharaoh, which I have put in thine hand: but I will harden his heart, that he shall not let the people go. [22]And thou shalt say unto Pharaoh, Thus saith the Lord, Israel is my son, even my firstborn: [23]and I say unto thee, Let my son go, that he may serve me: and if thou refuse to let him go, behold, I will slay thy son, even thy firstborn. [24]And it came to pass by the way in the inn, that the Lord met him, and sought to kill him. [25]Then Zippo'rah took a sharp stone, and cut off the foreskin of her son, and cast it at his feet, and said, Surely a bloody husband art thou to me. [26]So he let him go: then she said, A bloody husband thou art, because of the circumcision.

This passage is curious on several accounts. Aside from the obvious domestic quarrel between Moses and his wife, it is not at all clear why Jehovah threatened to kill Moses. Was the mountaintop deity outraged because Moses had failed to circumcise his son or was he just having another temper tantrum? Nor is it clear why Jehovah changed his mind about annihilating Moses after Moses' wife Zipporah cut off the foreskin of her young son's penis and threw it at Moses.

The most enigmatic aspect of the narrative is the fact that it relates an instance of a boy being circumcised long after the required eight days specifically set forth by Jehovah in his foreskin covenant with Abraham (see Chapter 34).

The explanation for this apparent inconsistency is found in a later passage in Joshua which explains that the rite of circumcision was temporarily suspended during the forty years of Israel's wandering in the wilderness, and for the second time in Israel's history, all the males, regardless of age, submitted themselves to this rite in order to fulfill the mandate of Jehovah's agreement with their progenitor Abraham. In this case, since there were so many boys and men involved, they were all quarantined in the camp until they had recuperated from the operation.

Considering the number of men and boys who were still intact after the two-generation hiatus in dick trimming, the "hill of the foreskins" mentioned here must have been quite a sight—a virtual mountain of flesh that might just as well have been called Prepuce Point!

Joshua 5:1–9 ¹And it came to pass, when all the kings of the Amorites, which were on the side of Jordan westward, and all the kings of the Canaanites, which were by the sea, heard that the Lord had dried up the waters of Jordan from before the children of Israel, until we were passed over, that their heart melted, neither was there spirit in them any more, because of the children of Israel. ²At that time the Lord said unto Joshua, Make thee sharp knives, and circumcise again the children of Israel the second time. ³And Joshua made him sharp knives, and circumcised the children of Israel at the hill of the foreskins. ⁴And this is the cause why Joshua did circumcise: All the people that came out of Egypt, that were males, even all the men of war, died in the wilderness by the way, after they came out of Egypt. ⁵Now all the people that came out were circumcised; but all the people that were born in the wilderness by the way as they came forth out of Egypt, them they had not circumcised. ⁶For the children of Israel walked forty years in the wilderness, till all the people that were men of war, which came out of Egypt, were consumed, because they obeyed not the voice of the Lord: unto whom the Lord sware that he would not show them the land, which the Lord sware unto their fathers that he would give us, a land that floweth with milk and honey. ⁷And their children, whom he raised up in their stead, them Joshua circumcised: for they were uncircumcised, because they had not circumcised them by the way. ⁸And it came to pass, when they had done circumcising all the people, that they abode in their places in the camp, till they were whole. ⁹And the Lord said unto Joshua, This day have I rolled away the reproach of Egypt from off you. Wherefore the name of the place is called Gilgal to this day.

Still another curiosity is the use of the word "feet." This word is used euphemistically in other places to stand for the genitals. One of the prophets predicted that, as the Israelites were to be carried off into exile, the Assyrian king who was their captor would shave both the hair of their heads as well as their pubic hair.

> **Isaiah 7:20** In the same day shall the Lord shave with a razor that is hired, namely, by them beyond the river, by the king of Assyria, the head, and the hair of the feet: and it shall also consume the beard.

In Chapter 10, the mother, in a period of great famine, was allowed to eat "her young one that cometh out from between her feet," and in Chapter 57, Ruth stealthily entered the barn where her husband-to-be Boaz was sleeping, and as she lay next to him, she uncovered his "feet."

In view of this tendency to substitute "feet" for "genitals," we have the amazing situation of the foreskin following a trajectory as it flew through the air of heading right for Moses' own cut cock almost as if it had a mind of its own and, knew exactly where it originally belonged!

DAVID CIRCUMCISES 200 PHILISTINE CORPSES

 AUL WAS BITTERLY ENVIOUS OF DAVID SINCE DAVID'S POPULARITY was greater than his own. His jealous rage resulted in two attempts to murder David, but Saul's javelin narrowly missed him both times.

> **I Samuel 18:6–11** ⁶And it came to pass as they came, when David was returned from the slaughter of the Philistine, that the women came out of all cities of Israel, singing and dancing, to meet king Saul, with tabrets, with joy, and with instruments of music. ⁷And the women answered one another as they played, and said, Saul hath slain his thousands, and David his ten thousands. ⁸And Saul was very wroth, and the saying displeased him; and he said, They have ascribed unto David ten thousands, and to me they have ascribed but thousands: and what can he have more but the kingdom? ⁹And Saul eyed David from that day and forward. ¹⁰And it came to pass on the morrow, that the evil spirit from God came upon Saul, and he prophesied in the midst of the house: and David played with his hand, as at other times: and there was a javelin in Saul's hand. ¹¹And Saul cast the javelin; for he said, I will smite David even to the wall with it. And David avoided out of his presence twice.

Saul was afraid of David because he felt that Jehovah favored and protected the youth. He subsequently got him out of the palace by demoting him to the rank of captain. Saul then offered his elder daughter Merab to David provided that he would prove himself to be a valiant soldier. His ulterior motive, of course, was that David would be killed in battle and that the Philistines, therefore, would do the dirty work of murdering David for him. In the end, however, Saul gave Merab in marriage to Adriel rather than to David.

I Samuel 18:12–19 [12]And Saul was afraid of David, because the Lord was with him, and was departed from Saul. [13]Therefore Saul removed him from him, and made him his captain over a thousand; and he went out and came in before the people. [14]And David behaved himself wisely in all his ways: and the Lord was with him. [15]Wherefore when Saul saw that he behaved himself very wisely, he was afraid of him. [16]But all Israel and Judah loved David, because he went out and came in before them. [17]And Saul said to David, Behold my elder daughter Merab, her will I give thee to wife: only be thou valiant for me, and fight the Lord's battles. For Saul said, Let not mine hand be upon him, but let the hand of the Philistines be upon him. [18]And David said unto Saul, Who am I? and what is my life, or my father's family in Israel, that I should be son-in-law to the king? [19]But it came to pass at the time when Merab Saul's daughter should have been given to David, that she was given unto Adri-el the Meho'lathite to wife.

Saul's younger daughter Michal loved David and this pleased the monarch no end since he was able to concoct a plan whereby he was virtually certain that David would be killed in battle: he asked David to slay one hundred Philistines and to bring their foreskins to him as a dowry for Michal's hand.

I Samuel 18:20–25 [20]And Michal Saul's daughter loved David: and they told Saul, and the thing pleased him. [21]And Saul said, I will give him her, that she may be a snare to him, and that the hand of the Philistines may be against him. Wherefore Saul said to David, Thou shalt this day be my son-in-law in the one of the twain. [22]And Saul commanded his servants, saying, Commune with David secretly, and say, Behold, the king hath delight in thee, and all his servants love thee: now therefore be the king's son-in-law. [23]And Saul's servants spake those words in the ears of David. And David said, Seemeth it to you a light thing to be a king's son-in-law, seeing that I am a poor man, and lightly esteemed? ²⁴And the servants of Saul told him, saying, On this manner spake David. ²⁵And Saul said, Thus shall ye say to David, The king desireth not any dowry, but a hundred foreskins of the Philistines, to be avenged of the king's enemies. But Saul thought to make David fall by the hand of the Philistines.

David was so intent on pleasing his future father-in-law that he and his men slew two hundred Philistines and brought their foreskins to the king in exchange for Michal's hand.

> **I Samuel 18:26–27** ²⁶And when his servants told David these words, it pleased David well to be the king's son-in-law: and the days were not expired. ²⁷Wherefore David arose and went, he and his men, and slew of the Philistines two hundred men; and David brought their foreskins, and they gave them in full tale to the king, that he might be the king's son-in-law. And Saul gave him Michal his daughter to wife.

Thanks to Sigmund Freud and to Women's Lib, nearly everyone is conversant with the concept of penis envy. I have coined the term "foreskin envy" here to describe the obsessive emphasis given in the Holy Writ on the rite of circumcision, especially when it reaches the extreme of being performed on the dead.

Surely there is no more grisly or more repulsive passage than this one in all the Scriptures. The true horror of it all does not really quite strike home until one pauses to reflect and to conjure up the macabre scene of David and his men dutifully performing necrophilic circumcision on the corpses of two hundred Philistine soldiers.

Saul understandably made this horrendous request because his jealousy and hatred of David were so intense that he wanted to insure that David would be killed in battle. Of course, when David showed up at the palace with double that number of foreskins, Saul's murderous intrigue was totally foiled and he was thereby compelled to give David Michal's hand.

Upon reading this passage, Voltaire, the great iconoclast, remarked with his characteristically acerbic and penetrating wit, that Michal might have been given her dowry in the form of a foreskin necklace!

Although the practice originated during the Biblical era, necrophilic circumcision is alive and well in present-day Israel. Enterprising rabbis there are making a financial killing by amputating the foreskins of cadavers of non-Jews prior to burial.

Part XI
THE LOWLY STATUS OF WOMEN

Bizarre Tests for Adultery and for Virginity

HE Hebrew law concerning adultery was clear and specific. It is the only sexual prohibition among the Ten Commandments. The Seventh Commandment reads:

Exodus 20:14 Thou shalt not commit adultery.

The penalty was prescribed in another dictum.

Leviticus 20:10 And the man that committeth adultery with another man's wife, even he that committeth adultery with his neighbor's wife, the adulterer and the adulteress shall surely be put to death.

A test was devised to determine whether or not a woman was guilty of adultery and if any quotation from the Scriptures reveals a people who were superstitious in the extreme, it is this fantastic prescription.

Numbers 5:11–31 [11]And the Lord spake unto Moses, saying, [12]Speak unto the children of Israel, and say unto them, If any man's wife go aside, and commit a trespass against him, [13]and a man lie with her carnally, and it be hid from the eyes of her husband, and be kept close, and she be defiled, and there be no witness against her, neither she be taken with the manner; [14]and the spirit of jealousy come upon him, and he be jealous of his wife, and she be defiled; or if the spirit of jealousy come upon him, and he be jealous of his wife, and she be not defiled: [15]then shall the man bring his wife unto the priest, and he shall bring her offering for her, the tenth part of an ephah of barley meal; he shall pour no oil upon it, nor put frankincense thereon; for it is an offering of jealousy, an offering of memorial, bringing iniquity to remembrance. [16]And the priest shall bring her near, and set her before the Lord: [17]and the priest shall take holy water in an earthen vessel; and of the dust that is in the floor of the tabernacle the priest shall take, and put it into the water: [18]and the priest shall set the woman before the Lord, and uncover the woman's head, and put the offering of memorial in her hands, which is the jealousy offering: and the priest shall have in his hand the bitter water that causeth the curse: [19]and the priest shall charge her by an oath, and say unto the woman, If no man have lain with thee, and if thou hast not gone aside to uncleanness with another instead of thy husband, be thou free from this bitter water that causeth the curse. [20]But if thou hast gone aside to another instead of thy husband, and if thou be defiled, and some man have lain with thee besides thine husband: [21]then the priest shall charge the woman with an oath of cursing, and the priest shall say unto the woman, The Lord make thee a curse and an oath among thy people, when the Lord doth make thy thigh to rot, and thy belly to swell; [22]and this water that causeth the curse shall go into thy bowels, to make thy belly to swell, and thy thigh to rot. And the woman shall say, Amen, amen. [23]And the priest shall write these curses in a book, and he shall blot them out with the bitter water: [24]and he shall cause the woman to drink the bitter water that causeth the curse: and the water that causeth the curse shall enter into her, and become bitter. [25]Then the priest shall take the jealousy offering out of the woman's hand, and shall wave the offering before the Lord, and offer it upon the altar: [26]and the priest shall take a handful of the offering, even the memorial thereof, and burn it upon the altar, and afterward shall cause the woman to drink the water. [27]And when he hath made her to drink the water, then it shall come to pass, that if she be defiled, and have done trespass against her husband, that the water that causeth the curse shall enter into her, and become bitter, and her belly shall swell, and her thigh shall rot: and the woman shall be a curse among her people. [28]And if the woman be not defiled, but be clean; then she shall be free, and shall conceive seed. [29]This is the law of jealousies, when a wife goeth aside to another instead of her husband, and is defiled; [30]or when the spirit of jealousy cometh upon him, and he be jealous over his wife, and shall set the woman before the Lord, and the priest shall execute upon her all this law. [31]Then shall the man be guiltless from iniquity, and this woman shall bear her iniquity.

Bible expositors do not know exactly what the "water of bitterness" was in the preceding narrative. What emerges clearly, however, is that the "suspicion offering" and the "law of jealousies" were designed to protect the interests of the husband, for there was never any such test for a man suspected of adultery.

In order to illustrate just how gullible the Hebrew psyche was in their belief in the efficaciousness of the test of bitter waters, L. M. Epstein relates in *Sex Laws and Customs in Judaism*, pp. 227–231, the following:

> If she is innocent, she emerges uninjured and in good spirits and goes back triumphantly to her husband and her home. If she is guilty, her face becomes yellow, her eyes bulge, her veins distend all over her body, her belly swells, her thigh falls, and she is quickly removed from the Temple court to die outside so as not to defile the sanctuary.
>
> Escape from the effects of the bitter water is impossible. Of one adulterous woman it is told that to escape the effects she substituted her identical twin sister to take the drink in her place. On the return of the sister from the ordeal, however, the guilty sister met her sister with embraces and kisses. it was through these kisses that the guilty wife inhaled the odor of the bitter water and died immediately,
>
> The humiliation of bitter water, if the wife be innocent, would add to her health if she was sickly, and give her beauty if she was homely. Not only would she become more prolific, but she would have easy labor. She would give birth to boys now instead of girls; she would have twins instead of single births; and the children she bore would be fair of complexion instead of dark, tall instead of short.

The test prescribed for determining virginity is not quite so bizarre as that for adultery. It is still a naive test at best and could hardly be considered a conclusive one in light of present gynecological knowledge of how easily a female's hymen can be ruptured by other-than-sexual means. The "tokens" of virginity mentioned here could only have been a bloodstained nightgown or bedding which the parents retained as physical evidence of their daughter's purity just in case an accusation to the contrary might occur. This custom is still widely practiced not only in the Middle East, but also in European countries. The paucity of virgins in Italy, for example, has led to cases of substituting tomato sauce for blood on the bridal sheet thrown over the balcony railing on the morning following the honeymoon night.

𝕯euteronomy 22:13–21 ¹³If any man take a wife, and go in unto her, and hate her, ¹⁴and give occasions of speech against her, and bring up an evil name upon her, and say, I took this woman, and when I came to her, I found her not a maid: [15]then shall the father of the damsel, and her mother, take and bring forth the tokens of the damsel's virginity unto the elders of the city in the gate: [16]and the damsel's father shall say unto the elders, I gave my daughter unto this man to wife, and he hateth her; [17]and, lo, he hath given occasions of speech against her, saying, I found not thy daughter a maid; and yet these are the tokens of my daughter's virginity. And they shall spread the cloth before the elders of the city. [18]And the elders of that city shall take that man and chastise him; [19]and they shall amerce him in a hundred shekels of silver, and give them unto the father of the damsel, because he hath brought up an evil name upon a virgin of Israel: and she shall be his wife; he may not put her away all his days. [20]But if this thing be true, and the tokens of virginity be not found for the damsel: [21]then they shall bring out the damsel to the door of her father's house, and the men of her city shall stone her with stones that she die; because she hath wrought folly in Israel, to play the whore in her father's house; so shalt thou put evil away from among you.

In the case of a priest's daughter, if she was found to have lost her virginity, the death penalty was still demanded, but in the form of incineration.

Leviticus 21:9   And the daughter of any priest, if she profane herself by playing the whore, she profaneth her father: she shall be burnt with fire.

Besides having the obligation to see to it that his daughter was kept sexually pure, a Hebrew priest could only marry a virgin and the law specifically forbade him from marrying anyone other than a virgin.

Leviticus 21:7   They shall not take a wife that is a whore, or profane: neither shall they take a woman put away from her husband: for he is holy unto his God.

Leviticus 21:10–15   [10]And he that is the high priest among his brethren, upon whose head the anointing oil was poured, and that is consecrated to put on the garments, shall not uncover his head, nor rend his clothes; [11]neither shall he go in to any dead body, nor defile himself for his father, or for his mother; [12]neither shall he go out of the sanctuary, nor profane the sanctuary of his

God; for the crown of the anointing oil of his God is upon him: I am the Lord. ¹³And he shall take a wife in her virginity. ¹⁴A widow, or a divorced woman, or profane, or a harlot, these shall he not take: but he shall take a virgin of his own people to wife. ¹⁵Neither shall he profane his seed among his people: for I the Lord do sanctify him.

Since Jehovah reputedly designed the female anatomy, as an omniscient deity, he certainly should have foreseen that the hymen would sometimes be completely absent at birth or easily torn before having intercourse for the first time. Therefore, to demand the death penalty for loss of virginity based on the absence of a ruptured maidenhead reveals a bloodthirsty, vindictive attitude toward his own creation. It is impossible of course, to estimate how many young female Israelites were butchered and sacrificed on the altar of this unconscionable and senseless edict.

Considering that the death penalty was exacted for loss of virginity, a curious variation on this theme occurs in the law. According to the edict, if a young lady loses her virginity in an out-of-the-way place, only her violator is subject to the death penalty since even if she had called for help, she presumably would not have been heard.

If, on the other hand, her violation occurred in a location that would have been within earshot of someone's assistance, she is considered just as guilty as her attacker and subject to the same fate.

> Deuteronomy 22:25–27   ²⁵But if a man find a betrothed damsel in the field, and the man force her, and lie with her: then the man only that lay with her shall die: ²⁶but unto the damsel thou shalt do nothing: there is in the damsel no sin worthy of death: for as when a man riseth against his neighbor, and slayeth him, even so is this matter: ²⁷for he found her in the field, and the betrothed damsel cried, and there was none to save her.

In summary, both the laws regarding adultery and those dealing with virginity should be considered as the Israelite's concept of property rights. Rather than being strictly moral issues, they were more a question of respect for another man's property so that an unfaithful wife or a promiscuous daughter was simply secondhand merchandise of less value to the husband or father, respectively.

Jephthah Offers His Daughter to Jehovah as a Human Sacrifice

AFTER JEPHTHAH THE BASTARD ROSE TO A POSITION OF GREAT prominence in Israel, he vowed to Jehovah that if he would give him victory over the Ammonites, upon his return, he would offer the first thing that would come out of his house as a sacrifice to Jehovah.

> **Judges 11:29–31** ²⁹Then the Spirit of the Lord came upon Jephthah, and he passed over Gil'e-ad, and Manas'seh, and passed over Mizpeh of Gil'e-ad, and from Mizpeh of Gil'e-ad he passed over unto the children of Ammon. ³⁰And Jephthah vowed a vow unto the Lord, and said, If thou shalt without fail deliver the children of Ammon into mine hands, ³¹then it shall be, that whatsoever cometh forth of the doors of my house to meet me, when I return in peace from the children of Ammon, shall surely be the Lord's, and I will offer it up for a burnt offering.

He was victorious over the Ammonites, and as he returned home from battle, his daughter came running out of the house to greet him.

> **Judges 11:32–34** ³²So Jephthah passed over unto the children of Ammon to fight against them; and the Lord delivered them into his hands. ³³And he smote them from Aro'er, even till thou come to Minnith, even twenty cities, and unto the plain of the vineyards, with a very great slaughter. Thus the children of Ammon were subdued before the children of Israel. ³⁴And Jephthah came to Mizpeh unto his house, and, behold, his daughter came out to meet him with timbrels and with dances: and she was his only child; beside her he had neither son nor daughter.

Since the young woman was Jephthah's only child, he repented of the vow he had made to Jehovah.

> **Judges 11:35** And it came to pass, when he saw her, that he rent his clothes, and said, Alas, my daughter! thou hast brought me very low, and thou art one of them that trouble me: for I have opened my mouth unto the Lord, and I cannot go back.

When Jephthah revealed to his daughter that he had made a promise unto Jehovah, she insisted that he fulfill the covenant, but she asked for two months to roam the mountains and to lament the fact that she would never be able to marry.

> **Judges 11:36–37** [36]And she said unto him, My father, if thou hast opened thy mouth unto the Lord, do to me according to that which hath proceeded out of thy mouth; forasmuch as the Lord hath taken vengeance for thee of thine enemies, even of the children of Ammon. [37]And she said unto her father, Let this thing be done for me: let me alone two months, that I may go up and down upon the mountains, and bewail my virginity, I and my fellows.

Jephthah agreed to her request. At the end of the two-month period, she returned and Jephthah then fulfilled his promise to Jehovah. Thereafter, it became the custom in Israel to spend four days each year lamenting the fate of Jephthah's daughter.

> **Judges 11:38–40** [38]And he said, Go. And he sent her away for two months: and she went with her companions, and bewailed her virginity upon the mountains. [39]And it came to pass at the end of two months, that she returned unto her father, who did with her according to his vow which he had vowed: and she knew no man. And it was a custom in Israel, [40]that the daughters of Israel went yearly to lament the daughter of Jephthah the Gil'eadite four days in a year.

This passage qualifies as being one of the most controversial in all the Holy Writ. Jehovah put Jephthah to a test similar to that demanded of Abraham when he was asked to sacrifice his son Isaac, but at the last minute, Jehovah stayed Abraham's knife-wielding hand from killing the boy and granted him a reprieve (Gen. 22:1–19).

In the case of Jephthah's daughter, however, there was no reprieve. But there is no dispute about the fact that Jephthah was not similarly spared by Jehovah. The difference of opinion centers on whether or not Jephthah actually burned his daughter to death as a human sacrifice to Jehovah or whether he merely consecrated her to Jehovah in a state of perpetual virginity.

The consensus of Biblical scholars seems to be that Jephthah allowed his daughter to live, but then insisted that she always remain a virgin. As prestigious an authority as Josephus, however, insists that she was burned to death by Jephthah. And if all Israel memorialized the fate of Jephthah's daughter on an annual basis, it hardly seems likely that they were simply memorializing her being confined to a perpetual state of virginity.

THE FEMALE HAND THAT FONDLES SHALL BE CUT OFF

F WE COULD GO BACK IN A TIME MACHINE TO THE BIBLICAL ERA and visit any one of the many nations surrounding Israel, and if we saw a handless woman, we would assume that, barring some type of birth defect, she had met with some sort of terrible accident. Not so in Israel!

If we were to see a handless female Israelite, we could rightly say, "Aha! We know where your hand has been and why it was cut off." The incomprehensibly bizarre and sexist injunction mandated that if a woman touched a man's genitals—even if she was trying to stifle the onslaught of an enemy against her own husband—her hand would be amputated. The extremely severe rule for females only provides still another example of the lowly status of the fair sex in Hebrew culture and embodies one more important Biblical watchword: Women, keep your hands to yourselves!

> Deuteronomy 25:11–12   11When men strive together one
> with another, and the wife of the one draweth near for to deliver
> her husband out of the hand of him that smiteth him and putteth
> forth her hand, and taketh him by the secrets: 12then thou shalt cut
> off her hand, thine eye shall not pity her.

It is so bemusing that the penalty should be so severe for a woman who touched a man's genitals for, although a man's generative organs were sacrosanct, an Israelite who was swearing an oath would customarily solemnize it by grasping the penis of the man to whom he was making the affirmation. This "penis-shake" or gropathon was almost as commonplace as our modern handshake.

When Abraham wanted to send his servant in search of a wife for his son Isaac, he made him take an oath by "putting his hand under his thigh," which means that the servant grasped Abraham's penis to solemnize the oath.

> Genesis 24:1–9   1And Abraham was old, and well stricken in
> age: and the Lord had blessed Abraham in all things. 2And
> Abraham said unto his eldest servant of his house, that ruled over

all that he had, Put, I pray thee, thy hand under my thigh: ³and I will make thee swear by the Lord, the God of heaven, and the God of the earth, that thou shalt not take a wife unto my son of the daughters of the Canaanites, among whom I dwell: ⁴but thou shalt go unto my country, and to my kindred, and take a wife unto my son Isaac. ⁵And the servant said unto him, Peradventure the woman will not be willing to follow me unto this land: must I needs bring thy son again unto the land from whence thou camest? ⁶And Abraham said unto him, Beware thou that thou bring not my son thither again. ⁷The Lord God of heaven, which took me from my father's house, and from the land of my kindred, and which spake unto me, and that sware unto me, saying, Unto thy seed will I give this land; he shall send his angel before thee, and thou shalt take a wife unto my son from thence. ⁸And if the woman will not be willing to follow thee, then thou shalt be clear from this my oath: only bring not my son thither again. ⁹And the servant put his hand under the thigh of Abraham his master, and sware to him concerning that matter.

The New Standard Bible Dictionary in an article on "Oath" on page 630 says: "In exceptional cases the hand might be placed under the thigh of the person imposing the oath as a sign of regard for the mystery of generation, whose source was God." The Encyclopedia Biblica says: "'Thigh' refers to the generative organ." (Vol. III, col. 3453, art. Oath) It becomes clear then that the man swearing an oath would grasp the penis or the testicles or both of the other male as part of the affirmation.

Before the death of Israel (Jacob), he called his son Joseph to his deathbed, and as Joseph grasped his father's penis, Israel made his son promise that he would take his remains out of Egypt and bury him in the land of his fathers. Joseph complied and thus sealed the oath to his father.

Genesis 47:29–31 ²⁹And the time drew nigh that Israel must die: and he called his son Joseph, and said unto him, If now I have found grace in thy sight, put, I pray thee, thy hand under my thigh, and deal kindly and truly with me; bury me not, I pray thee, in Egypt: ³⁰but I will lie with my fathers, and thou shalt carry me out of Egypt, and bury me in their buryingplace. And he said, I will do as thou has said. ³¹And he said, Swear unto me. And he sware unto him. And Israel bowed himself upon the bed's head.

An interesting account of this practice on a wholesale basis occurs in the account of the coronation of Solomon as king of all Israel.

> **I Chronicles 29:24**   And all the princes, and the mighty men, and all the sons likewise of king David, submitted themselves unto Solomon the king.

This veiled reference to the "penis-shake" could much more accurately be translated: "And all the princes, and the mighty men, and all the sons likewise of king David, grasped Solomon's penis and swore an oath." The scene presents us with the spectacle of a lineup of the mighty men of the kingdom awaiting their turn to participate in the royal "penis-shake" with Solomon.

After the death of Solomon, the elders of Israel came to Rehoboam, Solomon's son, to request that he lighten the burdens on them. Rehoboam's reply was:

> **I Kings 12:10**   And the young men that were grown up with him spake unto him saying, Thus shalt thou speak unto this people that spake unto thee, saying, Thy father made our yoke heavy, but make thou it lighter, unto us; thus shalt thou say unto them, My little finger shall be thicker than my father's loins.

In modern English, he was really saying, "You will feel my little finger more heavily upon you than my father's penis!"

This custom of grasping the male genitals when swearing a solemn oath reputedly survives to this day among the Rwala Bedouins in the Syrian Desert.

In English, both our words "testify" and "testament" are linguistically related to this quaint custom of swearing an oath.

Two Major Wife-Kidnapping Expeditions

 FTER THE BARBARIC RAPE AND MURDER OF THE LEVITE'S concubine-wife (see Chapter 16), the tribe of Benjamin had been virtually obliterated. The few hundred Benjaminites who remained were in need of wives, but the other tribes of Israel had considered Benjamin to be an accursed tribe and they were all refusing to let any of their daughters marry any of the Benjaminites.

Judges 21:1   Now the men of Israel had sworn in Mizpeh, saying, There shall not any of us give his daughter unto Benjamin to wife.

At a council meeting of the twelve tribes of Israel, one tribe had failed to send any representatives—the tribe of Jabesh-gilead. Therefore, in true-to-form reaction to this blatant breach of the Hebrew law, the entire tribe of Jabesh-gilead was condemned to death.

Judges 21:2–9   ²And the people came to the house of God, and abode there till even before God, and lifted up their voices, and wept sore; ³and said, O Lord God of Israel, why is this come to pass in Israel, that there should be today one tribe lacking in Israel? ⁴And it came to pass on the morrow, that the people rose early, and built there an altar, and offered burnt offerings and peace offerings. ⁵And the children of Israel said, Who is there among all the tribes of Israel that came not up with the congregation unto the Lord? For they had made a great oath concerning him that came not up to the Lord to Mizpeh, saying, He shall surely be put to death. ⁶And the children of Israel repented them for Benjamin their brother, and said, There is one tribe cut off from Israel this day. ⁷How shall we do for wives for them that remain, seeing we have sworn by the Lord, that we will not give them of our daughters to wives? ⁸And they said, What one is there of the tribes of Israel that came not up to Mizpeh to the Lord? And, behold, there came none to the camp from Ja'besh-gil'e-ad to the assembly. ⁹For the people were numbered, and, behold, there were none of the inhabitants of Ja'besh-gil'e-ad there.

Twelve thousand soldiers were sent against this tribe and they followed the usual pattern of slaying all the males and all the females who were not virgins. In this instance, they even slew all the children, both male and female, and spared only the virgins of marriageable age.

Judges 21:10–11   ¹⁰And the congregation sent thither twelve thousand men of the valiantest, and commanded them, saying, Go and smite the inhabitants of Ja'besh-gil'e-ad with the edge of the sword, with the women and the children. ¹¹And this is the thing that ye shall do, Ye shall utterly destroy every male, and every woman that hath lain by man.

The total bounty from this foray and massacre was four hundred virgins, and all four hundred were sent to the Benjaminites as a peace and goodwill offering so that they would now have wives to marry. The four hundred young women, however, were not quite enough to provide wives for all the Benjaminites.

Judges 21:12–15 ¹²And they found among the inhabitants of Ja'besh-gil'e-ad four hundred young virgins, that had known no man by lying with any male: and they brought them unto the camp to Shiloh, which is in the land of Canaan. ¹³And the whole congregation sent some to speak to the children of Benjamin that were in the rock Rimmon, and to call peaceably unto them. ¹⁴And Benjamin came again at that time; and they gave them wives which they had saved alive of the women of Ja'besh-gil'e-ad; and yet so they sufficed them not. ¹⁵And the people repented them for Benjamin, because that the Lord had made a breach in the tribes of Israel.

The council of the twelve tribes reconvened and tried to decide how they could provide wives for the remaining unmarried Benjaminites without allowing any of their daughters to marry them and without destroying still another tribe of Israel.

Judges 21:16–18 ¹⁶Then the elders of the congregation said, How shall we do for wives for them that remain, seeing the women are destroyed out of Benjamin? ¹⁷And they said, There must be an inheritance for them that be escaped of Benjamin, that a tribe be not destroyed out of Israel. ¹⁸Howbeit we may not give them wives of our daughters: for the children of Israel have sworn, saying, Cursed be he that giveth a wife to Benjamin.

A second expedition was then planned to kidnap prospective wives from among the women of Shiloh who were dancing in the vineyards as part of what was probably a delightful country festival. Any complaining fathers or brothers had to accept the explanation that this was simply an alternate plan rather than destroying still another tribe of Israel or allowing any daughters to willingly marry a Benjaminite.

Judges 21:19–22 ¹⁹Then they said, Behold, there is a feast of the Lord in Shiloh yearly, in a place which is on the north side of

Beth-el, on the east side of the highway that goeth up from Bethel to Shechem, and on the south of Lebo'nah. [20]Therefore they commanded the children of Benjamin, saying, Go and lie in wait in the vineyards; [21]and see, and, behold, if the daughters of Shiloh come out to dance in dances, then come ye out of the vineyards, and catch you every man his wife of the daughters of Shiloh, and go to the land of Benjamin. [22]And it shall be, when their fathers or their brethren come unto us to complain, that we will say unto them, Be favorable unto them for our sakes: because we reserved not to each man his wife in the war: for ye did not give unto them at this time, that ye should be guilty.

The kidnapping plan was executed as conceived, although the number of virgins who were thus abducted is not revealed.

Judges 21:23–25   [23]And the children of Benjamin did so, and took them wives, according to their number, of them that danced, whom they caught: and they went and returned unto their inheritance, and repaired the cities, and dwelt in them. [24]And the children of Israel departed thence at that time, every man to his tribe and to his family, and they went out from thence every man to his inheritance. [25]In those days there was no king in Israel: every man did that which was right in his own eyes.

VIRGINS AS SPOILS OF WAR

EHOVAH GAVE MOSES SPECIFIC INSTRUCTIONS TO RETALIATE against the Midianites for their having led the children of Israel into participation in pagan fertility rites (see Chapter 21). Moses' response was to send a massive army of 12,000 warriors against the Midianites.

After a total victory against the enemy, the Israelites brought all the spoils of war including the captives into the Israelite camp.

Moses was enraged when he saw that the Midianite women and children had been allowed to be taken as prisoners of war. He then gave the command to slay all the male children and any women who were not virgins. The total haul of virgins was an extraordinary 32,000!

Numbers 31:1–10   [1]And the Lord spake unto Moses, saying, [2]Avenge the children of Israel of the Mid'ianites: afterward shalt thou be gathered unto thy people. ³And Moses spake unto the people, saying, Arm some of yourselves unto the war, and let them go against the Mid'ianites, and avenge the Lord of Mid'ian. ⁴Of every tribe a thousand, throughout all the tribes of Israel, shall ye send to the war. ⁵So there were delivered out of the thousands of Israel, a thousand of every tribe, twelve thousand armed for war. ⁶And Moses sent them to the war, a thousand of every tribe, them and Phin'e-has the son of Ele-a'zar the priest, to the war, with the holy instruments, and the trumpets to blow in his hand. ⁷And they warred against the Mid'ianites, as the Lord commanded Moses; and they slew all the males. ⁸And they slew the kings of Mid'ian, beside the rest of them that were slain; namely, Evi, and Rekem, and Zur, and Hur, and Reba, five kings of Mid'ian: Ba'laam also the son of Be'or they slew with the sword. ⁹And the children of Israel took all the women of Mid'i-an captives, and their little ones, and took the spoil of all their cattle, and all their flocks, and all their goods. ¹⁰And they burnt all their cities wherein they dwelt, and all their goodly castles, with fire.

𝔑umbers 31:32–35   ³²And the booty, being the rest of the prey which the men of war had caught, was six hundred thousand and seventy thousand and five thousand sheep, ³³and threescore and twelve thousand beeves, ³⁴and threescore and one thousand asses, ³⁵and thirty and two thousand persons in all, of women that had not known man by lying with him.

If the wanton execution of male children and of women who were not virgins seems a bit extreme, there were two explicit edicts from Jehovah authorizing such carnage:

𝔇euteronomy 20:10–18   ¹⁰When thou comes nigh unto a city to fight against it, then proclaim peace unto it. ¹¹And it shall be, if it make thee answer of peace, and open unto thee, then it shall be, that all the people that is found therein shall be tributaries unto thee, and they shall serve thee. ¹²And if it will make no peace with thee, but will make war against thee, then thou shalt besiege it: ¹³and when the Lord thy God hath delivered it into thine hands, thou shalt smite every male thereof with the edge of the sword: ¹⁴but the women, and the little ones, and the cattle, and all that is in the city, even all the spoil thereof, shalt thou take unto thyself;

and thou shalt eat the spoil of thine enemies, which the Lord thy God hath given thee. ¹⁵Thus shalt thou do unto all the cities which are very far off from thee, which are not of the cities of these nations. ¹⁶But of the cities of these people, which the Lord thy God doth give thee for an inheritance, thou shalt save alive nothing that breatheth: ¹⁷but thou shalt utterly destroy them; namely, the Hittites, and the Amorites, the Canaanites, and the Per'izzites, the Hivites, and the Jeb'usites; as the Lord thy God hath commanded thee: ¹⁸that they teach you not to do after all their abominations, which they have done unto their gods; so should ye sin against the Lord your God.

Deuteronomy 21:10–14

¹⁰When thou goest forth to war against thine enemies, and the Lord thy God hath delivered them into thine hands, and thou hast taken them captive, ¹¹and seest among the captives a beautiful woman, and hast a desire unto her, that thou wouldest have her to thy wife; ¹²then thou shalt bring her home to thine house; and she shall shave her head, and pare her nails; ¹³and she shall put the raiment of her captivity from off her, and shall remain in thine house, and bewail her father and her mother a full month: and after that thou shalt go in unto her, and be her husband, and she shall be thy wife. ¹⁴And it shall be, if thou have no delight in her, then thou shalt let her go whither she will; but thou shalt not sell her at all for money, thou shalt not make merchandise of her, because thou hast humbled her.

In an unusual display of mercy, Jehovah decreed that once a man divested himself of a woman captured in war, he could not sell her as a slave. Even Jehovah recognized the fact that secondhand merchandise had little resale value!

In addition to Jehovah's proclamations concerning virgins as prisoners of war, he also indicated that the Israelites were free to ravish the wives of any defeated enemies.

Isaiah 13:11–16

¹¹And I will punish the world for their evil, and the wicked for their iniquity; and I will cause the arrogancy of the proud to cease, and will lay low the haughtiness of the terrible. ¹²I will make a man more precious than fine gold; even a man than the golden wedge of Ophir. ¹³Therefore I will shake the heavens, and the earth shall remove out of her place, in the wrath

of the Lord of hosts, and in the day of his fierce anger. ¹⁴And it shall be as the chased roe, and as a sheep that no man taketh up: they shall every man turn to his own people, and flee every one into his own land. ¹⁵<u>Every one that is found shall be thrust through; and every one that is joined unto them shall fall by the sword.</u> ¹⁶<u>Their children also shall be dashed to pieces before their eyes; their houses shall be spoiled, and their wives ravished.</u>

<u>Jehovah warned Israel in no uncertain terms that their wives would be given to others for sexual pleasure if they were to continue to be disobedient and hard of heart.</u>

Deuteronomy 28:28–30   ²⁸The Lord shall smite thee with madness, and blindness, and astonishment of heart: ²⁹and thou shalt grope at noonday, as the blind gropeth in darkness, and thou shalt not prosper in thy ways: and thou shalt be only oppressed and spoiled evermore, and no man shall save thee. ³⁰Thou shalt betroth a wife, and another man shall lie with her: thou shalt build a house, and thou shalt not dwell therein: thou shalt plant a vineyard, and shalt not gather the grapes thereof.

Jeremiah 6:11–14   ¹¹Therefore I am full of the fury of the Lord; I am weary with holding in: I will pour it out upon the children abroad, and upon the assembly of young men together: for even the husband with the wife shall be taken, the aged with him that is full of days. ¹²And their houses shall be turned unto others, with their fields and wives together: for I will stretch out my hand upon the inhabitants of the land, saith the Lord. ¹³For from the least of them even unto the greatest of them every one is given to covetousness; and from the prophet even unto the priest every one dealeth falsely. ¹⁴They have healed also the hurt of the daughter of my people slightly, saying, Peace, peace; when there is no peace.

Jeremiah 8:8–11   ⁸How do ye say, We are wise, and the law of the Lord is with us? Lo, certainly in vain made he it: the pen of the scribes is in vain. ⁹The wise men are ashamed, they are dismayed and taken: lo, <u>they have rejected the word of the Lord; and what wisdom is in them? ¹⁰Therefore will I give their wives unto others, and their fields to them that shall inherit them:</u> for every one from the least even unto the greatest is given to covetousness, from the prophet even unto the priest every one dealeth falsely. [11]For they have healed the hurt of the daughter of my people slightly, saying, Peace, peace; when there is no peace.

𝔷echariah 14:1–2 [1]Behold, the day of the Lord cometh, and thy spoil shall be divided in the midst of thee. [2]For I will gather all nations against Jerusalem to battle; and the city shall be taken, and the houses rifled, and the women ravished; and half of the city shall go forth into captivity, and the residue of the people shall not be cut off from the city.

WOMAN WAS MADE FOR MAN

 N THE FIRST CHAPTER, I MENTIONED THE TWO DECIDEDLY contradictory chronicles of the creation fable in Genesis. In the first account, man and woman are created simultaneously; in the second version, Eve is formed from one of Adam's ribs. Paul chose to reject the earlier narrative and to capitalize on the portrayal which put woman in an inferior role to that of man.

If ever there were an explanation of woman's inferior status in Occidental society, it is in the Scriptures. Paul delineates the importance of woman recognizing her "place" ad nauseam.

I Corinthians 11:3–12 [3]But I would have you know, that the head of every man is Christ; and the head of the woman is the man; and the head of Christ is God. [4]Every man praying or prophesying, having his head covered, dishonoreth his head. [5]But every woman that prayeth or prophesieth with her head uncovered dishonoreth her head: for that is even all one as if she were shaven. [6]For if the woman be not covered, let her also be shorn; but if it be a shame for a woman to be shorn or shaven, let her be covered. [7]For a man indeed ought not to cover his head, forasmuch as he is the image and glory of God: but the woman is the glory of the man. [8]For the man is not of the woman; but the woman of the man. [9]Neither was the man created for the woman: but the woman for the man. [10]For this cause ought the woman to have power on her head because of the angels. [11]Nevertheless neither is the man without the woman, neither the woman without the man, in the Lord. [12]For as the woman is of the man, even so is the man also by the woman; but all things of God.

I **Timothy** 2:8–15   [8]I will therefore that men pray every where, lifting up holy hands, without wrath and doubting. [9]In like manner also that <u>women adorn themselves in modest apparel,</u> with shame- facedness and sobriety; <u>not with braided hair, or gold, or pearls, or costly array;</u> [10]but (which becometh women professing godliness) <u>with good works.</u> [11]<u>Let the woman learn in silence with all subjection.</u> [12]<u>But I suffer not a woman to teach, nor to usurp authority over the man, but to be in silence.</u> [13]<u>For Adam was first formed, then Eve.</u> [14]<u>And Adam was not deceived, but the woman being deceived was in the transgression.</u> [15]Notwithstanding she shall be saved in childbearing, if they continue in faith and charity and holiness with sobriety.

I **Peter** 3:1–7   [1]Likewise, <u>ye wives, be in subjection to your own husbands;</u> that, if any obey not the word, they also may without the word be won by the conversation of the wives; [2]while they behold your chaste conversation coupled with fear. [3]Whose adorning, <u>let it not be that outward adorning of plaiting the hair, and of wearing of gold, or of putting on of apparel;</u> [4]but let it be <u>the hidden man of the heart, in that which is not corruptible, even the ornament of a meek and quiet spirit, which is in the sight of God of great price.</u> [5]For after this manner in the old time the holy <u>women</u> also, who trusted in God, a<u>dorned themselves, being in</u> subjection unto their own husbands: [6]even as <u>Sarah obeyed Abraham, calling him lord: whose daughters ye are,</u> as long as ye do well, and are not afraid with any amazement. [7]Likewise, ye husbands, dwell with them according to knowledge, <u>giving honor unto the wife, as unto the weaker vessel,</u> and as being heirs together of the grace of life; that your prayers be not hindered.

I **Corinthians** 14:34–36   [34]<u>Let your women keep silence in the churches: for it is not permitted unto them to speak; but they are commanded to be under obedience, as also saith the law.</u> [35]<u>And if they will learn any thing, let them ask their husbands at home; for it is a shame for women to speak in the church.</u> [36]What! came the word of God out from you? or came it unto you only?

Ephesians 5:22–33   [22]<u>Wives, submit yourselves unto your own husbands, as unto the Lord.</u> [23]For <u>the husband is the head of the wife, even as Christ is the head of the church;</u> and he is the saviour of the body. [24]Therefore as the church is subject unto Christ, so let the wives be to their own husbands in every thing. [25]Husbands, love your wives, even as Christ also loved the church, and gave himself for it; [26]that he might sanctify and cleanse it with the washing of water by the word, [27]that he might present it to himself a glorious church, not having spot, or wrinkle, or any such thing; but that it should be holy and without blemish. [28]So ought men to love their wives as their own bodies. He that loveth his wife loveth himself. [29]For no man ever yet hated his own flesh; but nourisheth and cherisheth it, even as the Lord the church: [30]for we are members of his body, of his flesh, and of his bones. [31]For this cause shall a man leave his father and mother, and shall be joined unto his wife, and they two shall be one flesh. [32]This is a great mystery: but I speak concerning Christ and the church. [33]Nevertheless, let every one of you in particular so love his wife even as himself and the wife see that she reverence her husband.

Colossians 3:18–19

[18]Wives, submit yourselves unto your own husbands, as it is fit in the Lord. [19]Husbands, love your wives, and be not bitter against them.

Much of what has already been written here indicates that the Hebrew culture was a patriarchal hierarchy par excellence and that women were merely valuable as property. Loss of virginity and acts of adultery were thus interpreted in light of the merchandise no longer having its former value. For that reason it was an affront to the female's father in the case of violating her virginity and the woman's husband in the case of committing adultery—economics, pure, plain and simple. Just a few quotations from the Old Testament will suffice to illustrate the point.

A husband was encouraged to fondle his wife and to exercise marital rights in particular with her bosom.

Proverbs 5:18–19

[18]Let thy fountain be blessed: and rejoice with the wife of thy youth. [19]Let her be as the loving hind and pleasant roe; let her breasts satisfy thee at all times; and be thou ravished always with her love.

Instant divorce was available to a man who was displeased with his wife. However, if a wife was displeased with her husband, she had no such option to send him away or simply to take leave of him. Yet an unhappy husband was free to get rid of an unwanted wife.

> **Deuteronomy 24:1–4** ¹When a man hath taken a wife, and married her, and it come to pass that she find no favor in his eyes, because he hath found some uncleanness in her: then let him write her a bill of divorcement, and give it in her hand, and send her out of his house. ²And when she is departed out of his house, she may go and be another man's wife. ³And if the latter husband hate her, and write her a bill of divorcement, and giveth it in her hand, and sendeth her out of his house; or if the latter husband die, which took her to be his wife; ⁴her former husband, which sent her away, may not take her again to be his wife.

An Israelite in financial straits was free to sell his daughter as a slave. It would have been unthinkable for him to have sold his son into slavery.

> **Exodus 21:7–11** ⁷And if a man sell his daughter to be a maidservant, she shall not go out as the menservants do. ⁸If she please not her master, who hath betrothed her to himself, then shall he let her be redeemed: to sell her unto a strange nation he shall have no power, seeing he hath dealt deceitfully with her. ⁹And if he have betrothed her unto his son, he shall deal with her after the manner of daughters. ¹⁰If he take him another wife, her food, her raiment, and her duty of marriage, shall he not diminish. ¹¹And if he do not these three unto her, then shall she go out free without money.

A man who violated a female slave was forgiven for the act provided that she had not as yet been given her freedom.

> **Leviticus 19:20–22** ²⁰And whosoever lieth carnally with a woman, that is a bondmaid, betrothed to a husband, and not at all redeemed, nor freedom given her; she shall be scourged: they shall not be put to death, because she was not free. ²¹And he shall bring his trespass offering unto the Lord, unto the door of the tabernacle of the congregation, even a ram for a trespass offering. ²²And the priest shall make an atonement for him with the ram of the trespass offering before the Lord for his sin which he hath done: and the sin which he hath done shall be forgiven him.

The most revealing custom relegating all women to second class citizenship was marriage, for it was almost invariably arranged by parents. If the son occasionally had some say in the matter, the daughter almost never did.

In Genesis 24, the marriage arrangement between Isaac and Rebekah is retold very touchingly and simply. Isaac's father, Abraham, had sent his steward to seek Rebekah's hand. She had never seen Isaac, but didn't hesitate to reply to the emissary.

> **Genesis 24:58**   And they called Rebekah, and said unto her, Wilt thou go with this man? And she said, I will go.

Rebekah accompanied the steward to the home of Abraham and was greeted by Isaac who was meditating in the fields as they arrived. They wasted no time in consummating their prearranged union.

> **Genesis 24:64–67**   ⁶⁴And Rebekah lifted up her eyes, and when she saw Isaac, she lighted off the camel. ⁶⁵For she had said unto the servant, What man is this that walketh in the field to meet us? And the servant had said, It is my master; therefore she took a vail, and covered herself. ⁶⁶And the servant told Isaac all things that he had done. ⁶⁷And Isaac brought her into his mother Sarah's tent, and took Rebekah, and she became his wife; and he loved her: and Isaac was comforted after his mother's death.

From such quaint customs emerged the lowly status of women reinforced rather than diminished in the New Testament and on into our own age. Along the way there was help from the early church fathers like Tertullian who declared:

> You are the devil's gateway: You are the unsealer of that forbidden tree: You are the first deserter of the divine law: You are she who persuaded him whom the devil was not valiant enough to attack. You destroyed so easily God's image, man. On account of your desert—that is, death—even the Son of God had to die.

With very good reason, then, America's great suffragist, Elizabeth Cady Stanton had this to say: "The Bible and the Church have been the greatest stumbling blocks in the way of women's emancipation."

To this very day, male Orthodox Jews recite this prayer of thanksgiving from the Talmud: "Blessed art Thou, O Lord God, King of the universe, who hast not made me a woman."

The notion that women are subservient to men forms a common link among Islam, Judaism and fundamentalist Christianity. The battered-wife syndrome of spousal abuse is much higher in these three groups than in the general population because religious "true believers" preach violence against women. In a meticulously researched and documented article "Unholy Matrimony: Why Bible Beaters Become Wife Beaters," writer Lisa Collier Cool reports in the March, 1995 issue of *Penthouse* that, sad to say, the husbands feel entitled to brutalize their submissive wives and the victims have internalized the myth that they deserve this kind of treatment. Remember, the Bible tells us so!

Part XII

SCATOLOGY, BESTIALITY
AND CASTRATION

Jehovah's Anal Fetish

 T IS NOT TOO SURPRISING THAT EVEN COPROPHILIA IS INCLUDED in the Biblical repertory of sex practices. What is surprising, however, is that the principal scatological references involve Jehovah himself!

When Israel was in bondage in Egypt, Jehovah sent numerous varieties of pestilence to torment Pharaoh into relenting and finally letting his captives go.

When Israel was rebellious, Jehovah threatened them with a new type of plague: "emerods" or in today's parlance "hemorrhoids."

> **Deuteronomy 28:27**   The Lord will smite thee with the botch of Egypt, and with the emerods, and with the scab, and with the itch, whereof thou canst not be healed.

Jehovah actually did send emerods or hemorrhoids as a plague to make the enemy suffer and they were inflicted "in their secret parts" which is to say "in their anus."

> **I Samuel 5:6–12**   ⁶But the hand of the Lord was heavy upon them of Ashdod, and he destroyed them, and smote them with emerods, even Ashdod and the coasts thereof. ⁷And when the men of Ashdod saw that it was so, they said, The ark of the God of Israel shall not abide with us: for his hand is sore upon us, and upon Dagon our god. ⁸They sent therefore and gathered all the lords of the Philistines unto them, and said, What shall we do with the ark of the God of Israel? And they answered, Let the ark of the God of Israel be carried about unto Gath. And they carried the ark of the God of Israel about thither. ⁹And it was so, that after they had carried it about, the hand of the Lord was against the city with a very great destruction: and he smote the men of the city, both small and great, and they had emerods in their secret parts. ¹⁰Therefore they sent the ark of God to Ekron. And it came to pass, as the ark of God came to Ekron, that the Ekronites cried out, saying, They have brought about the ark of the God of Israel to us, to slay us and our people. ¹¹So they sent and gathered together all the lords of the Philistines, and said, Send away the ark of the God of Israel, and let it go again to his own place, that it slay us not, and our people: for there was a deadly destruction

throughout all the city; the hand of God was very heavy there. [12]And the men that died not were smitten with the emerods: and the cry of the city went up to heaven.

The Philistines were willing to do anything to have the plague removed, and it was revealed to them that they should return the ark, but that they should not return it without an offering to accompany it. As a trespass offering, they were able to make golden images of the mice and of the hemorrhoids which had been inflicted in the plague. Voltaire, that incomparable wit, referred to these golden hemorrhoids as "golden anuses."

I Samuel 6:1–18   [1]And the ark of the Lord was in the country of the Philistines seven months. [2]And the Philistines called for the priests and the diviners, saying, What shall we do to the ark of the Lord? tell us wherewith we shall send it to his place. [3]And they said, If ye send away the ark of the God of Israel, send it not empty; but in any wise return him a trespass offering: then ye shall be healed, and it shall be known to you why his hand is not removed from you. [4]Then said they, What shall be the trespass offering which we shall return to him? They answered, Five golden emerods, and five golden mice, according to the number of the lords of the Philistines: for one plague was on you all, and on your lords. [5]Wherefore ye shall make images of your emerods, and images of your mice that mar the land; and ye shall give glory unto the God of Israel: peradventure he will lighten his hand from off you, and from off your gods, and from off your land. [6]Wherefore then do ye harden your hearts, as the Egyptians and Pharoah hardened their hearts? when he had wrought wonderfully among them, did they not let the people go, and they departed? [7]Now therefore make a new cart, and take two milch kine, on which there hath come no yoke, and tie the kine to the cart, and bring their calves home from them: [8]and take the ark of the Lord, and lay it upon the cart; and put the jewels of gold, which ye return him for a trespass offering, in a coffer by the side thereof; and send it away, that it may go. [9]And see, if it goeth up by the way of his own coast to Beth-she'mesh, then he hath done us this great evil: but if not, then we shall know that it is not his hand that smote us; it was a chance that happened to us. [10]And the, men did so; and took two milch kine, and tied them to the cart, and shut up their calves at home: [11]and they laid the ark of the Lord upon the cart, and the coffer with the mice of gold and the images of their emerods. [12]And the kine took the straight way to the way of Beth-she'mesh, and went along the highway, lowing as they went, and turned not aside to the right hand or to the left; and the lords of the Philistines went after them unto the border of Beth-she'mesh. [13]And they of Beth-she'mesh were reaping their wheat harvest in the valley: and they lifted up their eyes, and saw the ark, and rejoiced to see it. [14]And the cart came into the field of Joshua, a Beth-she'mite, and stood there, where there was a great stone: and they clave the wood of the cart, and offered the kine a burnt offering unto the Lord. [15]And the Levites took down the ark of the Lord, and the coffer that was with it, wherein the jewels of gold were, and put them on the great stone: and the men of Beth-she'mesh offered burnt offerings and sacrificed sacrifices the same day unto the Lord. [16]And when the five lords of the Philistines had seen it, they returned to Ekron the same day. [17]And these are the golden emerods which the Philistines returned for a trespass offering unto the Lord; for Ashdod one, for Gaza one, for As'kelon one, for Gath one, for Ekron one; [18]and the golden mice, according to the number of all the cities of the Philistines belonging to the five lords, both of fenced cities, and of country villages, even unto the great stone of Abel, whereon they set down the ark of the Lord: which stone remaineth unto this day in the field of Joshua, the Beth-she'mite.

No one was ever permitted to look inside of the ark, of course. But some of the heathen who were not familiar with this prohibition did look inside. Jehovah smote them and, according to the account in the King James Version, 50,070 men died that day because of having looked inside the ark. However, most Biblical critics concur that the 50,000 number was a mistake which was due to a scribal error and most translators indicate, therefore, that only seventy men perished that day. Perhaps this revised tally does portray Jehovah as being a little more merciful.

I Samuel 6:19–21 [19]And he smote the men of Beth-she'mesh, because they had looked into the ark of the Lord, even he smote of the people fifty thousand and threescore and ten men: and the people lamented, because the Lord had smitten many of the people with a great slaughter. [20]And the men of Beth-she'mesh said, Who is able to stand before this holy Lord God? and to whom shall he go up from us? [21]And they sent messengers to the inhabitants of Kir'jath-je'arim, saying, The Philistines have brought again the ark of the Lord; come ye down, and fetch it up to you.

Jehovah's idea of contaminating bread must surely be a first for all time. The bread is baked with human excrement as fuel and then the Israelites are later to eat this defiled bread when they mingle with the Gentiles. Upon hearing Ezekiel's objection to this defilement, Jehovah graciously substituted cow's manure for human feces.

Ezekiel 4:10–17 ¹⁰And thy meat which thou shalt eat shall be by weight, twenty shekels a day: from time to time shalt thou eat it. ¹¹Thou shalt drink also water by measure, the sixth part of a hin: from time to time shalt thou drink. ¹²And thou shalt eat it as barley cakes, and thou shalt bake it with dung that cometh out of man, in their sight. ¹³And the Lord said, Even thus shall the children of Israel eat their defiled bread among the Gentiles, whither I will drive them. ¹⁴Then said I, Ah Lord God! behold, my soul hath not been polluted: for from my youth up even till now have I not eaten of that which dieth of itself, or is torn in pieces; neither came there abominable flesh into my mouth. ¹⁵Then he said unto me, Lo, I have given thee cow's dung for man's dung, and thou shalt prepare thy bread therewith. ¹⁶Moreover he said unto me, Son of man, behold, I will break the staff of bread in Jerusalem: and they shall eat bread by weight, and with care; and they shall drink water by measure, and with astonishment: ¹⁷that they may want bread and water, and be astonished one with another, and consume away for their iniquity.

Besides the contaminated bread which would cause internal pollution, Jehovah also dreamed up a method of external pollution—smearing feces over the faces of the disobedient and rebellious Israelites.

Malachi 2:1–3 ¹And now, O ye priests, this commandment is for you. ²If ye will not hear, and if ye will not lay it to heart, to give glory unto my name, saith the Lord of hosts, I will even send a curse upon you, and I will curse your blessings: yea, I have cursed them already, because ye do not lay it to heart. ³Behold, I will corrupt your seed, and spread dung upon your faces, even the dung of your solemn feasts; and one shall take you away with it.

"Behold, I will corrupt your seed, and spread dung upon your faces"

Perhaps the foregoing quotations which reveal a deity who is anally fixated will explain why, on Mount Sinai, Jehovah chose not to reveal his face to Moses, but rather allowed Moses to see only his "back parts."

Exodus 33:20–23 [20]And he said, Thou canst not see my face: for there shall no man see me, and live. [21]And the Lord said, Behold, there is a place by me, and thou shalt stand upon a rock: [22]and it shall come to pass, while my glory passeth by, that I will put thee in a cleft of the rock, and will cover thee with my hand while I pass by: [23]and I will take away mine hand, and thou shalt see my back parts; but my face shall not be seen.

A terrible famine is described in the Old Testament and during this famine in Samaria, the people were so desperate for food that they ate the feces of doves, which item sold for five pieces of silver, or in today's currency for about three dollars a pint. This same passage describes an incident of cannibalism among the Samarians—a son boiled alive by his mother to provide food.

II Kings 6:24–29 [24]And it came to pass after this, that Ben-ha'dad king of Syria gathered all his host, and went up, and besieged Samaria. [25]And there was a great famine in Samaria: and, behold, they besieged it, until an ass's head was sold for fourscore pieces of silver, and the fourth part of a cab of dove's dung for five pieces of silver. [26]And as the king of Israel was passing by upon the wall, there cried a woman unto him, saying, Help, my lord, O king. [27]And he said, If the Lord do not help thee, whence shall I help thee? out of the barnfloor, or out of the winepress? [28]And the king said unto her, What aileth thee? And she answered, This woman said unto me, Give thy son, that we may eat him today, and we will eat my son tomorrow. [29]So we boiled my son, and did eat him: and I said unto her on the next day, Give thy son, that we may eat him: and she hath hid her son.

Several of the Old Testament writers and prophets continue this scatological tradition.

I Samuel 25:22 So and more also do God unto the enemies of David, if I leave of all that pertain to him by the morning light any that pisseth against the wall.

I Samuel 35:34   For in very deed, as the Lord God of Israel liveth, which hath kept me back from hurting thee, except thou hadst hasted and come to meet me, surely there had not been left unto Nabal by the morning light any that pisseth against the wall.

I Kings 14:7–10   ⁷Go, tell Jerobo'am, Thus saith the Lord God of Israel, Forasmuch as I exalted thee from among the people, and made thee prince over my people Israel, ⁸and rent the kingdom away from the house of David, and gave it thee: and yet thou hast not been as my servant David, who kept my commandments, and who followed me with all his heart, to do that only which was right in mine eyes; ⁹but hast done evil above all that were before thee: for thou hast gone and made thee other gods, and molten images, to provoke me to anger, and hast cast me behind thy back: ¹⁰therefore, behold, I will bring evil upon the house of Jerobo'am, and will cut off from Jerobo'am him that pisseth against the wall, and him that is shut up and left in Israel, and will take away the remnant of the house of Jerobo'am, as a man taketh away dung, till it be all gone.

I Kings 16:8–11   ⁸In the twenty and sixth year of Asa king of Judah began Elah the son of Ba'asha to reign over Israel in Tirzah, two years. ⁹And his servant Zimri, captain of half his chariots, conspired against him, as he was in Tirzah, drinking himself drunk in the house of Arza steward of his house in Tirzah. ¹⁰And Zimri went in and smote him, and killed him, in the twenty and seventh year of Asa king of Judah, and reigned in his stead. ¹¹And it came to pass, when he began to reign, as soon as he sat on his throne, that he slew all the house of Ba'asha: he left him not one that pisseth against a wall, neither of his kinsfolk, nor of his friends.

I Kings 21:21–22   ²¹Behold, I will bring evil upon thee, and will take away thy posterity, and will cut off from Ahab him that pisseth against the wall, and him that is shut up and left in Israel, ²²and will make thine house like the house of Jerobo'am the son of Nebat, and like the house of Ba'asha the son of Ahijah, for the provocation wherewith thou hast provoked me to anger, and made Israel to sin.

II Kings 9:8–10   ⁸For the whole house of Ahab shall perish: and I will cut off from Ahab him that pisseth against the wall, and him that is shut up and left in Israel: ⁹and I will make the house of Ahab like the house of Jerobo'am the son of Nebat, and like the house of Ba'asha the son of Ahijah: ¹⁰and the dogs shall eat Jezebel in the portion of Jezreel, and there shall be none to bury her. And he opened the door, and fled.

II Kings 18:26–27   ²⁶Then said Eli'akim the son of Hilki'ah, and Shebna, and Jo'ah, unto Rab-sha'keh, Speak, I pray thee, to thy servants in the Syrian language; for we understand it: and talk not with us in the Jews' language in the ears of the people that are on the wall. ²⁷But Rab-sha'keh said unto them, Hath my master sent me to thy master, and to thee, to speak these words? hath he not sent me to the men which sit on the wall, that they may eat their own dung, and drink their own piss with you?

Nehemiah 2:11–13   ¹¹So I came to Jerusalem, and was there three days. ¹²And I arose in the night, I and some few men with me; neither told I any man what my God had put in my heart to do at Jerusalem: neither was there any beast with me, save the beast that I rode upon. ¹³And I went out by night by the gate of the valley, even before the dragon well, and to the dung port, and viewed the walls of Jerusalem, which were broken down, and the gates thereof were consumed with fire.

Isaiah 36:11–12   ¹¹Then said Eli'akim and Shebna and Jo'ah unto Rab-sha'keh, Speak, I pray thee, to thy servants in the Syrian language; for we understand it: and speak not to us in the Jews' language, in the ears of the people that are on the wall. ¹²But Rab-sha'keh said, Hath my master sent me to thy master and to thee to speak these words? hath he not sent me to the men that sit upon the wall, that they may eat their own dung, and drink their own piss with you?

Jeremiah 8:1–2   ¹At that time, saith the Lord, they shall bring out the bones of the kings of Judah, and the bones of his princes, and the bones of the priests, and the bones of the prophets, and the bones of the inhabitants of Jerusalem, out of their graves: ²and they shall spread them before the sun, and the moon, and all the host of heaven, whom they have loved, and whom they have served, and after whom they have walked, and whom they have sought, and whom they have worshipped: they shall not be gathered, nor be buried; they shall be for dung upon the face of the earth.

Lamentations 4:5   They that did feed delicately are desolate in the streets; they that were brought up in scarlet embrace dunghills.

Nahum 3:5–6   ⁵Behold, I am against thee, saith the Lord of hosts; and I will discover thy skirts upon thy face, and I will show the nations thy nakedness, and the kingdoms thy shame. ⁶And I will cast abominable filth upon thee, and make thee vile, and will set thee as a gazingstock.

One text even refers to intestinal gas passing in musical fashion from the bowels of the prophet.

Isaiah 16:11   Wherefore my bowels shall sound like a harp for Moab, and mine inward parts for Kir-ha'resh.

Some of this coprophilic heritage spilled over into the New Testament, for even Paul makes a passing scatological reference. Paul compared the things of this world with dung, but this indecorous phrase is translated in modern versions as simply "less than nothing."

Philippians 3:7–11   ⁷But what things were gain to me, those I counted loss for Christ. ⁸Yea doubtless, and I count all things but loss for the excellency of the knowledge of Christ Jesus my Lord: for whom I have suffered the loss of all things, and do count them but dung, that I may win Christ, ⁹and be found in him, not having mine own righteousness, which is of the law, but that which is through the faith of Christ, the righteousness which is of God by faith: ¹⁰that I may know him, and the power of his resurrection, and the fellowship of his sufferings, being made conformable unto his death; ¹¹if by any means I might attain unto the resurrection of the dead.

Forbidden Intimacies with Animals

HROUGHOUT RECORDED HISTORY, SOLITARY AND ISOLATED shepherds have often been inclined to do much more than just tend their sheep. The disease syphilis got its name from the eponymous shepherd boy who reputedly was so intimate with some of his flock that he literally pulled their wool over more than just his eyeballs.

Sociologists and anthropologists assert that the severity of a law in a given culture directly relates to the frequency of the offense. Judging by that maxim, bestiality must have been quite prevalent in ancient Israel for it to join our growing list of sexual capital offenses and it gives us a whole new slant on the meaning of animal husbandry.

In Kinsey's monumental study of sexual behavior in the human male, he concluded that bestiality is much more widespread among rural males than it is among urban ones. However, he felt that were city boys in as frequent daily contact with animals as farm boys are, the incidence of animal intimacies would be quite stable for the entire male population.

Since Israel was a nomadic people, it is quite natural to expect that a lonely shepherd might fall into the temptation of engaging in animal intercourse. What is surprising and unexpected, though, is the existence of explicit prohibitions for females as well as males and Bible commentators are at a loss to explain why.

Exodus 22:19   Whosoever lieth with a beast shall surely be put to death.

Leviticus 18:23   Neither shalt thou lie with any beast to defile thyself therewith: neither shall any woman stand before a beast to lie down thereto: it is confusion.

Deuteronomy 27:21   Cursed be he that lieth with any manner of beast: and all the people shall say, Amen.

What is particularly astonishing about the Hebrew conception of the seriousness of bestiality is that the law insisted not only on the death of the human offender, but also on the death of the dumb animal.

Leviticus 20:15–16   [15]And if a man lie with a beast, he shall surely be put to death: and ye shall slay the beast. [16]And if a woman approach unto any beast, and lie down thereto, thou shalt kill the woman, and the beast: they shall surely be put to death; their blood shall be upon them.

In *Sex Laws and Customs in Judaism*, L. M. Epstein gives a lucid if difficult-to-accept explanation for this mistreatment of innocent animals. (pp. 133–134):

> The Bible itself rules that the penalty for contact with a beast is death both for the human and the beast . . . the rabbis deduce that the death penalty intended . . . is that of stoning, provided the offender be of the age of majority. The animal, too, is killed by stoning, provided the contact was with a human male above nine years and a day, or a human female above three years and a day, for below that age male and female respectively have no sexual status at all.
>
> The execution of the animal presents a moral problem to the rabbis, especially when the female animal is attacked by a human male, for the animal has not sinned, since it has no code of morality and particularly since it has been the passive object of a human crime. They believe, however, that the law is justified in executing the beast because it served as a tool for the downfall of a human being; more so because the recollection of the crime and the human criminal is focused on the beast, whose execution could cut memory short.

Unfortunately, there was no Biblical humane society to intercede for the poor animals!

Self-Castration, the Supreme Sexual Sacrifice

𝔐𝔞𝔱𝔱𝔥𝔢𝔴 19:12   For there are some eunuchs, which were so born from their mother's womb: and there are some eunuchs, which were made eunuchs of men: and there be eunuchs, which have made themselves eunuchs for the kingdom of heaven's sake. He that is able to receive it, let him receive it.

This quotation of Christ's is manifestly an endorsement of self-castration, but is greatly at variance with the Hebrew law and explicitly countermands and contravenes the Old Testament declaration:

Deuteronomy 23:1   He that is wounded in the stones, or hath his privy member cut off, shall not enter into the congregation of the Lord.

"Stones" here means "testicles" and "privy member" means "penis." It was not only clear in the Hebrew law that any male with mutilated genitals was cut off from the congregation of Jehovah, but this prohibition also applied even if the mutilation had been the result of an accident.

Jehovah himself declared that he would not accept an offering from a man whose testicles were crushed or mutilated. He gave the message to Moses who was to give it to Aaron specifically regarding an offering of bread in the sanctuary. The prohibition against the mutilated male is in verse 20 and, once again, "testicles" is rendered by the older English term "stones."

Leviticus 21:16–21   [16]And the Lord spake unto Moses, saying, [17]Speak unto Aaron, saying, Whosoever he be of thy seed in their generations that, hath any blemish, let him not approach to offer the bread of his God. [18]For whatsoever man he be that hath a blemish, he shall not approach: a blind man, or a lame, or he that hath a flat nose, or any thing superfluous, [19]or a man that is brokenfooted, or broken handed, [20]or crookbacked, or a dwarf, or that hath a blemish in his eye, or be scurvy, or scabbed, or hath his stones broken; [21]no man that hath a blemish of the seed of Aaron the priest shall come nigh to offer the offerings of the Lord made by fire: he hath a blemish; he shall not come nigh to offer the bread of his God.

Through the prophet Isaiah, Jehovah seemingly contradicted himself by saying that eunuchs who are true believers will, in the long run, receive rewards surpassing having sons and daughters.

Isaiah 56:3–5   [3]Neither let the son of the stranger, that hath joined himself to the Lord, speak, saying, The Lord hath utterly separated me from his people: neither let the eunuch say, Behold, I am a dry tree. [4]For thus saith the Lord unto the eunuchs that keep my sabbaths, and choose the things that please me, and take hold of my covenant; [5]Even unto them will I give in mine house and within my walls a place and a name better than of sons and of daughters: I will give them an everlasting name, that shall not be cut off.

In the story of the overthrow of the rebellious queen Jezebel, her demise came about through the efforts of eunuchs. (see p. 106)

> **II Kings 9:31–33** ³¹And as Jehu entered in at the gate, she said, Had Zimri peace, who slew his master? ³²And he lifted up his face to the window, and said, Who is on my side? who? And there looked out to him two or three eunuchs. ³³And he said, Throw her down. So they threw her down: and some of her blood was sprinkled on the wall, and on the horses: and he trode her under foot.

All together, there are at least forty references to eunuchs in the Scriptures. The story of Esther (see Chapter 53) indicates that the most frequent use of eunuchs was to serve as "harem keeper."

Israel's sexual naivete comes into bold relief once again with the use of eunuchs to protect and guard harem women. In most cases, a eunuch was castrated by removing the testicles only. This left the penis intact. Modern endocrinology states that the loss of the testes alone does not impair sexual function—it only assures sterility and freedom from baldness because of the elimination of the male sex hormone testosterone. This means that sexual excitation, including erection, is possible in a castrated male—only true ejaculation is impossible. An enterprising eunuch entrusted with the job of caring for the women in a harem really had it made since he could enjoy sex without the fear or risk of discovery through an embarrassing pregnancy.

In cases where castration involved removal of both the testes and the penis, all sexual activity was out of the question, of course, but the former type of castration seemed to be the rule rather than the exception.

Returning to Christ's putative recommendation of castration as a sign of supreme sexual sacrifice, it was taken quite literally as Christianity developed in the first few centuries of the early Church.

Among the early church fathers, the best known of those who inflicted self-castration upon themselves was Origen (A.D. 185–254). Contemporaneous with Origen was a sect which was so enthusiastically addicted to the practice that, in addition to requiring castration of all its members, they also castrated any guest who was rash enough to stay under their roof. The sect, known as Valesians, performed their castrations with a hot piece of metal, referring to the act appropriately as a "baptism of fire."

From the pen of Lucian, we get a vivid picture of the nature of the ceremonies during which self-castration often took place.

On certain days a multitude flocks to the temple, and the Galli in great numbers, sacred as they are, perform the ceremonies of the men and gash their arms and turn their backs to be lashed. Many bystanders play on the pipes, while many beat drums; others sing divine and sacred songs. All this performance takes place outside the temple . . . As the Galli sing and celebrate their orgies, frenzy falls on some of them, and many who had come as mere spectators afterwards are found to have committed the great act. I shall narrate what they do. Any young man who has resolved on this action, strips off his clothes and with a loud shout bursts into the midst of the crowd and picks up a sword from a number of swords which I suppose have been kept ready for many years for this purpose. He takes it and castrates himself, and runs wild through the city bearing in his hands what he has cut off. He casts it into any house at will, and from this house he receives women's raiment and ornaments.

Origen, the early church father of Alexandria, reacted to Christ's exhortation about eunuchs by cutting off his own balls for the kingdom of heaven.

The tonsure of the early priests of Christianity is a recognized symbol of castration and the skirted cassock worn by priests is, at least in part, an imitation of the many religions competing with early Christianity which required that their priests don only female attire after they were castrated.

A horrific modern example of cutting off your balls for the kingdom of heaven was the aptly named Heaven's Gate mass suicide in San Diego in the spring of 1997, the largest mass suicide ever to occur on American soil. Autopsies on the bodies of the 39 cult members revealed that not only had the middle-aged cult leader been surgically castrated, but also many of the younger men still in their sexual prime. What a waste in a futile attempt to enter Paradise through their own Heaven's Gate!

art XIII
ILLEGITIMACY, CELIBACY
AND VIRGIN BIRTH

PITY THE POOR BASTARD

Deuteronomy 23:2   A bastard shall not enter into the congregation of the Lord; even to his tenth generation shall he not enter into the congregation of the Lord.

Jehovah's anathema befell not only a bastard, but the bastard's descendants through ten succeeding generations. It is all the more remarkable, in this light, that Jephthah rose to a real position of prominence in Israel, for not only was his illegitimacy a well-known fact, but his mother had been a prostitute and thus he had a double stigma to overcome in his rise to the top. In Chapter 38, we learned of his sacrifice of his daughter to Jehovah. This brief account tells how he achieved prominence in Israel:

Judges 11:1–11   ¹Now Jephthah the Gil'eadite was a mighty man of valor, and he was the son of a harlot; and Gil'e-ad begat Jephthah. ²And Gil'e-ad's wife bare him sons; and his wife's sons grew up, and they thrust out Jephthah, and said unto him, Thou shalt not inherit in our father's house; for thou art the son of a strange woman. ³Then Jephthah fled from his brethren, and dwelt in the land of Tob: and there were gathered vain men to Jephthah, and went out with him. ⁴And it came to pass in process of time, that the children of Ammon made war against Israel. ⁵And it was so, that when the children of Ammon made war against Israel, the elders of Gil'e-ad went to fetch Jephthah out of the land of Tob: ⁶and they said unto Jephthah, Come, and be our captain, that we may fight with the children of Ammon. ⁷And Jephthah said unto the elders of Gil'e-ad, Did not ye hate me, and expel me out of my father's house? and why are ye come unto me now when ye are in distress? ⁸And the elders of Gil'e-ad said unto Jephthah, Therefore we turn again to thee now, that thou mayest go with us, and fight against the children of Ammon, and be our head over all the inhabitants of Gil'e-ad. ⁹And Jephthah said unto the elders of Gil'e-ad, If ye bring me home again to fight against the children of Ammon, and the Lord deliver them before me, shall I be your head? ¹⁰And the elders of Gil'e-ad said unto Jephthah, The Lord be witness between us, if we do not so according to thy words. ¹¹Then Jephthah went with the elders of Gil'e-ad, and the people made him head and captain over them; and Jephthah uttered all his words before the Lord in Mizpeh.

AN X-RATED KING SOLOMON FOR KIDS

T ALWAYS FASCINATES ME TO LEAF THROUGH THE MYRIAD volumes of Bible stories for children that populate every bookstore. The familiar fable of King Solomon's wisdom invariably appears in each and every collection, but the severely sanitized adaptation bears very little resemblance to the original text as found in I Kings 3:16–28. In the very unlikely event that I might decide to write an *X-Rated Bible Stories for Children* some day, here is how the popular parable might unfold:

KING SOLOMON AND THE LITTLE BASTARD

Once upon a time, there was a very wise man, King Solomon. This king was very rich. In fact, he had so much money that he married seven hundred wives and he also had three hundred concubines. A concubine was a woman who lived with a man without being married to him. Today, if a man and a woman live together without being married, we say that they are living in sin because they are guilty of fornication. Fornication is having sex with someone you are not married to, but God doesn't want us to do that anymore.

Also, today, if you have more than one wife or husband, you are called a bigamist and bigamy is against the law. And of course, if your daddy cheats on your mommy and has a secret girlfriend, or if your mommy cheats on your daddy and has a secret boyfriend, that is called adultery, and God doesn't want us to do that either. The Bible tells us that if people commit adultery, we should throw stones at them and kill them because God thinks it is much better to murder someone than to commit adultery.

Now, in Solomon's day, it was OK to have as many wives as you could afford to support because that was the time of the Old Dispensation which was God's Plan A for the world. But today, we are living under the New Dispensation which is also known as God's Plan B.

One day, two prostitutes came to see King Solomon. A prostitute is a woman who sells her body for sex, and God never wants us to do that. These two women brought a baby boy with them who was illegitimate. That means that no one knew for sure who the father of the child was. Since these two prostitutes had sex with so many different men, they could never know for sure which one of those men made them pregnant. Being pregnant means that their belly swelled up and got very big with a baby developing inside.

But this little bastard (another word for a child whose parents never got married) had a double problem. Not only was there doubt about who his father was, there was also some doubt as to which of the two prostitutes was his mother.

One of the whores (another word for prostitute) explained to the king that she and the other whore lived together in the same house. The first prostitute had a baby just three days before the other one also gave birth. But the second whore's baby died one night when she accidentally rolled over on it while asleep and smothered it to death. Then she got up and stole the baby from the other mother while she was sound asleep and put the corpse of her dead son in the place of the living child.

When the first mother awoke and was ready to nurse her son with the milk from her breast, she realized that the dead infant was not hers and she accused the other whore of kidnapping (child stealing).

As the two prostitutes argued back and forth before King Solomon, each one claimed to be the real mother of the little bastard. The king asked for a sword because he was going to cut the living child into two pieces and give one half to each of them. The woman who cried out and begged him not to do that turned out to be the real mother.

When the people heard about Solomon's decision for the two prostitutes and their little bastard, they soon realized what a really wise king they had. Now boys and girls, wasn't that a wonderful story?

PAUL, THE COMPULSIVE CELIBATE

 N THE OLD TESTAMENT, THERE IS ONLY ONE MENTION OF celibacy and it surfaces in the book of Jeremiah as a direct command from Jehovah for the prophet not to marry.

> **Jeremiah 16:1–2** ¹The word of the Lord came also unto me, saying ²Thou shalt not take thee a wife, neither shalt thou have sons nor daughters in this place.

Paul's recommendation of celibacy must be viewed as an adjunct to his eschatological views—so says virtually every Bible scholar. In plain, everyday language, this means that Paul believed that the end of the world was imminent and for that reason felt that there were much more important matters which needed attention than matters of the flesh!

> **I Corinthians 7:1–9** ¹Now concerning the things whereof ye wrote unto me: It is good for a man not to touch a woman. ²Nevertheless, to avoid fornication, let every man have his own wife,

and let every woman have her own husband. ³Let the husband render unto the wife due benevolence: and likewise also the wife unto the husband. ⁴The wife hath not power of her own body, but the husband: and likewise also the husband hath not power of his own body, but the wife. ⁵Defraud ye not one the other, except it be with consent for a time, that ye may give yourselves to fasting and prayer; and come together again, that Satan tempt you not for your incontinency. ⁶But I speak this by permission, and not of commandment. ⁷For I would that all men were even as I myself. But every man hath his proper gift of God, one after this manner, and another after that. ⁸I say therefore to the unmarried and widows, It is good for them if they abide even as I. ⁹But if they cannot contain, let them marry: for it is better to marry than to burn.

At least Paul recognized that not everyone could easily repress libidinous urges and that marriage was a viable alternative to their "burning" with lust, but for himself, he chose the ascetic path of denial. This view of his has had an enormous impact on the enforced celibacy of the Roman Catholic Church and on the narrow view of sexuality of the Judeo-Christian tradition and ethic.

Paul had much to say on the subject of sex in general and his interpretation of how sex should be handled in particular. I have already discussed his opinions on homosexuality (see Chapter 13). Let us now examine some of his other impressions.

ON INCEST

There had been an incident of incest reported from the Church at Corinth, and Paul let the believers there know, in no uncertain terms, that incest was wrong and that appropriate action should be taken against the church member who was guilty.

I Corinthians 5:1–5   ¹It is reported commonly that there is fornication among you, and such fornication as is not so much as named among the Gentiles, that one should have his father's wife. ²And ye are puffed up, and have not rather mourned, that he that hath done this deed might be taken away from among you. ³For I verily, as absent in body, but present in spirit, have judged already, as though I were present, concerning him that hath so done this deed, ⁴in the name of our Lord Jesus Christ, when ye are gathered together, and my spirit, with the power of our Lord Jesus Christ, ⁵to deliver such a one unto Satan for the destruction of the flesh, that the spirit may be saved in the day of the Lord Jesus.

ON DIVORCE

Paul insisted that his doctrine was not Jehovah's but only his own. He allowed no exception for divorce except if the spouse had been wed to an unbeliever. This allowed the individual to be free to marry again without being guilty of adultery. This interpretation of Paul's statement is what the consensus of Bible scholars feels although some think that the person so excused from the marriage bond was only free to live in a separated state and not to remarry.

Romans 7:1–3 ¹Know ye not, brethren, (for I speak to them that know the law,) how that the law hath dominion over a man as long as he liveth? ²For the woman which hath a husband is bound by the law to her husband so long as he liveth; but if the husband be dead, she is loosed from the law of her husband. ³So then if, while her husband liveth, she be married to another man, she shall be called an adulteress: but if her husband be dead, she is free from that law; so that she is no adulteress, though she be married to another man.

I Corinthians 7:12–16 ¹²But to the rest speak I, not the Lord: If any brother hath a wife that believeth not, and she be pleased to dwell with him, let him not put her away. ¹³And the woman which hath a husband that believeth not, and if he be pleased to dwell with her, let her not leave him. ¹⁴For the unbelieving husband is sanctified by the wife, and the unbelieving wife is sanctified by the husband: else were your children unclean; but now are they holy. ¹⁵But if the unbelieving depart, let him depart. A brother or a sister is not under bondage in such cases: but God hath called us to peace. ¹⁶For what knowest thou, O wife, whether thou shalt save thy husband? or how knowest thou, O man, whether thou shalt save thy wife?

It is instructive to compare the judgment of divorce in the Gospels with that of Paul. John is completely silent on the subject. Mark and Luke allow no exception whatever for remarrying after a divorce.

Mark 10:2–12 ²And the Pharisees came to him, and asked him, Is it lawful for a man to put away his wife? tempting him. ³And he answered and said unto them, What did Moses command you? ⁴And they said, Moses suffered to write a bill of divorcement, and to put her away. ⁵And Jesus answered and said unto them, For the hardness of your heart he wrote you this precept. ⁶But from the beginning of the creation God made them male and female. ⁷For this cause shall a man leave his father and mother, and cleave to his wife; ⁸and they twain shall be one flesh: so then they are no more twain, but one flesh. ⁹What therefore God hath joined together, let not man put asunder. ¹⁰And in the house his disciples asked him again of the same matter. ¹¹And he saith unto them, Whosoever shall put away his wife, and marry another, committeth adultery against her. ¹²And if a woman shall put away her husband, and be married to another, she committeth adultery.

Luke 16:18   Whosoever putteth away his wife and marrieth another, committeth adultery: and whosoever marrieth her that is put away from her husband committeth adultery.

Matthew refers twice to the subject of divorce and in both instances he indicates that it is permissible to remarry after a divorce, provided that the reason for the divorce was unfaithfulness. The fact that Mark and Luke do not allow this exception causes many Bible commentators to regard Matthew's exception as a later interpolation to try to soften the harsh and narrow law of the other Gospels.

Matthew 5:32   But I say unto you, That whosoever shall put away his wife, saving for the cause of fornication, causeth her to commit adultery: and whosoever shall marry her that is divorced committeth adultery.

Matthew 19:9   And I say unto you, Whosoever shall put away his wife, except it be for fornication, and shall marry another, committeth adultery: and whoso marrieth her which is put away doth commit adultery.

In tallying up the divergent views of divorce which are presented in the Gospels and in Paul's writings, we arrive at the following distressing moral paradigm:

MATTHEW   Divorce permissible; remarriage allowed provided that the divorce was based on adultery.
MARK   Divorce permissible; no remarriage allowed.
LUKE   Divorce permissible; no remarriage allowed.

PAUL   Divorce permissible; remarriage allowed provided that the divorce was based on one spouse being an unbeliever.

ON PROSTITUTION, PRE-MARITAL AND EXTRA-MARITAL SEX

I Corinthians 6:12–20   [12]All things are lawful unto me, but all things are not expedient: all things are lawful for me, but I will not be brought under the power of any. [13]Meats for the belly, and the belly for meats: but God shall destroy both it and them. Now the body is not for fornication, but for the Lord; and the Lord for the body. [14]And God hath both raised up the Lord, and will also raise up us by his own power. [15]Know ye not that your bodies are the members of Christ? shall I then take the members of Christ, and make them the members of a harlot? God forbid. [16]What! know ye not that he which is joined to a harlot is one body? for two, saith he, shall be one flesh. [17]But he that is joined unto the Lord is one spirit. [18]Flee fornication. Every sin that a man doeth is without the body; but he that committeth fornication sinneth against his own body. [19]What! know ye not that your body is the temple of the Holy Ghost which is in you, which ye have of God, and ye are not your own? [20]For ye are bought with a price: therefore glorify God in your body, and in your spirit, which are God's.

Galatians 5:19–21   [19]Now the works of the flesh are manifest, which are these, adultery, fornication, uncleanness, lasciviousness, [20]idolatry, witchcraft, hatred, variance, emulations, wrath, strife, seditions, heresies, [21]envyings, murders, drunkenness, revelings, and such like: of the which I tell you before, as I have also told you in time past, that they which do such things shall not inherit the kingdom of God.

Ephesians 5:1–7   [1]Be ye therefore followers of God, as dear children; [2]and walk in love, as Christ also hath loved us, and hath given himself for an offering and a sacrifice to God for a sweet-smelling savor. [3]But fornication, and all uncleanness, or covetousness, let it not be once named among you, as becometh saints; [4]neither filthiness, nor foolish talking, nor jesting, which are not convenient: but rather giving of thanks. [5]For this ye know, that no whoremonger, nor unclean person, nor covetous man, who is an idolater, hath any inheritance in the kingdom of Christ and of God. [6]Let no man deceive you with vain words: for because of these things cometh the wrath of God upon the children of disobedience. ⁷Be not ye therefore partakers with them.

Colossians 3:5–8
⁵Mortify therefore your members which are upon the earth; fornication, uncleanness, inordinate affection, evil concupiscence, and covetousness, which is idolatry: ⁶for which things' sake the wrath of God cometh on the children of disobedience: ⁷in the which ye also walked sometime, when ye lived in them. ⁸But now ye also put off all these; anger, wrath, malice, blasphemy, filthy communication out of your mouth.

I Thessalonians 4:1–8
¹Furthermore then we beseech you, brethren, and exhort you by the Lord Jesus, that as ye have received of us how ye ought to walk and to please God, so ye would abound more and more. ²For ye know what commandments we gave you by the Lord Jesus. ³For this is the will of God, even your sanctification, that ye should abstain from fornication: ⁴that every one of you should know how to possess his vessel in sanctification and honor; ⁵not in the lust of concupiscence, even as the Gentiles which know not God: ⁶that no man go beyond and defraud his brother in any matter: because that the Lord is the avenger of all such, as we also have forewarned you and testified. ⁷For God hath not called us unto uncleanness, but unto holiness. ⁸He therefore that despiseth, depiseth not man, but God, who hath also given unto us his Holy Spirit.

I Corinthians 7:5
Defraud ye not one the other, except it be with consent for a time, that ye may give yourselves to fasting and prayer; and come together again, that Satan tempt you not for your incontinency.

Paul undoubtedly would have had even more to say on the subject of sex, but he felt that it was corrupting even to speak of the subject and therefore limited himself to what he felt was necessary for his fellow believers to have for their moral instruction.

Ephesians 5:12
For it is a shame even to speak of those things which are done of them in secret.

In the book of Revelation, John joined Paul in extolling celibacy, for in a passage where he describes mortals entering the celestial realm, he refers to the 144,000 privileged men as being virgins who had not defiled themselves with women and had observed Paul's admonition that "it is good not to touch a woman."

Revelation 14:1–5

[1]And I looked, and, lo, a Lamb stood on the mount Zion, and with him a hundred forty and four thousand, having his Father's name written in their foreheads. [2]And I heard a voice from heaven, as the voice of many waters, and as a voice of a great thunder; and I heard the voice of harpers harping with their harps: [3]and they sung as it were a new song before the throne, and before the four beasts, and the elders: and no man could learn that song but the hundred and forty and four thousand, which were redeemed from the earth. [4]These are they which were not defiled with women; for they are virgins. These are they which follow the Lamb whithersoever he goeth. These were redeemed from among men, being the first fruits unto God and to the Lamb. [5]And in their mouth was found no guile: for they are without fault before the throne of God.

In Revelation 22:14–15, John also indicated that among those who would be excluded from the eternal city of heaven would be whoremongers. (See Chapter 13 for the quoted text.)

Paul's teachings on sex mark the advent of the philosophical view known as dualism. Prior to Pauline writings, the Hebrews espoused the philosophy of naturalism—that is, they considered the person, both body and soul, as a unity and sex was merely part of that whole. Putting aside completely the Hebrew view that the natural order of things was ordained of God, dualism split the world down the middle and created division everywhere. Since the physical world was evil and sensual, only the spiritual world was real and good. The body with its animal passions and desires belonged to the physical world and was nothing more than a wicked illusion. For believers to be spiritual, they had to renounce the world and the cravings of the body, with particular emphasis on sexual abstinence.

There was now a declaration of war between the body and the spirit with Satan fighting constantly to win the battle of the flesh over the "higher" sensibilities. The net result of this wholesale acceptance of dualism was to make believers aware that they were to be constantly on guard within themselves so that they could wage this struggle allowing good to triumph over evil. And the credit for this radical and ultimately defeatist change in emphasis goes to none other than Paul, the compulsive celibate.

H. L. Mencken must have had the apostle Paul in mind when he penned his now-famous definition of a Puritan: a person who has the terrible fear that someone, somewhere is having a good time.

Paul ranted and raved that "it is good for a man not to touch a woman," but he readily admitted that not everyone was able to "contain" as he could. However, he was also vehemently opposed to a man touching another man or a woman touching another woman, or, horror of horrors, to anyone touching oneself. As a Jew, Paul was well-versed in the rabbinical prohibition against touching himself, even when urinating, since it just might lead to bigger and better things. He had not yet been exposed to the newer and more liberal rabbinical teaching that if God did not want us to masturbate, he would have made our arms shorter.

Paul decided that it is better to marry than to "burn" with unfulfilled lust and he considered it essential to seek a spouse in order to avoid the terrible sin of fornication. Yet his message provides no solution for widows and widowers, for all single persons, and especially for sexually mature and capable youth with a fully-blossomed and urgent sex drive and for whom marriage is definitely out of the question.

We have all become unwitting victims or survivors of this negative, puritanical conditioning. The unrelenting theme song and distillation of all of Paul's ascetic writings comes to us as a most depressing Biblical moral guide: If it feels good, for God's sake, don't do it!

THE IMMACULATE DECEPTION

 VERY COMMON MISCONCEPTION ABOUT THE IMMACULATE Conception is that it describes the virgin birth of Christ. Those who have not had the benefit (?) of Roman Catholic catechism understandably think that since Jesus had no human father, his birth did not involve the dirty deed of regular carnal intercourse and therefore was unspotted or immaculate.

In Roman Catholic theology, however, the virgin birth applies only to Christ's conception without a human father and the subsequent perpetual virgin state of Mary; the Immaculate Conception refers only to Mary herself having been conceived without the stain of original sin that contaminates the rest of us. It was not until 1854 that Pope Pius IX issued the declaration elevating Mary to this unique status.

Only someone thoroughly indoctrinated by Roman Catholic programming could look at an infant in the arms of a proud mother and accept the dogma that that bundle of innocence was already corrupted by original sin because of Adam's disobedience in the Garden of Eden. The exorcism pronounced as part of the Roman Catholic baptismal ceremony purportedly drives out the devil of original sin and wipes the slate clean, ensuring the salvation of the baby's soul.

Now let us turn our attention to the background of the dogma of the virgin birth.

> **Isaiah 7:14** Therefore the Lord himself shall give you a sign; Behold, a virgin shall conceive, and bear a son, and shall call his name Imman'u-el.

The controversial Hebrew word used here sometimes means "virgin" and sometimes "young woman." A circular argument is provided by many apologists to explain why they feel it should mean "virgin." They quote from Matthew a text which plainly refers back to the Isaiah text:

> **Matthew 1:22–23** ²²Now all this was done, that it might be fulfilled which was spoken of the Lord by the prophet, saying, ²³Behold, a virgin shall be with child, and shall bring forth a son, and they shall call his name Imman'u-el.

There are some scholars, however, who view the Matthew text as a possible interpolation to show that Christ was indeed the Messiah and that he came in fulfillment of the Isaiah text. When the Revised Standard Version of the Bible first appeared, a genuine furor developed because the translators had rendered the word in question as "young woman" in the Isaiah text, relying on the original Hebrew rather than the Greek translation of the Hebrew used by the King James translators.

Luke also refers to the virgin birth in his gospel, but Mark and John are strangely silent on the issue.

At any rate, after Mary became pregnant, Joseph was prepared to keep her from public view since he thought that her condition was due to an affair with another man.

> **Matthew 1:18–19** ¹⁸Now the birth of Jesus Christ was on this wise: When as his mother Mary was espoused to Joseph, before they came together, she was found with child of the Holy

AND NOT WILLING TO MAKE HER A PUBLIC EXAMPLE

Ghost. ¹⁹Then Joseph her husband, being a just man, and not willing to make her a public example, was minded to put her away privily.

It was then explained to Joseph by an angel that his wife was to give birth to the Messiah.

Matthew 1:20–21 ²⁰But while he thought on these things, behold, the angel of the Lord appeared unto him in a dream, saying, Joseph, thou son of David, fear not to take unto thee Mary thy wife: for that which is conceived in her is of the Holy Ghost. ²¹And she shall bring forth a son, and thou shalt call his name Jesus: for he shall save his people from their sins.

The next section indicates that Joseph did not have sex with Mary until after the birth of Christ. But verse 25 effectively demolishes the Roman Catholic doctrine of perpetual virginity for Mary.

Matthew 1:24–25 ²⁴Then Joseph being raised from sleep did as the angel of the Lord had bidden him, and took unto him his wife: ²⁵And knew her not till she had brought forth her first-born son: and he called his name Jesus.

Once Christ was born, Mary was required to observe the same purification rites that any Hebrew mother had to follow. It is also noteworthy that the purification rite of circumcision was performed on the Christ child on the eighth day just as with any other Hebrew male infant.

Luke 2:21–24 ²¹And when eight days were accomplished for the circumcising of the child, his name was called Jesus, which was so named of the angel before he was conceived in the womb. ²²And when the days of her purification according to the law of Moses were accomplished, they brought him to Jerusalem, to present him to the Lord; [23](as it is written in the law of the Lord, Every male that openeth the womb shall be called holy to the Lord;) [24]and to offer a sacrifice according to that which is said in the law of the Lord, A pair of turtledoves, or two young pigeons.

If the conception of Christ in Mary's womb had truly been asexual, one wonders why she had to perform the same ceremonial purification rites as any other ordinary Hebrew mother.

Modern genetics teaches that virgin birth is not only entirely possible, but much more common that previously imagined. The scientific term is "parthenogenesis" and an article by Roy J. Harris, Jr. entitled "The Birds and Bees Can't Explain the Birth of Certain Turkeys" in the *Wall Street Journal* in July, 1973, explained: "In parthenogenesis, an outside agent—possibly a virus—apparently triggers duplication of the mother's set of chromosomes. This, in turn, touches off embryonic development."

In *Utopian Motherhood: New Trends in Human Reproduction*, Robert T. Francoeur makes the mind-boggling statement that "virgin births" occur as often as twins and twice as often as identical twins among white Americans meaning that in one case in ten thousand births, the eggs might have divided of their own accord, without any contact with spermatozoa.

Such revelations have comforted fundamentalists because they offer a rational explanation of a phenomenon which many have doubted for centuries. But geneticists offer a further explanation that dumbfounds all fundamentalists: in parthenogenesis or "virgin birth," the offspring can only be female since the male genetic code is lacking!

During the early centuries of Christendom, it was widely held that Christ had been born by emerging either through Mary's breast or navel in order to avoid contact with what the Germans call to this very day "the parts of shame." So widespread did this belief become that a book was written by Ratramnus attempting to prove that Christ had been born through the normal channels.

A concomitant issue in the Catholic Church was that of deciding whether Christ was divine from the moment of his conception or only at some later point during his intra-uterine development. It was not resolved until 1856 in favor of the "moment of conception" dogma.

It was, of course, difficult for many to accept the notion that Mary could have been impregnated by the Holy Ghost and still remain a virgin. The myth obtained that she had been impregnated through the ear. In some early paintings, the Holy Ghost, in the form of a dove, is seen descending with the sperm in its bill. Still another painting shows a lily through which the seminal words pass before entering Mary's ear. One early carving even shows a tube going from Gabriel's mouth to Mary's body, but under her skirts.

The Virgin's first systematic theologian, Francisco Suarez, helped to dispel all myths by explaining the virgin birth:

> The Blessed Virgin in conceiving a son neither lost her virginity nor experienced any venereal pleasure . . . it did not befit the Holy Spirit without any cause or utility to produce such an effect, or to excite any unbecoming movement of passion . . . On the contrary the effect of his overshadowing is to quench the fire of original sin . . . (*The Dignity and Virginity of the Mother of God*, p. 41).

For an engrossing and comprehensive account of the history of Mariolotry, read *Alone of All Her Sex: The Myth and the Cult of the Virgin Mary* by Marina Warner. And for a fascinating account of how the founders of all the world's leading religions were spawned by other-than-sexual means, read Kersey Graves' illuminating and brilliant analysis in *The World's Sixteen Crucified Saviors*.

The best reduction I have ever encountered of this preposterous ecclesiastical fairy tale sums it all up very neatly. The Virgin Mary gave birth to the little babe Jesus, the innocent lamb of God destined to be slain for the sins of all humankind. Consequently, Christian theology at its simplest and most fundamental level boils down to this very basic formula: Mary had a little lamb!

art XIV
SEXUAL BETRAYAL

A Honeymoon with the Wrong Bride

ISAAC TOLD JACOB THAT HE SHOULD NOT MARRY A CANAANITE woman, but rather that he should journey to Padan-aram where his Uncle Laban lived and there marry one of his cousins.

Jacob obediently traveled to his uncle's domain and upon arriving there, met Laban's daughter Rachel whom he fell in love with immediately,

Genesis 29:1–12 ¹Then Jacob went on his journey, and came into the land of the people of the east. ²And he looked, and behold a well in the field, and, lo, there were three flocks of sheep lying by it; for out of that well they watered the flocks: and a great stone was upon the well's mouth. ³And thither were all the flocks gathered: and they rolled the stone from the well's mouth, and watered the sheep, and put the stone again upon the well's mouth in his place. ⁴And Jacob said unto them, My brethren, whence be ye? And they said, Of Haran are we. ⁵And he said unto them, Know ye Laban the son of Nahor? And they said, We know him. ⁶And he said unto them, Is he well? And they said, He is well: and, behold, Rachel his daughter cometh with the sheep. ⁷And he said, Lo, it is yet high day, neither is it time that the cattle should be gathered together: water ye the sheep, and go and feed them. ⁸And they said, We cannot, until all the flocks be gathered together, and till they roll the stone from the well's mouth; then we water the sheep. ⁹And while he yet spake with them, Rachel came with her father's sheep: for she kept them. ¹⁰And it came to pass, when Jacob saw Rachel the daughter of Laban his mother's brother, and the sheep of Laban his mother's brother, that Jacob went near, and rolled the stone from the well's mouth, and watered the flock of Laban his mother's brother. ¹¹And Jacob kissed Rachel, and lifted up his voice, and wept. ¹²And Jacob told Rachel that he was her father's brother, and that he was Rebekah's son: and she ran and told her father.

Laban warmly welcomed Jacob into his home and after just one month, they made a pact whereby Jacob agreed to work for Laban for seven years in order to earn the hand of Rachel in marriage. The intensity of Jacob's love for Rachel can be measured by his statement that the seven years seemed to him as but a few days.

Genesis 29:13–20   ¹³And it came to pass, when Laban heard the tidings of Jacob his sister's son, that he ran to meet him, and embraced him, and kissed him, and brought him to his house. And he told Laban all these things. ¹⁴And Laban said to him, Surely thou art my bone and my flesh. And he abode with him the space of a month. ¹⁵And Laban said unto Jacob, Because thou art my brother, shouldest thou therefore serve me for nought? tell me, what shall thy wages be? ¹⁶And Laban had two daughters: the name of the elder was Le'ah, and the name of the younger was Rachel. ¹⁷Le'ah was tender eyed; but Rachel was beautiful and well-favored. ¹⁸And Jacob loved Rachel; and said, I will serve thee seven years for Rachel thy younger daughter. ¹⁹And Laban said, It is better that I give her to thee, than that I should give her to another man: abide with me. ²⁰And Jacob served seven years for Rachel; and they seemed unto him but a few days, for the love he had to her.

At the end of the seven-year period, the marriage took place at a wedding feast held by Laban.

Genesis 29:21–22   ²¹And Jacob said unto Laban, Give me my wife, for my days are fulfilled, that I may go in unto her. ²²And Laban gathered together all the men of the place, and made a feast.

On that wedding night, Jacob was awaiting his new bride in the bridal chamber, but Laban brought Rachel's older sister Leah to the chamber instead. In an era of no electric lights, it was not until the next morning that Jacob discovered the trick Laban had played on him. He demanded an explanation from Laban for his actions.

Genesis 29:23–25   ²³And it came to pass in the evening, that he took Le'ah his daughter, and brought her to him; and he went in unto her. ²⁴And Laban gave unto his daughter Le'ah Zilpah his maid for a handmaid. ²⁵And it came to pass, that in the morning, behold, it was Le'ah: and he said to Laban, What is this thou hast done unto me? did not I serve with thee for Rachel? wherefore then hast thou beguiled me?

Laban explained that it was the custom among his people always to marry off the older daughter before the younger one, a practice which he certainly should have taken the trouble to explain to Jacob seven years previously. Then a new pact was made giving Rachel to Jacob at the end of the bridal week with Leah, but only on the condition that he remain yet another seven years for the privilege. The "bridal week" was the seven-day celebration held in order to feast and make merry in honor of the joyous occasion.

> **Genesis 29:26–30** ²⁶And Laban said, It must not be so done in our country, to give the younger before the firstborn. ²⁷Fulfil her week, and we will give thee this also for the service which thou shalt serve with me yet seven other years. ²⁸And Jacob did so, and fulfilled her week: and he gave him Rachel his daughter to wife also. ²⁹And Laban gave to Rachel his daughter Bilhah his handmaid to be her maid. ³⁰And he went in also unto Rachel, and he loved also Rachel more than Le'ah, and served with him yet seven other years.

A little later in Israel's history, Jacob would have been entitled to one full year of leisure. The Hebrew law subsequently stipulated that a newly married male was exempt from military service for one full year and also from the responsibilities of making a livelihood. What a lengthy honeymoon!

> **Deuteronomy 24:5** When a man hath taken a new wife, he shall not go out to war, neither shall he be charged with any business: but he shall be free at home one year, and shall cheer up his wife which he hath taken.

The later Hebrew law would also have made both Laban and Jacob guilty of allowing two sisters to marry the same man. The Hebrew canon decreed that no Israelite could marry a second sister as long as the first sister was still alive.

> **Leviticus 18:18** Neither shalt thou take a wife to her sister, to vex her, to uncover her nakedness, besides the other in her life time.

ABRAHAM AND ISAAC,
TWO DOUBLE-DEALING PIMPS

 braham journeyed to Egypt with his wife Sarah, but he admonished her to pretend that she was his sister so that the Egyptians would not kill him in order to steal his wife.

Genesis 12:10–13 ¹⁰And there was a famine in the land: and Abram went down into Egypt to sojourn there; for the famine was grievous in the land. ¹¹And it came to pass, when he was come near to enter into Egypt, that he said unto Sarai his wife, Behold now, I know that thou art a fair woman to look upon: ¹²therefore it shall come to pass, when the Egyptians shall see thee, that they shall say, This is his wife: and they will kill me, but they will save thee alive. ¹³Say, I pray thee, thou art my sister: that it may be well with me for thy sake; and my soul shall live because of thee.

When they arrived in Egypt, Sarah's beauty was immediately noticed and she was taken into Pharaoh's household which of course meant that she was added to his great harem. Pharaoh compensated Abraham generously for his "sister." As part of the ruler's harem, she undoubtedly did what every other harem member did to please the king.

Genesis 12:14–16 ¹⁴And it came to pass, that, when Abram was come into Egypt, the Egyptians beheld the woman that she was very fair. ¹⁵The princes also of Pharaoh saw her, and commended her before Pharaoh: and the woman was taken into Pharaoh's house. ¹⁶And he entreated Abram well for her sake: and he had sheep, and oxen, and he asses, and menservants, and maidservants, and she asses, and camels.

Jehovah was displeased with Pharaoh for taking Sarah away from Abraham and he sent plagues to punish him for his acts. The monarch finally became aware of Abraham's deception and released Sarah and sent her and Abraham out of Egypt. Nothing in the narrative indicates that Abraham returned any of the munificence which Pharaoh had bestowed on him—sheep, oxen, donkeys, camels and servants.

Genesis 12:17–20   ¹⁷And the Lord plagued Pharaoh and his house with great plagues, because of Sarai, Abram's wife. ¹⁸And Pharaoh called Abram, and said, What is this that thou has done unto me? why didst thou not tell me that she was thy wife? ¹⁹Why saidst thou, She is my sister? so I might have taken her to me to wife: now therefore behold thy wife, take her, and go thy way. ²⁰And Pharaoh commanded his men concerning him: and they sent him away, and his wife, and all that he had.

Some time later, Abraham and Sarah set off on another journey. This time, the same hoax was perpetrated on King Abimelech. But in a dream, Jehovah revealed to Abimelech that Abraham and Sarah were married and he exonerated Abimelech of any wrongdoing in this instance since he had acted in good faith and since he had not as yet fornicated with Sarah.

Genesis 20:1–8   ¹And Abraham journeyed from thence toward the south country, and dwelt between Kadesh and Shur, and sojourned in Gerar. ²And Abraham said of Sarah his wife, She is my sister: and Abim'elech king of Gerar sent, and took Sarah. ³but God came to Abim'elech in a dream by night, and said to him, Behold, thou art but a dead man, for the woman which thou has taken; for she is a man's wife. ⁴But Abim'elech had not come near her: and he said, Lord, wilt thou slay also a righteous nation? ⁵Said he not unto me, she is my sister? and she, even she herself said, He is my brother: in the integrity of my heart and innocency of my hands have I done this. ⁶And God said unto him in a dream, Yea, I know that thou didst this in the integrity of thy heart; for I also withheld thee from sinning against me: therefore suffered I thee not to touch her. ⁷Now therefore restore the man his wife; for he is a prophet, and he shall pray for thee, and thou shalt live: and if thou restore her not, know thou that thou shalt surely die, thou, and all that are thine. ⁸Therefore Abim'elech rose early in the morning, and called all his servants, and told all these things in their ears: and the men were sore afraid.

King Abimelech then confronted Abraham over his attempted treachery, and Abraham revealed to the monarch that Sarah really was his half-sister since they both had the same father.

Genesis 20:9–13 ⁹Then Abim'elech called Abraham, and said unto him, What hast thou done unto us? and what have I offended thee, that thou hast brought on me and on my kingdom a great sin? thou hast done deeds unto me that ought not to be done. ¹⁰And Abim'elech said unto Abraham, What sawest thou, that thou hast done this thing? ¹¹And Abraham said, Because I thought, Surely the fear of God is not in this place; and they will slay me for my wife's sake. ¹²And yet indeed she is my sister; she is the daughter of my father, but not the daughter of my mother; and she became my wife. ¹³And it came to pass, when God caused me to wander from my father's house, that I said unto her, This is thy kindness which thou shalt show unto me; at every place whither we shall come, say of me, He is my brother.

Abimelech then demonstrated his generosity by lavishing gifts on Abraham. Among the gifts were 1,000 pieces of silver.

Genesis 20:14–16 ¹⁴And Abimelech took sheep, and oxen, and menservants, and womenservants, and gave them unto Abraham, and restored him Sarah his wife. ¹⁵And Abim'elech said, Behold, my land is before thee: dwell where it pleaseth thee. ¹⁶And unto Sarah he said, Behold, I have given thy brother a thousand pieces of silver: behold, he is to thee a covering of the eyes, unto all that are with thee, and with all other; thus she was reproved.

Jehovah had mysteriously chosen to punish Abimelech for accepting Abraham's offer of Sarah and the punishment meted out was sterility for all the women in the king's household. Although the text implies that their sojourn with Abimelech was very brief, it must have endured for some time in order for the curse of sterility imposed by Jehovah to become evident.

Abraham then entreated Jehovah to reconsider the plague of sterility which had befallen Abimelech's wife and all the women in his harem. Jehovah responded to Abraham's plea by rescinding the sex hex and Abimelech's wife and all the women in his harem became fertile once again.

Genesis 20:17–18 ¹⁷So Abraham prayed unto God: and God healed Abim'elech, and his wife, and his maidservants; and they bare children. ¹⁸For the Lord had fast closed up all the wombs of the house of Abim'elech, because of Sarah, Abraham's wife.

BEHOLD ISAAC WAS SPORTING WITH REBEKAH HIS WIFE

Like father, like son! Isaac used his wife Rebekah to deceive a king with the same ruse that his father Abraham had contrived with Sarah. Once again, the fraud was perpetrated on King Abimelech who surely should have heard the rumor of what had happened to his fellow monarch, Abimelech of Gerar. In this instance, the monarch discovered the subterfuge when he looked out of his palace window and saw Isaac and Rebekah petting—the modern equivalent of "sporting" and the couple left the kingdom without Rebekah's ever getting to join the royal harem!

Genesis 26:6–11   ⁶And Isaac dwelt in Gerar. ⁷And the men of the place asked him of his wife; and he said, She is my sister: for he feared to say, She is my wife; lest, said he, the men of the place should kill me for Rebekah; because she was fair to look upon. ⁸And it came to pass, when he had been there a long time, that Abim'elech king of the Philistines looked out at a window, and saw, and, behold, Isaac was sporting with Rebekah his wife. ⁹And Abim'elech called Isaac, and said, Behold, of a surety she is thy wife: and how saidst thou, She is my sister? And Isaac said unto him, Because I said, Lest I die for her. ¹⁰And Abim'elech said, What is this thou hast done unto us? one of the people might lightly have lain with thy wife, and thou shouldest have brought guiltiness upon us. ¹¹And Abim'elech charged all his people, saying, He that toucheth this man or his wife shall surely be put to death.

Foxy Delilah Double-Crosses Superstud Samson

Y MEANS OF AN ANGEL-MESSENGER, JEHOVAH REVEALED TO the wife of Manoah that she would bear a son and that he was to be consecrated as a Nazarite. This meant that his hair was never to be cut and that he was never to touch strong drink.

Judges 13:2–5 ²And there was a certain man of Zorah, of the family of the Danites, whose name was Mano'ah; and his wife was barren, and bare not. ³And the angel of the Lord appeared unto the woman, and said unto her, Behold now, thou art barren, and bearest not: but thou shalt conceive, and bear a son. ⁴Now therefore beware, I pray thee, and drink not wine nor strong drink, and eat not any unclean thing: ⁵for, lo, thou shalt conceive, and bear a son; and no razor shall come on his head: for the child shall be a Nazarite unto God from the womb: and he shall begin to deliver Israel out of the hand of the Philistines.

Samson was born as promised and consecrated to Jehovah.

Judges 13:24 And the woman bare a son, and called his name Samson: and the child grew, and the Lord blessed him.

As Samson grew into manhood, he saw a Philistine woman that he wanted to marry, but his parents tried to discourage him.

Judges 14:1–3 ¹And Samson went down to Timnath, and saw a woman in Timnath of the daughters of the Philistines. ²And he came up, and told his father and his mother, and said, I have seen a woman in Timnath of the daughters of the Philistines: now therefore get her for me to wife. ³Then his father and his mother said unto him, Is there never a woman among the daughters of thy brethren, or among all my people, that thou goest to take a wife of the uncircumcised Philistines? And Samson said unto his father, Get her for me; for she pleaseth me well.

Samson married the Philistine woman anyway, but she betrayed him by enticing him to tell her the answer to a riddle which he had expounded to thirty Philistines who had gathered at the wedding feast.

Judges 14:16–17   [16]And Samson's wife wept before him, and said, Thou dost but hate me, and lovest me not: thou hast put forth a riddle unto the children of my people, and hast not told it me. And he said unto her, Behold, I have not told it my father nor my mother, and shall I tell it thee? [17]And she wept before him the seven days, while their feast lasted: and it came to pass on the seventh day, that he told her, because she lay sore upon him: and she told the riddle to the children of her people.

Samson was so enraged that he slew the thirty men, and leaving his wife behind, returned to his father's house. His wife was then given to the friend of Samson who had been the best man at Samson's wedding.

Judges 14:19–20   [19]And the Spirit of the Lord came upon him, and he went down to Ash'kelon, and slew thirty men of them, and took their spoil and gave change of garments unto them which expounded the riddle. And his anger was kindled, and he went up to his father's house. [20]But Samson's wife was given to his companion, whom he had used as his friend.

Samson later returned to visit his wife, but his father-in-law refused him entry into the house. He attempted to appease Samson by offering him his younger daughter, but Samson refused the offer and proceeded to burn the land of the Philistines. They, in turn, burned the house of Samson's father-in-law incinerating both the father and the daughter.

Judges 15:1–6   [1]But it came to pass within a while after, in the time of wheat harvest, that Samson visited his wife with a kid; and he said, I will go in to my wife into the chamber. But her father would not suffer him to go in. [2]And her father said, I verily thought that thou hadst utterly hated her; therefore I gave her to thy companion: is not her younger sister fairer than she? take her, I pray thee, instead of her. [3]And Samson said concerning them, Now shall I be more blameless than the Philistines, though I do them a displeasure. [4]And Samson went and caught three hundred foxes, and took firebrands, and turned tail to tail, and put a firebrand in the midst between two tails. [5]And when he had set the brands on fire, he let them go into the standing corn of the Philistines, and burnt up both the shocks and also the standing corn, with the vineyards and olives. [6]Then the Philistines said,

Who hath done this? And they answered, Samson, the son-in-law of Timnite, because he had taken his wife, and given her to his companion. And the Philistines came up, and burnt her and her father with fire.

After this and other exploits, Samson patronized a whore and shacked up with her for almost two days straight!

Judges 16:1–3 ¹Then went Samson to Gaza, and saw there a harlot, and went in unto her. ²And it was told the Gazites, saying, Samson is come hither. And they compassed him in, and laid wait for him all night in the gate of the city, and were quiet all the night, saying, In the morning, when it is day, we shall kill him. ³And Samson lay till midnight, and arose at midnight, and took the doors of the gate of the city, and the two posts, and went away with them, bar and all, and put them upon his shoulders, and carried them up to the top of a hill that is before Hebron.

He then fell in love with Delilah, and although she repeatedly betrayed him to the Philistines, he was too weak to resist her seductive charms and finally revealed to her the secret of his great strength.

The five heads of the Philistine nation had each offered Delilah 1,100 pieces of silver so that her total reward in today's money would have been about $5,000, certainly a handsome sum in view of Judas' later betrayal of Christ for only thirty pieces of silver.

Delilah tried desperately to get Samson to reveal the secret of his strength, but Samson led her off the track with a lie. At first, he told her that he would be totally incapacitated if his hands were tied with seven raw leather bowstrings (withes).

Judges 16:4–9 ⁴And it came to pass afterward, that he loved a woman in the valley of Sorek, whose name was Deli'lah. ⁵And the lords of the Philistines came up unto her, and said unto her, Entice him, and see wherein his great strength lieth, and by what means we may prevail against him, that we may bind him to afflict him: and we will give thee every one of us eleven hundred pieces of silver. ⁶And Deli'lah said to Samson, Tell me, I pray thee, wherein thy great strength lieth, and wherewith thou mightest be bound to afflict thee. ⁷And Samson said unto her, If they bind me with seven green withes that were never dried, then shall I be weak, and be as another man. ⁸Then the lords of the Philistines brought up to her seven green withes which had not been dried, and she bound him with them. ⁹Now there were men lying in wait, abiding with her in the chamber. And she said unto him, The Philistines be upon thee, Samson. And he brake the withes, as a thread of tow is broken when it toucheth the fire. So his strength was not known.

② He next told her that his strength would leave him if he were tied with brand new rope.

Judges 16:10–12 ¹⁰And Deli'lah said unto Samson, Behold, thou hast mocked me, and told me lies: now tell me, I pray thee, wherewith thou mightest be bound. ¹¹And he said unto her, If they bind me fast with new ropes that never were occupied, then shall I be weak, and be as another man. ¹²Deli'lah therefore took new ropes, and bound him therewith, and said unto him, The Philistines be upon thee, Samson. And there were liers in wait abiding in the chamber. And he brake them from off his arms like a thread.

③ The next fabrication was that his strength would wither if his hair were woven into a loom.

Judges 16:13–14 ¹³And Deli'lah said unto Samson, Hitherto thou hast mocked me, and told me lies: tell me wherewith thou mightest be bound. And he said unto her, If thou weavest the seven locks of my head with the web. ¹⁴And she fastened it with the pin, and said unto him, The Philistines be upon thee, Samson. And he awaked out of his sleep, and went away with the pin of the beam, and with the web.

Finally, Delilah nagged at Samson every day until he could stand it no longer and he confessed the true secret of his strength.

Judges 16:15–17 ¹⁵And she said unto him, How canst thou say, I love thee, when thine heart is not with me? Thou hast mocked me these three times, and hast not told me wherein thy great strength lieth. ¹⁶And it came to pass, when she pressed him daily with her words, and urged him, so that his soul was vexed unto death; ¹⁷that he told her all his heart, and said unto her, There hath not come a razor upon mine head; for I have been a Nazarite unto God from my mother's womb: if I be shaven, then my strength will go from me, and I shall become weak, and be like any other man.

She then betrayed him into the hands of the Philistines and collected her reward.

Judges 16:18–20   18And when Deli'lah saw that he had told her all his heart, she sent and called for the lords of the Philistines, saying, Come up this once, for he hath showed me all his heart. Then the lords of the Philistines came up unto her, and brought money in their hand. 19And she made him sleep upon her knees; and she called for a man, and she caused him to shave off the seven locks of his head; and she began to afflict him, and his strength went from him. 20And she said, The Philistines be upon thee, Samson. And he awoke out of his sleep, and said, I will go out as at other times before, and shake myself. And he wist not that the Lord was departed from him.

The Philistines blinded Samson and put him in prison and his hair began to grow again while he was there.

Judges 16:21–22   21But the Philistines took him, and put out his eyes, and brought him down to Gaza, and bound him with fetters of brass; and he did grind in the prison house. 22Howbeit the hair of his head began to grow again after he was shaven.

During a feast honoring the Philistine god Dagon, Samson was brought to the festival to provide the guests with some amusing diversion. At least one commentator argues cogently that since the Philistines were phallic worshippers, when they called for Samson to "make us sport," they were really asking for Samson to put on a jerk-off display for their amusement. (R. E. L. Masters in *The Cradle of Erotica*, p.113.) This same historian points out that the most logical reason for the Philistines to want to capture Samson was to have him provide stud service for any and all Philistine women in order to breed a nation of supermen. He views the whole Samson epic as the Near Eastern counterpart of the Hercules of Western mythology whose sexploits resulted from superhuman virility, prowess and potency.

Judges 16:23–25 ²³Then the lords of the Philistines gathered them together for to offer a great sacrifice unto Dagon their god, and to rejoice: for they said, Our god hath delivered Samson our enemy into our hand. ²⁴And when the people saw him, they praised their god: for they said, Our god hath delivered into our hands our enemy, and the destroyer of our country, which slew many of us. ²⁵And it came to pass, when their hearts were merry, that they said, Call for Samson, that he may make us sport. And they called for Samson out of the prison house; and he made them sport: and they set him between the pillars.

Samson asked permission to lean on the pillars of the house and it was granted. He called upon Jehovah to renew his strength and pulled the pillars down bringing about his own death as well as the death of all who were assembled there.

Judges 16:26–31 ²⁶And Samson said unto the lad that held him by the hand, Suffer me that I may feel the pillars whereupon the house standeth, that I may lean upon them. ²⁷Now the house was full of men and women; and all the lords of the Philistines were there; and there were upon the roof about three thousand men and women, that beheld while Samson made sport. ²⁸And Samson called unto the Lord, and said, O Lord God, remember me, I pray thee, and strengthen me, I pray thee, only this once, O God, that I may be at once avenged on the Philistines for my two eyes. ²⁹And Samson took hold of the two middle pillars upon which the house stood, and on which it was borne up, of the one with his right hand, and of the other with his left. ³⁰And Samson said, Let me die with the Philistines. And he bowed himself with all his might; and the house fell upon the lords, and upon all the people that were therein. So the dead which he slew at his death were more than they which he slew in his life. ³¹Then his brethren and all the house of his father came down, and took him, and brought him up, and buried him between Zorah and Eshta'ol in the buryingplace of Mano'ah his father. And he judged Israel twenty years.

And thus ends one of the most celebrated of all Bible love stories, for it has inspired operas, books, movies and paintings. It also is a favorite children's Bible tale, but only in a much bowdlerized version.

KING AHASUERUS DITCHES
QUEEN VASHTI FOR ESTHER

AHASUERUS WAS NONE OTHER THAN THE GREAT AND EXTRAVAGANT Persian emperor Xerxes. His queen was Vashti and at the conclusion of a six-month-long stag party, he commanded that Vashti promenade before his drunken guests so that they could appreciate her great beauty. This Vashti refused to do and Xerxes booted her out of the palace and sent a decree to all his kingdom so that all the young virgins of the empire might come to the royal palace and compete for Vashti's throne.

Esther 2:1–4   ¹After these things, when the wrath of king Ahasue'rus was appeased, he remembered Vashti, and what she had done, and what was decreed against her. ²Then said the king's servants that ministered unto him, Let there be fair young virgins sought for the king: ³and let the king appoint officers in all the provinces of his kingdom, that they may gather together all the fair young virgins unto Shushan the palace, to the house of the women, unto the custody of Hege the king's chamberlain, keeper of the women; and let their things for purification be given them: ⁴and let the maiden which pleaseth the king be queen instead of Vashti. And the thing pleased the king; and he did so.

Mordecai, who was already in the king's palace, brought his cousin Esther to the palace to enter the competition.

Esther 2:5–7   ⁵Now in Shushan the palace there was a certain Jew, whose name was Mor'decai, the son of Ja'ir, the son of Shim'e-i, the son of Kish, a Benjamite; ⁶who had been carried away from Jerusalem with the captivity which had been carried away with Jeconi'ah king of Judah, whom Nebuchadnez'zar the king of Babylon had carried away. ⁷And he brought up Hadas'sah, that is, Esther, his uncle's daughter: for she had neither father nor mother, and the maid was fair and beautiful; whom Mor'decai, when her father and mother were dead, took for his own daughter.

The eunuch in charge of the king's harem was Hegai and he favored Esther by giving her seven female attendants and a private apartment. Esther's cousin

AND WITH OTHER THINGS FOR THE PURIFYING OF WOMEN

Mordecai had warned Esther not to reveal that she was a Jewess and he visited her daily in her quarters.

Esther 2:8–11 [8]So it came to pass, when the king's commandment and his decree was heard, and when many maidens were gathered together unto Shushan the palace, to the custody of He'gai, that Esther was brought also unto the king's house, to the custody of He'gai, keeper of the women. [9]And the maiden pleased him, and she obtained kindness of him; and he speedily gave her her things for purification, with such things as belonged to her, and seven maidens, which were meet to be given her, out of the king's house: and he preferred her and her maids unto the best place of the house of the women. [10]Esther had not showed her people nor her kindred: for Mor'decai had charged her that she should not show it. [11]And Mor'decai walked every day before the court of the women's house, to know how Esther did, and what should become of her.

The purification and preparation rites engaged in are of especial interest: one full year, the first half of which was devoted to beauty treatments and the second half of which was a six-month stint of perfuming and application of ointments. After this one-year period of cosmetic foreplay, the virgin was finally ready to spend the night with the king who would normally sleep with her only once. Unless he found special delight in her charms and sexual prowess, she moved on into the second harem of the palace and remained there on tap.

Esther 2:12–14 [12]Now when every maid's turn was come to go in to king Ahasue'rus, after that she had been twelve months, according to the manner of the women, (for so were the days of their purifications accomplished, to wit, six months with oil of myrrh, and six months with sweet odors, and with other things for the purifying of the women,) [13]then thus came every maiden unto the king; whatsoever she desired was given her to go with her out of the house of the women unto the king's house. [14]In the evening she went, and on the morrow she returned into the second house of the women, to the custody of Sha-ash'gaz, the king's chamberlain, which kept the concubines: she came in unto the king no more, except the king delighted in her, and that she were called by name.

When Esther's turn came to go to bed with the king, she so pleased Ahasuerus that he set the royal crown on her head and immediately put her in Vashti's place. She must have been quite a bedroom virtuosa!

𝕰𝕾𝕿𝕳𝖊𝖗 2:15–18   [15]Now when the turn of Esther, the daughter of Ab'ihail the uncle of Mor'decai, who had taken her for his daughter, was come to go in unto the king, she required nothing but what He'gai the king's chamberlain, the keeper of the women, appointed. And Esther obtained favor in the sight of all them that looked upon her. [16]So Esther was taken unto king Ahasue'rus into his house royal in the tenth month, which is the month Tebeth, in the seventh year of his reign. [17]And the king loved Esther above all the women, and she obtained grace and favor in his sight more than all the virgins; so that he set the royal crown upon her head, and made her queen instead of Vashti. [18]Then the king made a great feast unto all his princes and his servants, even Esther's feast; and he made a release to the provinces, and gave gifts, according to the state of the king.

The story has a happy ending. Since Esther had not revealed to Xerxes that she was a Jewess, she was later able to exert her royal influence with the king and prevent an anti-Semitic bloodbath from occurring. And all she had sacrificed was her virginity!

Part XV
Sexual Potency and Rejuvenation

GIDEON SIRES SEVENTY-ONE SONS

Judges 8:28–32 ²⁸Thus was Mid'ian subdued before the children of Israel, so that they lifted up their heads no more. And the country was in quietness forty years in the days of Gideon. ²⁹And Jerubba'al the son of Jo'ash went and dwelt in his own house. ³⁰And Gideon had threescore and ten sons of his body begotten: for he had many wives. ³¹And his concubine that was in Shechem, she also bare him a son, whose name he called Abim'elech. ³²And Gideon the son of Jo'ash died in a good old age, and was buried in the sepulchre of Jo'ash his father, in Oph'-rah of the Abi-ez'rites.

Gideon is included in this section only because he is the namesake of the famous Society of Gideons responsible for placing Bibles in virtually every nook and cranny of every hotel and motel room in the hostelries of America and more than 145 foreign countries. Organized in 1898 in a Wisconsin hotel room, this group of fundamentalist businessmen dedicated itself to "sowing the precious Seed, the word of God, in the field of the world."

Gideon fathered seventy-one sons (no daughters?), and although this is certainly no dastardly act, he accomplished it with many wives and a concubine. Fundamentalists who make up groups like the Gideons always preach that morality is absolute, never relative. Yet if one were to ask them why men today cannot imitate Gideon and have a lot of wives plus a few mistresses here and there, the reply would doubtless be, "But times have changed and we are living under a new dispensation." If times have changed, then morality is relative and not absolute, or is it?

As we saw in Chapter 30, Gideon was responsible for setting up a phallic idol which so mesmerized the Israelites that they went "a whoring after it" and were enticed into the sex worship and idolatry which Jehovah wanted desperately for them to eschew.

Perhaps this overzealous group of Bible fans should consider renaming their organization before putting any more Bibles in any more inns!

SOLOMON'S THOUSAND AND ONE WOMEN

I Kings 11:1–3 ¹But king Solomon loved many strange women, together with the daughter of Pharaoh, women of the Moabites, Ammonites, Edomites, Zido'nians, and Hittites; ²of the nations concerning which the Lord said unto the children of

Israel, Ye shall not go in to them, neither shall they come in unto you: for surely they will turn away your heart after their gods: Solomon clave unto these in love. ³And he had seven hundred wives, princesses, and three hundred concubines: and his wives turned away his heart.

Solomon's harem included seven hundred wives and three hundred mistresses. If we add to that number the name of Abishag, the Shunammite, whom Solomon presumably memorialized in his great Song of Songs, he then had a total bevy of one thousand and one females.

In Biblical times, the only limitation on the number of wives or mistresses were a man's financial resources and the available supply of women. The law placed no limit on the number of wives. Solomon's father, David, married eight wives specifically and later added many more women to his court harem.

Biblical polygamy, therefore, must be considered as a matter more of prestige than of sensuality. Viewed in that light, it is not unlike the prestige afforded to the two-car family in today's America. But with such a stable of women readily at hand, Solomon surely must have indulged his passions more than he would have in a monogamous role.

KING DAVID'S REVIVAL WITH FEMALE BODY FRICTION

I Kings 1:1–4 ¹Now king David was old and stricken in years; and they covered him with clothes, but he gat no heat. ²Wherefore his servants said unto him, Let there be sought for my lord the king a young virgin: and let her stand before the king, and let her cherish him, and let her lie in thy bosom, that my lord the king may get heat. ³So they sought for a fair damsel throughout all the coasts of Israel, and found Ab'ishag a Shu'nammite, and brought her to the king. ⁴And the damsel was very fair, and cherished the king, and ministered to him: but the king knew her not.

When King David felt chilled in his sickbed and he needed to be warmed, the chronicler does not clarify why it was so urgent to have a young virgin brought to David's bed to revive him and to warm him. Although the text assures us that David did not "know" young Abishag, judging by his previous record, he assuredly would have ravished her if it had not been for his advanced age and his enfeebled condition—a hard-on was clearly out of the question!

David's elder son, Adonijah, fell deeply in love with Abishag and wanted to marry her. Despite the evidence that Abishag served David strictly as a nurse and slept with him for medical purposes only, Adonijah's desire for marriage was actually considered to be incestuous since Abishag really belonged to David.

After a period during which Adonijah tried to set up a kingdom independent of his father David, Adonijah's rebellion was quelled. He then went to Bathsheba in peace to ask her to intercede with Solomon, for Solomon was now officially the king.

AND CHERISHED THE KING AND MINISTERED TO HIM

Bathsheba told Solomon of Adonijah's desire to marry Abishag, but Solomon became so outraged that he ordered Adonijah's immediate execution.

There are really three explanations for this sadistic revenge of Solomon: I. Solomon considered Adonijah's request to be incestuous and therefore a serious infraction of the Hebrew moral law; 2. Adonijah's request to have Abishag was tantamount, in Solomon's eyes, to a request for half of David's kingdom which he now had for his very own and which he was not about to share with his rebellious elder brother; 3. Solomon himself was attracted to Abishag. Many commentators attribute the Song of Solomon to Solomon's deep and abiding love for Abishag which he therefore immortalized in that peerless love paean (see Chapter 58).

I Kings 2:13–25   13And Adoni'jah the son of Haggith came to Bath-she'ba the mother of Solomon. And she said, Comest thou peaceably? And he said, Peaceably. 14He said moreover, I have somewhat to say unto thee. And she said, Say on. 15And he said, Thou knowest that the kingdom was mine, and that all Israel set their faces on me, that I should reign: howbeit the kingdom is turned about, and is become my brother's: for it was his from the Lord. ¹⁶And now I ask one petition of thee, deny me not. And she said unto him, Say on. ¹⁷And he said, Speak, I pray thee, unto Solomon the king, (for he will not say thee nay) that he give me Ab'ishag the Shu'nammite to wife. ¹⁸And Bath-she'ba said, Well; I will speak for thee unto the king. ¹⁹Bath-she'ba therefore went unto king Solomon, to speak unto him for Adoni'jah. And the king rose up to meet her, and bowed himself unto her, and sat down on his throne, and caused a seat to be set for the king's mother; and she sat on his right hand. ²⁰Then she said, I desire one small petition of thee; I pray thee, say me not nay. And the king said unto her, Ask on, my mother; for I will not say thee nay. ²¹And she said, Let Ab'ishag the Shu'nammite be given to Adoni'jah thy brother to wife. ²²And king Solomon answered and said unto his mother, And why dost thou ask Ab'ishag the Shu'nammite for Adoni'jah? ask for him the kingdom also; for he is mine elder brother; even for him, and for Abi'-athar the priest, and for Jo'ab the son of Zeru-i'ah. ²³Then king Solomon sware by the Lord, saying, God do so to me and more also, if Adoni'jah have not spoken this word against his own life. ²⁴Now therefore, as the Lord liveth, which hath established me, and set me on the throne of David my father, and who hath made me a house, as he promised, Adoni'jah shall be put to death this day. ²⁵And king Solomon sent by the hand of Benai'ah the son of Jehoi'ada; and he fell upon him that he died.

Part XVI
IN PRAISE OF LOVE

Ruth Propositions Boaz and Shacks Up Overnight in a Barn

UTH WAS THE WIDOWED DAUGHTER-IN-LAW OF NAOMI. Naomi encouraged her to return to her people after the death of her husband, but Ruth insisted on staying on with the famous words:

Ruth 1:16–17   ¹⁶And Ruth said, Entreat me not to leave thee, or to return from following after thee: for whither thou goest, I will go; and where thou lodgest, I will lodge: thy people shall be my people, and thy God my God; ¹⁷where thou diest, will I die, and there will I be buried: the Lord do so to me, and more also, if aught but death part thee and me.

Naomi had a wealthy kinsman named Boaz and she felt that a match between Ruth and Boaz would be a good thing for them both. Naomi instructed Ruth to go to Boaz's barn and to wait until Boaz had retired before going to lie at his side and spend the night with him. Ruth agreed to carry out Naomi's instructions.

Ruth 3:1–5   ¹Then Na-o'mi her mother-in-law said unto her, My daughter, shall I not seek rest for thee, that it may be well with thee? ²And now is not Boaz of our kindred, with whose maidens thou wast? Behold, he winnoweth barley tonight in the threshingfloor. ³Wash thyself therefore, and anoint thee, and put thy raiment upon thee, and get thee down to the floor; but make not thyself known unto the man, until he shall have done eating and drinking. ⁴And it shall be, when he lieth down, that thou shalt mark the place where he shall lie, and thou shalt go in, and uncover his feet, and lay thee down; and he will tell thee what thou shalt do. ⁵And she said unto her, All that thou sayest unto me I will do.

That night, she went to the barn and lay down at Boaz's feet after Boaz had eaten and drunk. When Boaz turned in his sleep at midnight, he discovered Ruth there at his feet. He was delighted to learn that Ruth wanted to marry him instead of a younger man and he promised to take care of all details for the wedding.

Ruth 3:6–11 [6]And she went down unto the floor, and did according to all that her mother-in-law bade her. [7]And when Boaz had eaten and drunk, and his heart was merry, he went to lie down at the end of the heap of corn: and she came softly, and uncovered his feet, and laid her down. [8]And it came to pass at midnight, that the man was afraid, and turned himself: and, behold, a woman lay at

AND UNCOVERED HIS FEET AND LAID HER DOWN

his feet. [9]And he said, Who art thou? And she answered, I am Ruth thine handmaid: spread therefore thy skirt over thine handmaid; for thou art a near kinsman. [10]And he said, Blessed be thou of the Lord, my daughter: for thou hast showed more kindness in the latter end than at the beginning, inasmuch as thou followedst not young men, whether poor or rich. [11]And now, my daughter, fear not; I will do to thee all that thou requirest: for all the city of my people doth know that thou art a virtuous woman.

There was one problem confronting them both, however. Naomi had a closer living relative than Boaz and, according to the Hebrew custom, he must first be offered Ruth's hand in marriage.

Ruth 3:12–13 [12]And now it is true that I am thy near kinsman: howbeit there is a kinsman nearer than I. [13]Tarry this night, and it shall be in the morning, that if he will perform unto thee the part of a kinsman, well; let him do the kinsman's part: but if he will not do the part of a kinsman to thee, then will I do the part of a kinsman to thee, as the Lord liveth: lie down until the morning.

Ruth spent the entire night with Boaz. He sent her on her way before day-break in order to avoid any unnecessary gossip in the neighborhood. He made Ruth take with her about a bushel and a half of barley in her shawl.

> **Ruth 3:14–15** [14]And she lay at his feet until the morning: and she rose up before one could know another. And he said, Let it not be known that a woman came into the floor. [15]Also he said, Bring the veil that thou hast upon thee, and hold it. And when she held it, he measured six measures of barley, and laid it on her: and she went into the city.

When Ruth related all of these events to Naomi, she assured Ruth that Boaz was a man of his word and that he would resolve the situation that very day.

> **Ruth 3:16–18** [16]And when she came to her mother-in-law, she said, Who art thou, my daughter? And she told her all that the man had done to her. [17]And she said, These six measures of barley gave he me; for he said to me, Go not empty unto thy mother-in-law. [18]Then said she, Sit still, my daughter, until thou know how the matter will fall: for the man will not be in rest, until he have finished the thing this day.

The story has a happy ending, for when Naomi's nearest relative learned that the property belonging to Naomi's deceased son was for sale, he was interested in purchasing it. He declined the offer, however, when he discovered that purchasing the property would require his marriage to Ruth. This left Boaz free to seek Ruth's hand which he did, and they were happily married.

At least one modern writer refuses to believe that no sexual liberties took place between Ruth and Boaz. Rev. Tom Horner, writing in *Sex in the Bible*, p. 126, says:

> In the little book of Ruth there is a very unusual reference in which the word "feet" is clearly a euphemism for the male genitals . . . There in the middle of the night, she "uncovered his feet, and lay down." She was obviously making a marriage proposal to an older man who never dreamed that she would be interested in him. How do we know that it is a marriage proposal and not just a proposition? Because if Boaz had not received permission the next day from Ruth's nearest of kin to marry her, and if her escapade with him were later discovered through her

pregnancy, the poor girl would have been stoned as an adulteress. For she still belonged to her dead husband, so to speak, until given in marriage to another.

According to Horner's interpretation, Ruth propositioned Boaz by quite literally throwing herself at his "feet."

SOLOMON'S STEAMY SONG OF LOVE

T THE COUNCIL OF JAMNIA IN A.D. 100, THE SONG OF SONGS was firmly locked into the canon of the Holy Scriptures. The more prudish of Biblical apologists have attempted to represent the composition as an allegory of the love of Jehovah for Israel or of Christ for the Church. One must stretch the imagination somewhat to conceive of Israel or the Church with white skin, eyes like doves, the hair dyed black or purple with henna, even teeth, scarlet lips, a prominent nose, rosy temples, long straight hair, firm breasts, round full thighs, a round belly, a figure as erect as a palm tree and beautiful steps.

Other scholars of a more liberal bent have interpreted the Song of Songs as an ancient marriage cantata, sung by soloists and chorus antiphonally to celebrate a wedding. But realistic Bible commentators have admitted that it is just what it appears to be: a sensuous and sensual hymn praising the joys and ecstasies of carnal love, and here the sumptuous English of the King James Version only serves to intensify that analysis.

There are eight chapters in this exquisitely beautiful love poem, but only a few stanzas will suffice to reveal the earthy emphasis on physical love, the love Solomon felt for Abishag, the Shunammite.

KISSING, THE BEST FORM OF FOREPLAY

Song of Solomon 1:2 Let him kiss me with the kisses of his mouth: for thy love is better than wine.

ADMIRATION FOR WELL-FORMED BREASTS

Song of Solomon 4:5–6 ⁵Thy two breasts are like two young roes that are twins, which feed among the lilies. ⁶Until the day break, and the shadows flee away, I will get me to the mountain of myrrh, and to the hill of frankincense.

THY TWO BREASTS ARE LIKE TWO YOUNG ROES

Song of Solomon 7:6–9

[6]How fair and how pleasant art thou, O love, for delights! [7]This thy stature is like to a palm tree, and thy breasts to clusters of grapes. [8]I said, I will go up to the palm tree, I will take hold of the boughs thereof: now also thy breasts shall be as clusters of the vine, and the smell of thy nose like apples; [9]and the roof of thy mouth like the best wine for my beloved, that goeth down sweetly, causing the lips of those that are asleep to speak.

Song of Solomon 8:8–10

[8]We have a little sister, and she hath no breasts: what shall we do for our sister in the day when she shall be spoken for? [9]If she be a wall, we will build upon her a palace of silver: and if she be a door, we will enclose her with boards of cedar. [10]I am a wall, and my breasts like towers: then was I in his eyes as one that found favour.

VISUAL AND OLFACTORY STIMULANTS TO SEX

Song of Solomon 4:1

Behold, thou art fair, my love; behold, thou art fair; thou hast doves' eyes with thy locks: thy hair is as a flock of goats, that appear from mount Gil'e-ad.

Song of Solomon 6:5

Turn away thine eyes from me, for they have overcome me: thy hair is as a flock of goats that appear from Gil'e-ad.

Song of Solomon 4:10–11   [10]How fair is thy love, my sister, my spouse! How much better is thy love than wine! and the smell of thine ointments than all spices! [11]Thy lips, O my spouse, drop as the honeycomb: honey and milk are under thy tongue; and the smell of thy garments is like the smell of Lebanon.

ORAL EROTICISM (THE FRENCH, SOUL, OR TONGUE KISS)

Song of Solomon 4: 11   Thy lips, O my spouse, drop as the honeycomb: honey and milk are under thy tongue; and the smell of thy garments is like the smell of Lebanon.

APHRODISIACS AND OTHER SEX STIMULANTS

Song of Solomon 7:11–13   [11]Come, my beloved, let us go forth into the field; let us lodge in the villages. [12]Let us get up early to the vineyards; let us see if the vine flourish, whether the tender grape appear, and the pomegranates bud forth: there will I give thee my loves. [13]The mandrakes give a smell, and at our gates are all manner of pleasant fruits, new and old, which I have laid up for thee, O my beloved.

(For definition of "mandrakes," see Chapter 33.)

Song of Solomon 8:1–2   [1]O that thou wert as my brother, that sucked the breasts of my mother! when I should find thee without, I would kiss thee; yea, I should not be despised. [2]I would lead thee, and bring thee into my mother's house, who would instruct me: I would cause thee to drink of spiced wine of the juice of my pomegranate.

LONGING FOR AN ABSENT LOVER

Song of Solomon 3:1–4   [1]By night on my bed I sought him whom my soul loveth: I sought him, but I found him not. [2]I will rise now, and go about the city in the streets, and in the broad ways I will seek him whom my soul loveth: I sought him, but I found him not. [3]The watchmen that go about the city found me: to whom I said, Saw ye him whom my soul loveth? [4]It was but a little that I passed from them, but I found him whom my soul loveth: I held him, and would not let him go, until I had brought him into my mother's house, and into the chamber of her that conceived me.

Song of Solomon 8:3
His left hand should be under my head, and his right hand should embrace me.

Queen Victoria had obviously familiarized herself with this passage when she issued her famous statement about the duty of wives to accommodate their husbands in an era when women were never supposed to feel sexual desire or experience sexual gratification. The monarch's advice to her female subjects was, "Lie back, close your eyes and think of England!"

Today, we refer to the female-on-the-bottom posture as the "missionary position" but few seem to know the origin of the term. Hawaii and other Polynesian islands had a very sex-positive culture before the Christian missionaries arrived. The natives considered it an art form to be sure the female was sexually satisfied. Whether by trial and error or from pure intuition, they rarely had sex with the woman below the man. Consequently, when some of the natives peeked through the bedroom windows of the missionaries' huts to see if they could learn any new sex techniques from their spiritual mentors, they observed them humping away with the wife underneath. They deduced that the mountaintop deity Jehovah had in fact dictated an 11th Commandment to Moses an Mt. Sinai: "Thou shalt lie with the man on top!" From then on, this configuration was dubbed the missionary position.

art XVII

DEVIL SEX AND WITCHCRAFT

Cohabitation With Devils

Genesis 6:1–8 ¹And it came to pass, when men began to multiply on the face of the earth, and daughters were born unto them, ²that the sons of God saw the daughters of men that they were fair; and they took them wives of all which they chose. ³And the Lord said, My Spirit shall not always strive with man, for that he also is flesh: yet his days shall be a hundred and twenty years. ⁴There were giants in the earth in those days; and also after that, when the sons of God came in unto the daughters of men, and they bare children to them, the same became mighty men which were of old, men of renown. ⁵And God saw that the wickedness of man was great in the earth, and that every imagination of the thoughts of his heart was only evil continually. ⁶And it repented the Lord that he had made man on the earth, and it grieved him at his heart. ⁷And the Lord said, I will destroy man whom I have created from the face of the earth; both man, and beast, and the creeping thing, and the fowls of the air; for it repenteth me that I have made them. ⁸But Noah found grace in the eyes of the Lord.

John Milton's masterpiece *Paradise Lost* was based on this excerpt from Genesis as well as on a section from Revelation.

Revelation 12:7–9 ⁷And there was war in heaven: Michael and his angels fought against the dragon; and the dragon fought and his angels, ⁸and prevailed not; neither was their place found any more in heaven. ⁹And the great dragon was cast out, that old serpent, called the Devil, and Satan, which deceiveth the whole world: he was cast out into the earth, and his angels were cast out with him.

The "sons of God" mentioned above are the angels who rebelled along with Lucifer and who were cast out from heaven with him because of their disobedience. Just as Satan, alias Lucifer, took great delight in entering the Garden of Eden and in causing the downfall of Jehovah's latest venture in creation, so also did these fallen angels delight in choosing among the fairest of earth's women and, by cohabiting with them, populating the earth with so many immoral and rebellious creatures that Jehovah eventually repented of his earth experiment and vowed to blot out all earthlings and to start anew.

This decision led, of course, to singling out Noah and his clan as the only humans worthy of survival, to Noah's ark and to the Great Deluge which engulfed the then-known world.

One cannot help wonder why the omniscient Jehovah created humankind in the first place knowing full well that their wickedness would soon necessitate their own destruction.

WITCHES, WIZARDS, AND FAMILIAR SPIRITS

HE BIBLICAL CONDEMNATION OF WITCHES, WIZARDS AND THOSE who had familiar spirits is spelled out in unequivocal terms:

Exodus 22:18   Thou shalt not suffer a witch to live.

Leviticus 19:31   Regard not them that have familiar spirits, neither seek after wizards, to be defiled by them: I am the Lord your God.

Leviticus 20:6   And the soul that turneth after such as have familiar spirits, and after wizards, to go a whoring after them, I will even set my face against that soul, and will cut him off from among his people.

Leviticus 20:27   A man also or woman that hath a familiar spirit, or that is a wizard, shall surely be put to death: they shall stone them with stones; their blood shall be upon them.

Deuteronomy 18:10–11   [10]There shall not be found among you any one that maketh his son or his daughter to pass through the fire, or that useth divination, or an observer of times, or an enchanter, or a witch, [11]or a charmer, or a consulter with familiar spirits, or a wizard, or a necromancer.

It has been estimated that the above quotations decreeing death for witches have been responsible for as many as nine million executions!

But what has all of this to do with sex? Simply a radical change in viewpoint from Biblical times to the time of the Inquisition. In Biblical times, witches, wizards and those with familiar spirits were looked upon much as we look upon mediums and channelers today.

After Saul was estranged from Jehovah and did not know how to proceed in his battle against the Philistines, in desperation he consulted a witch. The account tells of his visiting a witch at the town of Endor and she merely conjured up the spirit of Samuel for Saul so that Saul could query the deceased prophet about what the best course of action was in proceeding against the Philistines (I Samuel 28:6–14).

But by the end of the Middle Ages, the Devil had taken on a specifically sexual quality and in a bull issued by Pope Innocent VIII, the Devil was henceforth to be regarded as a person and not merely as a symbol of error. His anatomy was described with special attention given to his penis which was always of enormous size and often even forked so that he could simultaneously penetrate a woman vaginally and anally. Attending the Devil was a host of lesser devils, and their exact number was given as 7,405,926.

The witch mania reached its zenith with its two high priests, Henry Kramer and James Sprenger. These Dominican friars saw evil in nearly every erotic manifestation and because of their twisted sexuality, they lavished on the human female the hatred generated within themselves by their enforced celibacy.

In 1484, Kramer and Sprenger published the despicable *Malleus Maleficarum* in their home town of Cologne, Germany. In *Malleus,* which has been the most influential work ever published on witchcraft, they expressed their general loathing for all women:

> She is an imperfect animal, she always deceives ... All witchcraft comes from carnal lust, which is in woman insatiable. Wherefore for the sake of fulfilling their lusts they consort even with devils.

R. E. L. Masters in his classical study of witchcraft, *Eros and Evil,* gives us a vivid picture of how earnestly the Biblical injunctions were now carried out:

> Predictably, those who hated the flesh became obsessed by the flesh. Inquisitors and others who dealt with witches doted upon every erotic detail of the confessions and testimony, encouraged the morbid and the sensational, examined naked witches for the Devil's Mark (shaving their bodies the better to find it), and in all displayed such shameless avidity in matters erotic as to provoke public criticism.

The Devil's Mark, which often resembled the foot of a hare or of a toad, was believed placed by Him on the flesh of each witch so that the witch could not attempt later to deny that a pact had been made. It was often concealed in the female genitals and in the rectum, and was anesthetic. To make certain that some blemish was in fact the Devil's Mark, long pins would be inserted into the flesh of the witch. One may well imagine that sadists were attracted to the work of driving pins into the breasts and genitalia and other sensitive body parts of witches.

In Bamberg, nine hundred persons were burned between 1609 and 1633, including the town's mayor, Johannes Julius, who wrote to his daughter: "It is all falsehood and invention. They never cease the torture until one says something." A bishop of Geneva burned five hundred in three months and a bishop of Wirzburg, nine hundred. The senate of the town of Savoy condemned eight hundred in a single body. Between 1404 and 1554, the Holy Office burned at least 30,000 witches. The bloodiest outbreak of witch mania was in Spain where Torquemada personally sent 10,220 persons to the stake and 97,371 to the galleys.

But the most important point to all of these statistics is the change in emphasis—no longer was witchcraft a question of the magical or the otherworldly; it was now exclusively a phenomenon of sexual congress with the Devil or with one of His Satanic Majesty's innumerable host. Clearly, this planet Earth now belonged to Satan and Jehovah's creation experiment had reached its nadir.

Epilogue

 E HAVE EXAMINED THE MANY AND VARIEGATED PASSAGES FROM the Bible on the subject of human sexuality and the unspeakably barbaric and draconian Hebrew moral code which so severely condemned sexual waywardness and nonconformity that it exacted the death penalty for mere sexual peccadilloes.

Those who doubt that what the Bible says about sex has any influence on our lives today need to recall a statement from *Sexual Behavior in the Human Male,* p. 487. Authors Kinsey, Pomeroy and Martin remind us that "the ancient religious codes are still the prime sources of the attitudes, the ideas, the ideals, and the rationalizations by which most individuals pattern their sexual lives."

As a fitting close, it is most appropriate to quote two Bible texts which reflect a sane, healthy and refreshingly hedonistic view on the subject of humankind's brief span on this earth and how our unmitigated enjoyment of sex might help to enhance our appreciation of this, the only life we can truly be assured of:

Ecclesiastes 4:11   Again, if two lie together, then they have heat: but how can one be warm alone?

Ecclesiastes 9:9–10   ⁹Live joyfully with the wife whom thou lovest all the days of the life of thy vanity, which he hath given thee under the sun, all the days of thy vanity: for that is thy portion in this life, and in thy labor which thou takest under the sun. ¹⁰Whatsoever thy hand findeth to do, do it with thy might; for there is no work, nor device, nor knowledge, nor wisdom, in the grave, whither thou goest.

AFTERWORD

M Y LINK TO A MISSING ATHEIST: THE MADALYN MURRAY O'Hair Connection

The October, 1965 issue of *Playboy* magazine featured an interview with Madalyn Murray which began: "'Why are you an atheist, Mrs. Murray?' Answer: 'Because religion is a crutch and only the crippled need crutches.'" Upon reading that remarkable article, I resolved to contact this outspoken, militant nonbeliever to convey to her how much her courage and candor had inspired me.

During the next several years, we corresponded, talked frequently by long distance and I eagerly joined her crusade for the separation of church and state. When I became a member of the faculty of USC in 1970, I was instrumental in having the now-remarried Madalyn Murray O'Hair invited to the university as a speaker for their Great Issues Forum. In 1972, she came to the campus and delivered a speech entitled "Freedom From Religion." Her most memorable comment was about how critically religion and government support, depend on and need each other. She expounded, "After all, if you can be taught to believe in the virgin birth, you can also be taught to believe in the Federal Reserve System."

Subsequent to her appearance in Los Angeles, publisher Jeremy Tarcher offered her a book contract to expand on the material of her freedom-from-religion theme and I immediately offered to go to Austin during my summer vacation that year to help with background research for the manuscript. I rented a small apartment near the general headquarters of American Atheists in order to be as close as possible to my heroine. The final result of our collaboration was *Freedom Under Siege: The Impact of Organized Religion on Your Liberty and Your Pocketbook* (1974).

At this point in my relationship with Madalyn, I felt she could do no wrong. I admired her with the same adulation accorded any cult leader by a gung-ho, zealous convert to the cause.

After my stint in Austin, I kept in close touch with her and when my completed manuscript of *The X-Rated Bible* received one rejection slip after another from numerous publishers, I proposed to Madalyn that she consider printing it at her own American Atheist Press. She responded enthusiastically to the offer, complimented me profusely on the contents (a rare act for a woman never generous with praise) and published my opus in 1985.

My sex spoof went on to become the all-time best-seller of the offerings at her firm, a rather amazing feat considering that it was available almost exclusively by mail order. Mainstream distributors and bookstores refused to carry any titles from such an offbeat, controversial house, especially since the public mind automatically associated it with the embattled and antagonistic atheist leader. Along with this reputation, she had gleefully garnered the epithet of "the most hated woman in America."

By the time the Murray-O'Hairs (Madalyn, son Jon and granddaughter Robin) mysteriously disappeared off the face of the earth in September, 1995, my relationship with them had deteriorated to the extent that they stopped paying me royalties and definitely considered me *persona non grata* in the atheist community.

Enter Adam Parfrey of Feral House. The publisher found my anthology in a used book store, liked what he read and felt that it deserved a reprint with much wider circulation and, for the first time, distribution through conventional outlets. The present volume brings that vision to fruition at long last.

Ben Edward Akerley
Los Angeles, California
November, 1998

BIBLICAL REFERENCES (ALPHABETICAL INDEX)

INDEX

Animation: Christian thought, & abortion, 113–114

Animism: in Israelite thought, 17–18, 22

Aphrodisiacs: mandrake believed to be, 119–120; in Song of Solomon, 217

Apostasy: alcohol linked with, 107–108; Israelites, 16, 68, 70–73, 94, 100–108

Aquinas, Saint Thomas: rape less sinful than masturbation, 15

Ark (of the Covenant): celebration of return, 74–76; David's exhibitionistic dance, 75–76; desecration of, punishments associated with, 74, 161–163

Arson: Samson's destruction of cornfields, 198

Asa (grandson of Rehoboam): phallic worship, suppression of, 104

Asherah: fertility god embraced by Jezebel, 106

Ashtoreth: idol representing, 105–106

Assault: parent, death penalty for, 45

Atkinson, Miles: circumcision, comments quoted, 130

Augustine, Saint: procreation, opinions on, 29

Baal: masochism of priests, 73; worship of, 105, 106–107

Babylon: Revelation image of, 111

Baptist, John the: see John (the Baptist).

Barrenness: see fertility, human.

Bastards and bastardy: see illegitimacy.

Bathsheba (M. David, Uriah): adultery of, & consequences, 58–63 asks for Abishag for Adonijah, 209–210

Behind the Mask of Medicine (Miles Atkinson): circumcision, comments quoted, 130

Belief systems: animism, Israelite: 17–18, 22

Benjaminites (tribe of Israel): gang-rape, murder of Levite's concubine, 50–54; intermarriage with other Israelites shunned, 147–150

Bennett, D. M.: A. Comstock entrapment of, xvii

Bestiality: death penalty for, 18, 169–170

Betrothment and Marriage, (A. de Smet): Onan, comments quoted, 18, 169–170

Bible: see religiously-based writings.

Bilhah (concubine of Jacob): children of, 119, 121; incest with Reuben, 45

"Birds and Bees Can't Explain the Birth of Certain Turkeys, The" (Roy J. Harris, Jr. article): parthenogenesis, comments quoted, 187

Birth control: methods, coitus interruptus. ineffectiveness of, 14–15; coitus interruptus, of Onan, results of, 13-14

Bisexuality: David & Jonathan, T. Horner quotation, 39

'Bitter waters': test for adultery, 138–140

Black people: alleged descendants of Ham & Canaan, 69

Blindness: men of Sodom punished with, 33–34. See also punishments.

Blood: food, forbidden as, 17; murder, sign of vengeance, Abel's death, 17. See also menstruation, 'purification'.

Boaz (M. Ruth): propositioned by Ruth, & marriage, 134, 212–215

'Born-again' Christians: see Christian religion.

British Journal of Venereal Diseases (R. R. Willcox article): syphilis of Miriam, possible, 25

British Medical Journal (G. S. Thompson article): circumcision, comments quoted,

Bryan, William Jennings: Scopes trial, defense of Bible in, 130

Cain (O. Adam, Eve): murder of Abel, 17; possible incest of, 1

Canaan (O. Ham): cursed by grandfather Noah, 68–69

Cannibalism: newborns, during famine, 28, 134; Samarian famine, 165

Capital punishment: abortion, death of mother due to spontaneous injury, 113; adultery, 18, 65–66, 138–140, 214–215; assaulting parent, 45; bestiality, 18, 169–170; coitus during menstruation, unclear reference, 18–19; cursing parent, 45; desecration of Ark of the Covenant, 74, 161–163; disobedience, 45–46; failure to circumcise, unclear reference, 124; fornication, 18, 84–85, 141; homosexual actions, 18, 40; incest, 45; rape, 49, 142; stealing slave 45; violation of tribal law, 147–148; witchcraft, 221–223. See also punishments.

Catholic Church: see Roman Catholic Church.

Celibacy: see abstinence.

Censorship: 'obscene' materials, A. Comstock actions, xvi–xvii; pro-censorship groups, listing, xv

Childbirth: amniotic fluid, as 'polluting' substance, 27; coitus forbidden after, 27; curse upon Eve, 26–28; non-vaginal birth of Christ posited, 187; salvation, part of, 155. See also fertility, human; 'purification'; procreation.

Children: Bible too salacious for, xvi, xviii

Christian religion: abortion and fetal animation, thought concerning, 113–114; abstinence recommended, 21, 28–29; castration, 127–129; circumcision controversy, 127–128; devotees, number of "born-again", U.S., 1976 Gallop poll, xi–xiii; divorce, 179–181; heaven, lack of sexual behaviors in, 15–16; homosexuality, condemnations of, 39–41; rape less sinful than masturbation, Aquinas opinion, 15; 'secret gospel of Mark', possible homosexuality of Christ, 42–43; sex as 'necessary evil', theological opinions, 28–29; Virgin Mary, cultus of, 187–188, witches, treatment of, 221–223; women, subjugation of, 154–156, 158–159, 222. See also Protestant religion; Roman Catholic Church.

Christian Response to the Sexual Revolution, The (David Mace): circumcision, comments quoted, 125–126

Christ, Jesus: adultery, comments on, 64–66; anointing at feast, 96–98; birth & circumcision of, 184–187; divinity at moment of conception, 187; healing, women with 'issue of blood', 26; heaven, no sexual behaviors in, 15–16; homosexual tendencies hypothesized, Morton Smith, quotation from, 43; non-vaginal birth posited, 187; prostitution, condemnation of, 95–96, 99; Samaritan woman,

condemnation of common-law bond, 95–96; sexuality of, 99–100

Christology Reconsidered (Norman Pittenger): sexuality of Christ, quotation, 99–100

Church and the Homosexual, The (John J. McNeill): Biblical interpretations, problems with, quotation, 41–42

Circumcision: see desexualization, religiously-based.

Circumcision: An American Health Fallacy (Edward Wallerstein): cited 131

Circumcision: The Painful Dilemma (Rosemary Romberg): cited, 131

Clemens, Samuel L. ('Mark Twain'): Bible & own works, comments on, xviii

Clement (of Alexandria): 'secret gospel of Mark' & possible homosexual tendencies of Christ, 42–43

Clitoridectomy: see desexualization, religiously-based.

Coitus: childbirth, forbidden after, 27; frequency, 'normal', 29–30; God, forbidden when expecting visit from, 21–22, Holy Ghost offended by, 29; menstruation, forbidden during, 18–19; 'necessary evil', Christian thought, 28–29; possibly 'forbidden fruit', Garden of Eden, 2. See also prostitution (cultic).

Coitus interruptus: see birth control.

Cole, Rev. William Graham: homosexuality of David & Jonathan challenged, quotation, 36; punishment, coitus during menstruation, quotation, 18

Communion, Holy: denied to non-abstinent couples, St. Jerome, 28

Comstock Act (obscenity): xvi

Comstock, Anthony: Bennett, D. M., entrapment of, xvii; puritanism of, O'Higgins & Reede quotation, xv

Conception, Immaculate: doctrine of Virgin Mary's, 114–184

Concubines and concubinage: Abraham's, 114–115, 117; Abishag, 208–209; Absalom's incest with David's, 6, 10–11, 62; Gideon's, 207; Jacob's, 118–119, 121; Levite's, & Gibeah rape/murder of, 50–54; Reuben's incest with Jacob's, 45.

See also harem; marriage and marriage customs.

Contamination [archaic, reflecting primitive thinking]: see 'purification'; sacrifice.

Continence: see abstinence.

Corinth (Christian church at): homosexuality condemned, Pauline epistle, 40; incest condemned, Pauline epistle, 178

Council of Jamnia: acceptance of Song of Solomon as canonical work, 215

Covenant, Ark of the: celebration of return, 74–76; David's exhibitionistic dance, 75–76; desecration of, punishments associated with, 74, 161–163

Cozbi (Midianite; M. Zimri): killed by Phinehas for intermarriage, 70

Crime: see adultery; arson; assault; bestiality; fornication; incest; kidnapping; murder; rape; seduction; slander; theft; torture. See also trials.

'Crimes against nature' [archaic usage, reflecting primitive thinking, for non-reproductively-oriented sexual behaviors]: masturbation vs. rape, Aquinas opinion, 15; Pauline epistles, references in, 39, 42. See also bestiality; homosexual actions.

Criminals: sexually 'immoral' people likened to, 40–41, 181

Cross-dressing: see transvestism.

Cultic prostitution: see prostitution.

"Cupid's Yokes" (E. H. Heywood; D. M. Bennett, publisher): A. Comstock action against, xvii

Cursing: parent, death penalty for, 45

Damnation, eternal: see hell.

Darrow, Clarence: Scopes trial, Bible analysis during, xviii

David (Israelite king; M. Bathsheba; P. Solomon): Abishag, relationship with, 208–209; adultery with Bathsheba, results of, 58–63; circumcises dead Philistines, 135–136; exhibitionism of, 75–76 incest of Amnon & Tamar, anger over, 5; incest, victim of Absalom's, 6, 10–11, 62; Joab, curse upon household of, 23, 24; Jonathan, relationship with,

36–39; Michal taken from husband by, 76–77; possible venereal disease of, 24, 25; Saul, relationship with, 36–38, 79, 106, 134–136; wives of, 61, 75–77, 135–136, 208

Death penalty: see capital punishment; see also punishments.

Delilah (promiscuous Philistine): Samson, association with, & betrayal, 199–201

Desexualization, religiously-based castration: Christ's comments, 170; circumcision as symbolic form, 127; Israelite law, 170–171; later Christian influence, 172–173; circumcision: Abraham, 123–124; age at, 27, 132; Christian tradition, significance in, 127–129; dead persons, 125, 135–136; death penalty, failure to perform, unclear reference, 124; lapses in ritual practice of, 132–133; medical practice, dubious value as, 130–131; purification of mother, reduction of time for, 27, 125; required for intermarriage, 47–48; sign of Jehovah's covenant, 123–124, 126–127, 129; clitoridectomy: 124

de Smet, Canon A: Onan & levirate law, comments quoted, 15

Devil & devils: medieval thought concerning, 222

Dietary taboos: blood forbidden as food, 17

Dignity and Virginity of the Mother of God, The (Francisco Suarez): Mary's conception of Christ, 188

Dinah (O. Jacob, Leah; S. '12 tribes'): rape of, & results, 46–50

Discrimination, gender-based: Christian thought, 154–156, 158–159, 222; menstruous females, 17–21; mother of female infant, extended period of 'defilement', 27. See also women.

Discrimination, handicapped: forbidden to offer sacrifices to Jehovah, 171

Disease: hemorrhoid plagues, 161–163; Israelite plague, for apostasy with Midianites, 70. See also venereal disease.

Disobedience: death penalty for, 45–46

Divorce: bill of divorcement, 156–157;

divorced pair forbidden to remarry, 157; New Testament on, 179–181; priest forbidden to marry divorcee, 141–142; rape victim, impossible for rapist to divorce, 49–50; war-captive wife not to be enslaved, but divorced, 152. See also concubines and concubinage; marriage and marriage customs.

Drunkenness: see alcohol use and abuse.

Dualism: compared to naturalism, 183–184

Ecclesiastical writings & statements: Innocent VIII, Devil as person, 222; Plus IX, doctrines promulgated by, 113–114, 184

Eden, Garden of: 'forbidden fruit' possibly coitus, 2

Ejaculation, premature: possible Biblical reference to, 24

Eli (priest; P. Hophni, Phinehas): lasciviousness of sons in temple, 100

Elijah (prophet): priests of Baal, confrontation with, 72–73

Elizabeth (M. Zacharias, P. John the Baptist): sterility & later pregnancy, 116

Encyclopedia Biblica: oaths, quotation concerning, 146

Encyclopedia of Jewish Religion: exceptions to circumcision, 125

Endor, witch of: Saul's consultation of, 222

Ephods: 'household gods', 105

Epstein, L. M.: bestiality, execution of animal, 170; bitter waters test, adultery, 140; circumcision, dead infants, 125; sexual rites & Israelite religion, 102

Er (M. Tamar; S. Onan, Shelah): slain by Jehovah, 13

Eros and Evil (R. E. L. Masters): witches, torture of, comments quoted, 222–223

Espionage: fall of Jericho, Rahab's part in, 88–92

Esther (cousin of Mordecai; M. Ahasuerus): enters harem, 203–205

Eunuchs: see desexualization, religiously-based; harems.

Evangelism: U. S., efforts in, 1976 Gallup poll results, xi–xiii

Eve (M. Adam; P. Abel; Cain, Seth): creation and mating of, 1–2; curse upon, 26, 28

Excommunication: abortion, Roman Catholic punishment for, 113; failure to circumcise, unclear reference, 124; incest, 6; coitus during menses, unclear reference, 18. See also punishments.

Excrement: food contamination, 113; bodily contamination, 124; general, 164–168

Exhibitionism: David, return of ark, 75–76; Noah, while drunk, 68–69. See also nudity.

'Fall' of man: sexual overtones in, 2

'Familiar spirits': see witches.

Famine: Abraham's Egyptian visit during, 193; cannibalism in, 28, 134, 165

Feces: see excrement.

Fertility cults: see pagan rituals & worship; phallic symbols; prostitution (cultic).

Fertility, human: Jacob's wives/concubines, 118–121; levirate marriage, to maintain lineage, 13–15; sterility: Abimelech's harem, 195; Elizabeth, 116; Hannah, 116; Manoah's wife, 116, 197; Sarah, 114–116; sterility, punishment for incest, 16. See also childbirth; procreation; 'purification'.

Fetus: religious thought concerning, 113

Fines: inducing miscarriage without death of woman, 113 rape of virgin, 49–50; slandering a virgin, 140–141. See also punishments.

Flood, Great: interbreeding as grounds for causation, 220–221

Food taboos: blood forbidden as food, 17

Fornication: betrothed female slave, laws concerning, 157; death penalty for, 18–19, 84–85, 141; Esther & Ahasuerus, 203–205; Judah & Tamar, 83–85; Paul's condemnations, 177–178

Francoeur, Robert T.: parthenogenesis, frequency of, 187

Gallup poll (1976): 'born-again Christians', statistics on, in U. S., xi–xiii

Garden of Eden: 'forbidden fruit' possibly coitus, 2

Gay people: see homosexual actions.

Genocide: Hivites, 48–49; Jabesh-Gilead

tribe, 148; Jericho townspeople, 91;
sanctioned by Jehovah, 151–152

Ghost, Holy: see Holy Ghost.

Gibeah (city): mob rape/murder of concubine
& attempted homosexual rape, 52–53

Gideon: children of, 207; idols, treatment
of, 21–22

Gideons (society): 207

God/gods: coitus forbidden, when expecting
appearance by, 21–22; interbreeding
with humans, 220; non-sexual origins
of, Graves cited, 188. See also Ashteroth;
Baal; Jehovah; pagan rituals & worship,
sacrifices & offerings.

Gods of Love: Creative Process in Early Religion
(T. Clifton Longworth): sexual emblems,
mistranslation of references, quotation, 103

Gomer (M. Hosea): adultery of, 93–94

Gomorrah (city): destruction of, 7, 9, 32,
34–35

Gonorrhea: 24

Gospel of Philip: Christ, marriage to Mary
Magdalene, 99

Graves, Kersey: book cited, 188

'Great Whore' (Revelation): 110–111

Guide for the Perplexed (Moses Maimonides):
quotation on desexualization effect of
circumcision, 129

Hadassah: see Esther.

Hagar (concubine to Abraham; P. Ishmael):
impregnation of, & banishment,
114–115, 117

Ham (O. Noah; S. Japheth, Shem; P. Canaan):
curse of father upon offspring, 68–69

Hamor (P. Shechem); betrothal of Dinah
& Shechem proposed: 46–48

Handicapped: offerings to Jehovah
unacceptable, 171

Hannah (P. Samuel): sterility followed by
pregnancy, 116

Harem: Abimelech, Sarah taken for,
194–195; Ahasuerus', 203–205;
David's, 207; eunuchs and, 170–172;
Pharoah, Sarah taken for, 193–194;
Solomon's, 207. See also concubines &
concubinage; marriage & marriage customs.

Harris, Roy J., Jr.: parthenogenesis,

comments quoted, 187

Hayes, Rutherford B.: pardon of D. M.
Bennett, xvii

Heaven [used for religionist concept of
pleasant afterlife]: sexual behavior
lacking in, 15–16

Heaven's Gate, mass suicide and surgical
castration of cult members, 173

Hebrew Iliad, The (R. H. Pfeiffer): translation
of II Samuel 3:29: 23, 24

Hegai [Hege] (keeper of royal harem):
preparation of Esther, 203–205

Hell [religionist concept of unpleasant
afterlife]: Babylon, 111; rebellious angels,
35; sexually 'immoral' condemned to,
40–41, 178

Hemorrhoids: Philistine plague of, 161–163

Herod (king; M. Herodias): death of John
the Baptist through Salome's influence,
80–81

Herodias (M. Herod; P. Salome): John the
Baptist, hatred of, & results, 80–81

Heywood, E. H.: "Cupid's Yokes", A.
Comstock actions against, xvii

Hirah (Adullamite friend of Judah): tries to
redeem Judah's pledge to prostitute, 84

Holy Communion: denied to non-abstinent
couples, Jerome, 28

Holy Ghost: offended by marital coitus, 29

Homicide: see murder.

Homosexual behavior: Biblical interpretations,
problems of, J. J. McNeill quotation, 41;
Christ, odd acts of, M. Smith quotation,
42–43; David & Jonathan, posited,
36–39; death penalty, 18, 40; Gibeah
residents, demand to rape guest, 52;
Ham & Noah, posited, 69; Ishmael,
possible molestation of Isaac, 117; Paul,
comment in epistles, 39–40; prostitutes,
41; Sodom mob, attempt to rape guests,
32–33

Hophni (O. Eli): lascivious actions during
temple service, 100

Horner, Rev. Tom: David & Jonathan,
bisexuality of, quoted, 39; Ruth & Boaz,
relationship of, 214–215

Hosea (prophet): marriage to whore, 93–94

Mark (Gospel writer): divorce, remarriage not permitted after, 179–180

Mark, 'secret gospel': homosexual tendencies of Christ, M. Smith hypothesis, 42–43

Marriage & marriage customs: abstinence in, Pauline epistles, 177–178; arranging of, 158; Benjamin, tribe of, problems finding mates, 147–150; celebration customs, 191–192, 197–198; divorced couple forbidden to remarry, 157; exemption of groom from work, war, 64, 192; harem, eunuchs & women in, 172; heaven, non-existence in, 15–16; kidnapping of brides, 148150; levirate marriage, 13–16, 83, 85; Masters, W. E., & V. Johnson, sexual dysfunction & religious orthodoxy, xix; monogamy encouraged, 177–178, 180; near kinsman, role, Ruth's case, 213–214; polygamy, duty to both wives, 157; polygamy, limits on, 207; polygamy, sharing of husband, 120; priests, acceptable mates for, 141–142; Samaritan woman, common-law bond condemned, Christ, 95–96; siblings, marriage of, 4, 6; sisters, marriage forbidden to, 192; virginity, importance of, 18, 140–142, 152; war captive, marriage to, 152; women, subjugation in Christian thought, 154–156, 158. See also concubines & concubinage; divorce; harem; intermarriage.

Mary (of Bethany): anointing of Christ, 96–98

Mary Magdalene: anointing of Christ, 96–98; possible sexual relations with Christ, Phipps comments, 99

Mary, Virgin: Immaculate Conception, doctrine, 114, 184; Joseph, relations with, 185–186; non-vaginal impregnation & birth of Christ posited, 187–188; immaculately conceived,184; 187–188; purification of, 186–187; Warner book cited, 188

Masochism: priests of Baal, 72–73

Masters, R. E. L.: Samson, comparison with Hercules, 201; witches, torture of, comments quoted, 222–223

Masters, W. E., & V. Johnson: religious orthodoxy & sexual dysfunction, xix

Masturbation: coitus interruptus mistaken for, 13; 'pollution' caused by, 22–23; sacred images used for, posited, 106; worse than sin of rape, Aquinas opinion, 15

Matthew (Gospel writer): remarriage permitted if divorce based on adultery, 180

McNeill, Fr. John J.: homosexuality, problems of Biblical interpretation, comments quoted, 41–42

Mencken, H. L.: definition of Puritan, 184

Menstruation: attitudes towards sex & discomfort, religiously-affiliated women, 20–21; coitus forbidden during, 18–19; 'purification' rituals, Biblical, 17–21; 'purification' rituals, modern Orthodox Judaism, 21; 'sin' aspect of, 28. See also 'purification'; sacrifices & offerings.

Merab (O. Saul): offered to David, 135

Micah (prophet): prophesying while naked, 79–80

Michal (O. Saul; M. David): deception of envoys with idol, 106; exhibitionism of David, disgust over, 75–76; foreskin dowry, 135–136; taken from second husband & given to David, 7677

Midianites: apostasy of Israel with, 71; retaliation against, 150–151

Milton, John: *Paradise Lost,* basis for 220

Minnesota Supreme Court: man committed as sexual psychopath, Kinsey case, 30

Miriam (S. Aaron, Moses): disease of, possible explanations of, 25

Miscarriage: see abortion.

"Monkey Trial", Bible, inerrancy challenged in, xviii

Monogamy: encouraged in Christian thought, 177–178, 180

Mordecai (cousin of Esther): sends Esther to king's harem, 203

Moses (S. Aaron, Miriam): product of incest, 2; commandments to Israelites on abstinence, 21–22; life saved by son's circumcision, 132; orders slaughter of pagan worshippers, 70, 71–72

'Mother of Harlots' (Revelation reference):
110–111

Murder (attempted): David, by Saul, 37,
106, 134–135; Gazites, of Samson,
199; Isaac, as sacrifice by Abraham, 144

Murder: Abel, by Cain, 17; Absalom, by
Joeb, 11; Adonijah, by Solomon's orders,
210; alleged witches, by Inquisition,
222–223; Amnon, by Absalom's orders,
5–6; Hivites, genocide of, 48–49;
Israelites engaging in pagan worship,
70–71; Jabesh-gilead tribe, genocide of,
148; Jephthah's daughter, as vow,
143–144; Jericho residents, genocide of,
91–92; John the Baptist, by will of
Herodias, 80–81; Levite's concubine,
Gibeah gang rape, 53–54; Midianites,
genocide of, 150–151; non-virgins, in
war, 148–149, 150–151; Philistines, by
Samson, 198; Samaritan woman's son
killed as food, 165; Samson's father-in-
law & wife, by Philistines, 198–199;
Uriah, by David's orders, 60–62; Zimri
& Cozbi, by Phinehas, 70–71

Naomi (mother-in-law, Ruth): helps Ruth
to proposition Boaz, 212–215

Nathan (prophet): David denounced by, &
prophecies, 62–63; incest of Absalom
predicted, 10

Naturalism: compared with dualism,
183–184

Nature, 'crimes' against [archaic usage,
reflecting primitive thinking, for non-
reproductively-oriented sexual behaviors]:
masturbation vs. rape, Aquinas opinion,
15; Pauline epistles, references in,
39–40, 42. See also bestiality;
homosexual actions.

Nazarite: restrictions upon, 197

Negroes: see black people.

New Standard Bible Dictionary, The: oaths,
quotation, 146

Noah (P. Ham, Japheth, Shem): drunkenness
of, & curse of ,son, 68–69

NOCIRC (National Organization of
Circumcision Information Resource
Centers): address and phone number, 131

Nocturnal emissions: 'pollution' caused by,
22–23

Nudity: during prophecy, 79–80; Israelite
culture, prudery in, 68–69; pagan rituals
&, 71. See also exhibitionism.

Oaths & vows: Abraham's servant's vow,
145–146; Israelite vow to kill all not at
Mizpeh, 148; Jephthah's vow to sacrifice, 143–145; Joseph's oath to Jacob,
146–147; Nazarite's vows, 197–201;
solemnization of, 156–159

'Obscene' materials: censorship by A.
Comstock, xvii

Offerings: see sacrifices & offerings.

O'Higgins, H. and E. Reede: A. Comstock
& puritanism, quotation, xi–xii

Oholah & Oholibah: symbols of Israel's
apostasy, 109–110

Onan (O. Judah; S. Er, Shelah; M. Tamar):
coitus interruptus of, mistaken for
masturbation, 14; death of, for disobedience, 14–15

"Open Letter to Jesus Christ, An" (D. M.
Bennett, publisher): A. Comstock
reaction to, xvii

Opinion polls: Gallop (1976), "born-again
Christians", xi

Origen: castration and, 173

Original sin: see sin.

Pagan rituals & worship (used for non-
Jehovistic worship): Elijah's challenge
to priests of Baal, 72–73; genocide of
pagans sanctioned, 151–152; Israelite
interest in, 16, 68, 70, 94, 101–109;
nudity &, 70–72, 80; suppression of,
101–102, 107, 108. See also idols;
phallic symbols; prostitution (cultic).

Paige, Karen E.: menstruation, perceptions
of & discomfort, modern U. S.
women, 20

Paine, Thomas: Bible, comments on, xiv

Papal infallibility: doctrine of, 113

Paradise Lost (John Milton): basis for, 220

Parthenogenesis: Bible prophecies, translation
problems in, 185; modern information
concerning, 187–188; Virgin Mary,
alleged, 184–188

Patai, Raphael: coitus during menstruation, punishments for, quotation, 19

Paul (formerly Saul; apostle): abstinence, commendation of, 177–178; circumcision, teachings concerning, 127–130; 'crimes' against nature, comments on, 39, 42; divorce of unbelieving spouse permitted, 179, 180–181; female inferiority, opinions concerning, 154–156; general condemnation of sexuality, 181–182; homosexuality, condemnation of, 39–40; incest, in Corinth, comments on, 178–180; monogamy encouraged, 93, 180; Rahab praised by, 92

Pearly Gates Syndrome or How to Sell Real Estate in Heaven (C. M. Smith): Bible, 'racy material' in, xix

Pederson, Johannes: sexual rites Israelite religion, comments quoted, 102

Penthouse (Lisa Collier Cool article): spousal abuse, high incidence of among fundamentalists, 159

Peter (apostle): circumcision, teachings concerning, 128–129

Pfeiffer, R. H.: II Samuel 3:29, translation of: 23, 24

Phallic symbols: Israelite interest in, 16, 102, 103–108; suppression of, 104–105, 106, 108–109. See also idols; pagan rituals & worship; prostitution (cultic).

Phaltiel (M. Michal): Michal taken away from & given to David, 76

Pharez (O. Judah, Tamar): incestuous birth of, 85

Pharoah (Egyptian king): deceived by Abraham & Sarah, 193

Philip, Gospel of: Christ, marriage to Mary Magdalene, 80

Philistines: capture of Ark of the Covenant, & hemorrhoid plague, 161–163; Samson, capture of, 199–202

Philosophy: animism, 17, 22; dualism vs. naturalism, 183–184

Phinehas: murder of Cozbi & Zimri for intermarriage, 70

Phinehas (O. Eli): lasciviousness in temple services, 100–101

Phipps, William E.: Christ, sexuality of, comments quoted, 99

Pittenger, Norman: Christ, sexuality of, comments quoted, 99

Pius IX, Pope: doctrines promulgated by, 113, 184

Polls, opinion: Gallop (1976), 'born-again Christians' statistics, xiii

Polygamy: duties to each wife, 157; limits on, 207–208; sharing of husband, 119

Popes: Innocent VIII, Devil declared to be real personal being, 222; Pius IX, doctrines promulgated by, 113, 184

Pornography: groups opposed to, xi, xiii

Potiphar (captain of Pharoah's guard): wife's attempts to seduce Joseph, 56–58

Premature ejaculation: possible Biblical reference, 24

Priests & priesthood: acceptable mates, 141; daughters must be virgins, 141; lasciviousness, 100–101; masochism, priests of Baal, 72–73; nudity forbidden, 71. see also pagan ritual & worship; prostitution (cultic); sacrifices & offerings.

Procreation: Augustine, opinions on, 29; Eve, curse of, 26, 28; homosexuality possibly condemned for interference with, 71; Jerome, opinions on, 28; Roman Catholic view, importance of, 15. See also abstinence; fertility, human.

Prophecy: Absalom's incest predicted, 10, 118–119; death of David's son predicted, 62–63; nudity during, 79–80

Prostitutes: Gomer, 93; 'Great Whore' of Revelation, 110–111; Israel likened to, 108–110; male, 41–42; mother of Jephthah, 175; Oholah & Oholibah, as symbols of Israel's apostasy, 109–110; priests forbidden to marry, 141; Rahab, & fall of Jericho, 88–92; Samaritan woman, condemned by Christ, 95–96; Samson's attraction to, 199–201; Solomon's judgment of true mother, 176; Tamar masquerades as, 83–85; warnings against, 61–62, 86–88

Prostitution: Christ, condemnation by, 95–97, 99; cultic, 16, 41, 68, 70–71,

94, 100–102, 106–110; general admonitions against, 61–62, 86–88; male, 40–41; Paul, condemnation of, 181. See also idols; pagan ritual & worship; phallic symbols.

Protestant religion: attitudes towards sex & menstrual discomfort, U. S. women, 20; 'born-again' phenomenon, in U. S., xi–xii

Prudery: in Israelite culture, 68–69

Psychology Today (Karen E. Paige article): menstruation, perceptions of, & attitudes towards sex, U. S., 20

Punishments: amputation, damaging testicles in fight, 145–146; blindness, men of Sodom, 33; death penalty, abortion, killing woman via injury in spontaneous accident, 113; adultery, 18, 64–65, 138–140, 215; assault of parent, 45; bestiality, 169–170; coitus during menstruation, unclear reference, 18–19; cursing of parent, 45; desecration of Ark of the Covenant, 74, 161–169; disobedience, 45–46; failure to circumcise, unclear reference, 124; fornication, 15, 84, 141; homosexual acts, 40–41; incest, 45; rape, 142; theft of slave, 45; witchcraft, 221–223; disease, desecration of ark, 161–169; excommunication, abortion, Roman Catholic church, 114; coitus during menstruation, unclear reference, 18–19; failure to circumcise, unclear reference, 124; incest, 6; fines, inducing miscarriage without death of women, 113; rape, 49–50; slandering a virgin, 140-141; forced marriage, rape, 49–50; genocide, violation of tribal law, 148–149; sterility, incest, 16; whipping, sexual contact with betrothed slave, 157–158. See also hell.

Purification, ceremonial: Bathsheba, before adultery, 58; childbearing, after, 26–27, 186–187; circumcision as rite for new mother, 27, 125; coitus, after, 21; ejaculation, after, 21–24; flesh, after 'issue' of, 24–25; menstruation, after, 17–21; variations in time needed to accomplish, explanations, 23–24, 27, 125; Virgin

Mary, after childbirth, 186–187; women, harem of Ahasuerus, 204–205

Puritanism: xi–xii

Quotations: Atkinson, Miles, circumcision, 130; Augustine, procreation, 29; Clemens, Samuel L., Bible & own works, xviii; Cole, William Graham, coitus during menstruation, punishments for, 18; Cole, homosexuality of David & Jonathan challenged, 36; de Smet , A., Onan's sin, 15; *Encyclopedia Biblica*, oaths, 146; Epstein, L. M., bitter water test for adultery, 140; Epstein, execution of animals in bestiality cases, 170; Epstein, sexual rites & Israelite religion, 102; Harris, Roy J., Jr., parthenogenesis, 187; Horner, Tom, bisexuality of David & Jonathan, 39; Horner, sexual relations of Ruth & Boaz, 214–215; Ingersoll, Robert G., Bible, xvii; *Interpreter's Bible*, Noah probably assaulted by Ham, 69; Jerome, sexual behaviors, 28; Johnson, V., & W. E. Masters, sexual dysfunction & religious orthodoxy, xix; Kramer, Henry, witches, 222; Longworth, T. Clifton, mistranslation of sexual refer-ences, 103; Lucian, castration ceremony, 172; Luther, Martin, on sexuality, 29; Mace, David, circumcision, 125; Masters, R. E. L., torture of witches, 222; Masters, W. E., & V. Johnson, sexual dysfunction & religious orthodoxy, xix; McNeill, John J., Biblical interpretations of homosexuality, 41; *New Standard Bible Dictionary*, oaths, 146; O'Higgins, H., and E. Reede, puritanism & A. Comstock, xi–xii; Paige, Karen E., attitudes towards menstruation in U. S., 20; Paine, Thomas, Bible, xiv; Patai, Raphael, coitus during menstruation, punishments for, 19; Pederson, Johannes, sexual rites & Israelite religion, 102; Phipps, William E., sexuality of Christ, 80; Pittenger, Norman, sexual life of Christ, 99; Reede, E. & H. O'Higgins, puritanism & A. Comstock, xi–xii; Smet, A. de, Onan's sin, 15; Smith, Charles M., Bible, 'racy material' in, xix; Smith, Morton, possible homosexual tendencies of Christ, 42; Sprenger, James, witches, 222; Stanton, Elizabeth Cady, religion as bar to women's freedom, 158; Suarez, Francisco, Mary's conception of Christ, 188; Taylor, Gordon Rattray, cultic prostitution, 101; Tertullian, condemnation of women, 158; Thompson, G. S., circumcision, 130; Twain, Mark, Bible & own works, xviii. See also Biblical references in separate listing.

Rachel (O. Laban; S. Leah; M. Jacob): betrothal and marriage, 190–192; sells Jacob's sexual favors to Leah, 119–120; sterility & later childbearing of, 118, 121; theft of household gods from father, 104

Rahab (prostitute): hiding of Israelite spies, 88–89

Rape: betrothed slave, laws concerning, 157–158; death penalty for, 142; Dinah, victim of Shechem, 46–50; homosexual rape attempted, Gibeah, 52; homosexual rape attempted, Sodom, 32–33; Israelite law concerning, 49–50, 142; less sinful than masturbation, Aquinas opinion, 16; Levite's concubine, Gibeah incident, 53–54; Lot's daughters offered for, 7, 32; Noah, possibly attacked by son, 68–69; Potiphar's wife, false charge against Joseph, 57–58; Shiloh women, by Benjaminite tribe, 149–150

Tamar, victim of Amnon, 3–6; victim cannot be divorced by rapist, 50

Rebekah (M. Isaac): betrothal & marriage, 158–159; passed off as Isaac's sister, 190

Reede, Edward, & Henry O'Higgins: A. Comstock and puritanism, quotation, xi–xii

Rehoboam (O. Solomon): burdens upon Israelites, 147; phallic worship, support for, 104

Religiosity (used for measurable characteristics, religious behaviors): 1976 Gallop poll, U. S., xi–xiii

Religiously-based writings, analysis/criticisms: Bible, Bennett, D. M., suggestion that it

be treated as actionable 'obscene' material, xvi; circulation figures, xviii; Clemens, Samuel L., comments on, xviii; 1976 Gallop Poll results, as 'inspired' word of God, xi–xii; Ingersoll, Robert G., comments, xvii; Jefferson, Thomas, rewriting of, xvi; mistranslations in, Longworth comments quoted, 103; mistranslations, McNeill comments, 40; Paine, Thomas, comments on, xiv; 'racy material' in, C. M. Smith, xix; Scopes trial, inerrancy challenged in, xiv; Twain, Mark, comments on, xviii; *Secret Gospel of Mark,* Morton Smith analysis, possible homosexual tendencies of Christ, 42–43; Talmud, superstitions concerning menstruation, 20

Religiously-oriented groups: pornography, groups opposed to, xv

Religiously-oriented persons: menstrual discomfort & attitudes toward sex, U. S. women, 20–21

Religious orthodoxy, sexual dysfunctions &, xix

Religious prostitution: see prostitution, cultic.

Remarriage: see divorce; marriage and marriage customs.

Reuben (O. Jacob, Leah; S. progenitors of other 11 'tribes', Dinah): incest of, 45

Rituals, religious: see 'purification'; sacrifices & offerings

Roman Catholic religion: abortion as grave offense, 114; abstinence recommended during menstruation, 21; attitudes towards sex & menstrual discomfort, U. S. women, 20–21; "born-again Christians", Gallup poll figures, xiii; Christ's divinity, dogma of, 187; sexuality & procreation, theological opinions on, 15, 28–29; Virgin Mary, cultus of, 188

Romberg, Rosemary: circumcision, book cited, 131

Rome (Christian church): homosexuality condemned, Pauline epistle, 39–40

Rome (city): 'Great Whore' of Revelation, 110

Ruth (daughter-in-law of Naomi, M. Boaz): propositions & marries Boaz, 134, 212–215

Sacrifices & offerings: Ark of the Covenant, returned by Philistines, 75; childbirth, after, 26–28, 125, 186; circumcision as, 124, 126, 129; Elijah's challenge, priests of Baal, 72–73; human sacrifice, 143; 'issue' of flesh, after, 24–25; jealousy test, women accused of adultery, 138–139, menstruation, after, 20, 28; offering of handicapped unacceptable to Jehovah, 171; pagan deities, by Israelites, 94, 103, 104–108; Philistines, golden mice & hemorrhoids, 162–163; rape of betrothed slave, sin offering for, 157–158

Salome (O. Philip, Herodias): dance for Herod, & results, 80–81

Samson: birth to formerly sterile mother, 116, 197; Delilah, relationship with, & betrayal, 199–200; marriage & revenge, 197–199; Nazarite vow of, 197–200

Samuel: born to formerly sterile mother, 116; spirit conjured by witch of Endor, 222

Sarah ('Sarai'; M. Abraham; P. Isaac): Hagar, relations with, 114–115; passed off as Abraham's sister, 115, 193–195; sterility of, and later pregnancy, 114, 115–116

Sarai: see Sarah.

Saul (Israelite king; P. Jonathan): hatred of David, 36–39, 79, 106, 134–136; prophesying while naked, 79; witch of Endor consulted, 222

Saul (Christian convert): see Paul.

Scopes Trial: Bible, inerrancy of, challenged in, xviii

Secret Gospel: the Discovery and Interpretation of the Secret Gospel According to Mark (Morton Smith): possible homosexuality of Christ, comments quoted, 42

Seduction: betrothed slave, laws concerning, 157–158; Boaz & Ruth, 212–215; Judah, by Tamar, 83–85; Potiphar's wife's attempts with Joseph, 56–58

Self-abuse [archaic]: see masturbation.

Semen: as 'polluting' substance, 21–24

Sex and Family in the Bible and the Middle East (R. Patai): coitus, during menstruation, punishment for, quotation, 19

Sex and Love in the Bible (W. G. Cole): coitus, during menstruation, punishment for, quotation, 19; homosexuality of David & Jonathan challenged, quotation, 36

Sex in History (Gordon Rattray Taylor): cultic prostitution, comments quoted, 101

Sex in the Bible (Tom Horner): David & Jonathan, bisexuality of, comments, 39; Ruth & Boaz, sexual relationship posited, 214–215

Sex Laws and Customs in Judaism (L. M. Epstein): bestiality, execution of animal involved, explanation, 169–170; bitter water test for suspected adultery, quotation, 140; circumcision of dead infants, 125; sexual rites & Israelite religion, quotation, 102

Sexual behavior: attitudes towards, & menstrual discomfort, 20–21; lacking in the Christian heaven, 15; 'necessary evil', Christian thought, 28. See also abstinence; bestiality; birth control; coitus; concubines & concubinage; fornication; harem; homosexuality; marriage & marriage customs; masturbation; procreation.

Sexual dysfunctions: premature ejaculation, 24; religious orthodoxy, contributing factor in, xix

Sexual intercourse: see coitus.

Sexuality of Jesus, The (William E. Phipps): comments, 99

'Sexual psychopathy': laws, Kinsey case, 30

Shechem (Hivite man): rape of Dinah, & consequences, 46–50

Shelah (O. Judah; S. Er, Onan): promised to Tamar as husband, 83, 85

Shem (O. Noah; S. Ham, Japheth): covers father's nudity, 68–69

Simeon (O. Jacob S. Dinah, progenitors of the 11 other 'tribes'): murder of Hivites, 48–49

Sin: all conceived in, psalmist's view, 26; masturbation a worse sin than rape, Aquinas opinion, 15; sexual overtones in 'original sin', 2

Slander: good name of virgin, punishment for, 140–141

Uriah (military commander; m. Bathsheba): adultery of wife, 59–60; murdered by David's command, 60–61

Urine: see excrement.

Utopian Motherhood: New Trends in Human Reproduction: parthenogenesis, comments (Francoeur), 187

Uzzah (O. Abinadeb): struck dead for touching the Ark of the Covenant, 74

Vashti (M. Ahasuerus): dethroning of, 203

Valesians: castration practiced by, 172

VD: see venereal disease.

Venereal disease: 24–26

Victoria (Queen): advice to female subjects, 218

'Virgin birth': see parthenogenesis.

Virgin Mary: see Mary, Virgin.

Virgins and virginity: importance of, 18, 140–142, 156; Jephthah's daughter kept as, hypothesis, 144–145; non-virgins considered of little value, 142, 148–149, 150–152; offered for rape, 7, 32, 53; signs of, 140–141

Vows: see oaths & vows.

Wallerstein, Edward: circumcision, book cited, 131

Wall Street Journal (Roy J. Harris, Jr. article): parthenogenesis, comments quoted, 187

Warner, Marina: Virgin Mary, book cited, 188

Wars & war-related action: abstinence of soldiers during, 63–64; incidents of, 148–152; human sacrifice for victory, 143–145; Israelite-Hivite, 48–49; Jehovah's rules concerning, 151–152; Jericho, fall of, 88–92; Uriah's death in, 60–61; women, treatment in, 148–149, 150–152

Was Jesus Married? (William Phipps): Christ, marriage to Mary Magdalene, 99

'Wet dreams': see nocturnal emissions.

Whipping: sexual contact with betrothed slave, 157–158; see also punishments.

"Why Do Marsupials Propagate Their Kind?" (D. M. Bennett, publisher): A. Comstock reaction to, xviii

Widows: adultery possible for, 85, 214; priests forbidden to marry, 142

Willcox, R. R.: syphilis, of Miriam, possible, 25

Witches & witchcraft: death penalty, Biblical, 221–223; Endor, witch consulted by Saul, 222; Inquisition, 222–223

Withdrawal (as contraceptive method): see birth control.

Wizards: see witches.

Women: amputation as punishment, 145; childbearing as part of salvation of, 155; Christian thought concerning, 154–156, 158, 222; harem life, 172–173; kidnapping, 149–150; non-virgins considered of little value, 140–142, 148–149, 150–152; property of male relatives, 32–33, 35, 53, 142, 157; slave, status as, 152, 157–159; 'uncleanness' alleged, 17–21, 26–28, 125; witchcraft alleged, 222–223. See also concubines & concubinage; discrimination, gender-based; divorce; marriage & marriage customs.

'Women Learn to Sing the Menstrual Blues' (K. E. Paige): 20

World's Sixteen Crucified Saviors, The (Kersey Graves): cited, 188

Xerxes: see Ahasuerus.

Zarah (O. Judah, Tamar): incestuous birth of, 85

Zilpah (servant of Jacob; P. Gad, Asher): childbearing of, 119, 121

Zimri (M. Cozbi the Midianite): killed by Phinehas for intermarriage, 70

Zipporah (M. Moses): circumcision of son, 132

Zoar (city): Lot's family flees to, 7, 34

Zoophilia: death penalty for, 18, 169–170

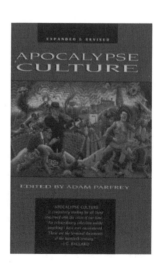